D0617696

Faces of Jesus
in Africa

FAITH AND CULTURES SERIES
An Orbis Series on Contextualizing Gospel and Church
General Editor: Robert J. Schreiter, C.PP.S.

The *Faith and Cultures Series* deals with questions that arise as Christian faith attempts to respond to its new global reality. For centuries Christianity and the church were identified with European cultures. Although the roots of Christian tradition lie deep in Semitic cultures and Africa, and although Asian influences on it are well documented, that original diversity was widely forgotten as the church took shape in the West.

Today, as the churches of the Americas, Asia, and Africa take their place alongside older churches of Mediterranean and North Atlantic cultures, they claim their right to express Christian faith in their own idioms, thought patterns, and cultures. To provide a forum for better understanding this situation, the Orbis *Faith and Cultures Series* publishes books that illuminate the range of questions that arise from this global challenge.

Orbis and the *Faith and Cultures Series* General Editor invite the submission of manuscripts on relevant topics.

Also in the Series

Hispanic Devotional Piety: Tracing the Biblical Roots, C. Gilbert Romero.

FAITH AND CULTURES SERIES

Faces of Jesus
in Africa

Edited by
Robert J. Schreiter, C.PP.S.

ORBIS BOOKS

Maryknoll, New York 10545

Third Printing, January 1995

Library of Congress Cataloging-in-Publication Data

Faces of Jesus in Africa / edited by Robert J. Schreiter.
   p. cm.
  ISBN 0-88344-768-1
  1. Jesus Christ—History of doctrines—20th century. 2. Jesus Christ—Person and offices. 3. Africa, Sub-Saharan—Religious life and customs. I. Schreiter, Robert J.
BT 198.F33   1991
232′.096′0904—dc20   91-16678
                                    CIP

Contents

Introduction

Jesus Christ in Africa Today

ROBERT J. SCHREITER

Africa is the fastest growing Christian continent in the world today. Sometime in the 1980s its numbers surpassed those of Christians in North America, making it the third most populous Christian continent in the world after Latin America and Europe. It is estimated that Africa will have nearly 325 million Christians by the year 2000.

Within that teaming, bustling continent one finds the full range of questions facing Christianity as a world church today. Much of the continent still staggers under the burden of colonialism and the disappointments of "flag democracy"—political independence but continued economic subordination to the powerful cultures in Europe, East Asia, and North America. The opportunity to develop the resources of the country remains elusive in so many places. The AIDS epidemic in central Africa threatens to decimate the human resources for growth and development in a way that the slave trade did in earlier centuries. The northeastern segment of the continent continues to struggle with civil war, drought, and recurring famine. The southern sections find their struggles to be against a different kind of enemy—overcoming apartheid and establishing a new social and political order. And countries throughout the continent have to cope with national boundaries drawn by colonial powers that do not coincide with the natural social units of cultures. There have been over seventy political coups and numerous civil wars in Africa since the independence movements of the 1960s—often representing the clash between nineteenth-century conceptions of the nation-state and much older political and social realities.

But to dwell on the problems that plague contemporary Africa is to see only some of the faces it presents to the world today. Its breathtaking landscapes, the warmth and dignity of its peoples, its incomparable religious sense, the lure of its values of family, promotion of life and mutual care— values that have resisted the corrosions of modernity—all of these seem to mitigate the daunting problems Africa faces and reveal the tremendous human resources that Africa is bringing to bear on its future. One cannot escape the feeling that a fulsome energy underlies what is going on in Africa today, both in the problems it confronts and the prospects it displays.

The Christian church, too, mirrors the vigor and energies of the continent. Forms of religiosity run the range from continuing the European missionary patterns of half a century or better ago to the many thousands of so-called independent churches that reflect recurring preoccupations with healing, the spirit world, and ecstatic prayer. Thus one encounters an astonishing range of expressions of Christianity in Africa today. Some have suggested that the independent churches show what a genuinely inculturated Christianity might look like in Africa, were inculturation left to Africans alone. These independent churches are not simply reactions to the clash of African and North Atlantic cultures; they often show a keenly refined sense of the liberation people need, as has been the case with some of the independent churches in South Africa. Even though the European-derived Christian churches would not bring themselves to adapt as far as these independent churches have gone, they feel themselves committed to a greater sense of inculturation into African life and to a fuller participation in the liberation of their people.

Indeed, as Charles Nyamiti points out in the lead article in this collection, the twin themes of inculturation and liberation shape many of the concerns preoccupying African Christian theology today. Inculturation of the Gospel remains a prime, if not the prime, item on Africa's agenda. For too long, embracing Christ and his message meant rejection of African cultural values. Africans were taught that their ancient ways were deficient or even evil and had to be set aside if they hoped to become Christians. But it is clear today that that process of Christianization was too often a process of Europeanization. The bitter irony, as African theologians have pointed out, is that African values and customs are often closer to the Semitic values that pervade the Scriptures and the story of Jesus than the European Christian values that have been imposed upon them. Colonial patterns of domination have undermined African Christians in two ways: by demeaning their own sense of worth and dignity as Africans, and interposing European cultural values between them and the Gospel message. Thus a style of Christianity needs to emerge that does not bifurcate the African Christian—making the African Christian reject a cultural heritage and identity in order to become a Christian. Popes Paul VI and John Paul II have reiterated the theme of being authentically African and authentically Christian in their visits to Africa. But as the contributors to this volume note, the intentions at this point far supersede the reality. Inculturation remains more a wish than a realized fact.

Hand in hand with inculturation goes a liberation from the manifold sufferings of the peoples of Africa. The African preoccupation with healing, set forth especially by Cécé Kolié in this volume, but echoed by Anne

Nasimiyu-Wasike and Laurenti Magesa, grows out of this profound sense of all the things and social forms from which Africans seek liberation. John Waliggo's contribution to this volume is an eloquent litany of all the various kinds of suffering that Africans today must undergo. He also establishes a profound link between liberation from suffering and inculturation. He sees a wrenching motif of rejection pervading African society that eats deep into Africans' sense of self-esteem and draws natural and social calamities into its network. Liberation will only be achieved when Africans are again made whole. And that involves more than relief from illness and famine, security from civil strife, and deliverance from economic corruption and exploitation. It has to do with the soul of Africans, their participation in the fullness of life that links them both to the yet unborn and to the ancestors as well as the living communities around them. It is only in such integrity that liberation is fully achieved. Thus the transformation of political and economic structures must go hand in hand with a reconstruction of African cultures and self-esteem—not as some antiquarian or folkloric curio that generates tourist revenues, but a living, vibrant cultural reality that can work closely in creating a new order in Africa.

But where is Jesus Christ in the midst of all of this? The understanding of who Jesus is mirrors in many ways the challenges that Africa faces today. Efoé Julien Pénoukou from Benin reflects on the state of christology in the villages, using his uncle as an example—orthodox creedal formulations can be reproduced, but do they really touch the souls, the concrete lives of people? Zablon Nthamburi, Kolié, and Waliggo echo these sentiments, particularly Waliggo in his survey of Ugandan seminarians. Christ is still a largely distant figure for many Africans, but as the seminarians' response shows, that need not be the case. There are aspirations of who Jesus might become for them—walking with a suffering people and sharing their pain and struggles.

But alongside this relative pessimism about how incarnate Christ has become in African soil, one finds striking images that contribute not only to the building up of genuinely African theologies (and for a continent so vast and culturally diverse, one must speak in the plural), but also making distinct contributions to the understanding of Christ for the whole church. This collection of essays has been assembled to show not only the problems that christology in Africa is facing, but also the stunning contributions it is making to the world church. Africa has important things to teach and recall to the minds of the rest of the church, and these need to be celebrated alongside the difficulties with which it struggles.

Given a continent so large and diverse as Africa, no portrayal of the faces of Jesus that Africa is now discerning can hope to be complete. This collection focuses on two areas: francophone western Africa, and anglophone eastern Africa. It does not take into account the ancient churches of Egypt and Ethiopia whose traditions predate most of those of western Europe. Nor does it take into account those now-extinct churches of northern Africa—the churches of Tertullian, Cyprian, and Augustine—that contributed so much to Western European Christianity's understanding of itself. Likewise, it alludes only indirectly to the christological situation in southern Africa where the struggle to create a new society overshadows other concerns. And even within central Africa, the focus is largely upon Bantu cultures.

While this would seem to limit severely the scope of African Christianity surveyed, it has two distinct advantages. First of all, it stands as a reminder that Africa in all its diversity is not easily encompassed, and that we should be loathe to generalize too quickly about its realities. Second, this concentration on the Bantu midsection of the continent displays something of the rough coherence that does prevail in that part of Africa. The francophone and anglophone distinctions grow more out of colonial heritage than present realities. And the contributions included here, which grew out of two conferences on christology reflect, as it were, that coherence. Most of the authors, but not all, are Roman Catholics. The ease with which all the authors here cite both Roman Catholic and Protestant literature shows something of an ecumenical consensus undergirding these efforts at constructing theology today.

This collection is in two parts. The first part tries to take the wider view of what is happening in christology today. In the opening essay, Charles Nyamiti notes the plethora of christological literature in Africa today, calling it the best-developed area of theological reflection on that continent. He goes on to develop a typology of different approaches to christology—moving from the tradition to the African reality, and from African reality to the tradition—and highlights in the latter the preoccupations with inculturation and liberation. He notes in concluding that much continues to need to be done, and that trinitarian and ecclesiological themes in christology should not be neglected.

The work of one theologian that Nyamiti singles out for praise is that of Julien Pénoukou, whose contribution forms the second essay. Pénoukou's essay lives up to Nyamiti's assessment. With a strong grasp of the way that cultural frameworks shape theological thought, Pénoukou shows the limitations of some Western categories for expressing the reality of Jesus and shows the fittingness of African ones: the limitations of Western understandings of death, the reduction of salvation to individualist and decisionist models, and the need to develop a relationalist ontology over against the more individualist or monadic varieties that haunt Eurocentric theologies. Pénoukou offers an excellent example of how African theologies are not only presenting a viable theology suited to local realities, but also how they can help reshape a larger theological discussion among the cultures in the world church.

Douglas W. Waruta's essay takes a slightly different tack. He begins with biblical data and church tradition to show how the medieval understanding of the threefold offices of Christ as priest, prophet, and king can be under-

stood in the African context today. This represents something of Nyamiti's
first typology of moving from the Christian tradition to the cultural reality.
While this does not always create the same engaging kind of theology that
movement in the opposite direct provides, it serves two important purposes:
it helps outsiders to the African scene gain some entry into cultures that
may not be familiar to them, and it can give Africans a sense that their
theological formulations can stand tall alongside and within the Great Tradition.

Zablon Nthamburi's and Anne Nasimiyu-Wasike's offerings take a look
at what it means for African men and women to reflect on the reality of
Jesus in their contexts today. Nthamburi surveys some of the images that
have been suggested by theologians and suggests that the African way will
need to focus on the praxis of Jesus. Sensitive to the needs of African
peoples, Nthamburi calls for a christology that emphasizes Christ's solidarity with all peoples, especially those who suffer, who hunger, who are
weak. Christ has to be more than a friend of the middle and upper classes.

Anne Nasimiyu-Wasike begins by reminding her readers that until about
twenty-five years ago, all African theology was written by men and from a
male perspective. She notes the growing number of women who are theologians in Africa and are changing this view of African theology. She begins
with a reflection on women's experience in Africa, working sixteen to eighteen hours a day to provide the basic necessities of life for their families.
This leaves precious little time for the luxury of reflection. Yet there is
much that grows out of women's experience that provides the basis for
theology: women as the bearers and nurturers of life, their profound sense
of the union between the supernatural and everyday life, their ability to
harmonize their own lives with the divine. She then goes on to relate wom-
en's experience to the stories of Jesus about women in the Gospels, and
concludes with how African women's experiences relate to different
approaches to christology. All in all her essay suggests many possibilities
that might be developed further into a vibrant christology that unfolds a
holistic sense of life.

The second part of this collection turns to what Anselme Sanon (quoting
E. Sambou), notes as the prime task in African theology today: " 'in most
African countries the prime theological urgency consists in discovering the
true face of Jesus Christ, that Christians may have the living experience of
that face, in depth and according to their own genius.' " To see the face of
a person is the beginning of engaging that person in genuinely human
relationship. Sanon explores one face of Jesus, as master of initiation. He
unfolds the meaning of initiation as the ongoing process from childhood to
ancestorhood that makes us progressively more fully human. Jesus, as master of initiation, has gone before us in the process and knows all that we
must endure. Sanon goes on to sketch out the stages in a manner reminiscent of Clement of Alexandria's *Christ the Teacher* or the mystagogic catecheses of Cyril of Jerusalem or Ambrose. Sanon's essay represents an

important retrieval of an ancient image that not only resonates with African sensibilities, but with all peoples trying to regain cultural ways that have been denied to them (one thinks of native peoples in North America) or secularized peoples looking for guidance in the welter of moral possibilities offered to them by societies of wealth and abundance.

François Kabasélé explores in detail another face of Jesus that has been touched upon by other authors in this collection, Jesus as chief. Some have noted that this image has become outdated and obsolete in some areas of Africa where this position of leadership has lost its power. Others caution against negative implications of this symbol, especially the domineering aspects that sometimes accompany being a chief. But as Kabasélé points out, this does not disqualify the possible inclusion of this symbol as a way of identifying the face of Jesus. It simply reminds us that chief does not mean the same thing in every culture, African or otherwise (nor does ancestor, healer, or priest), and that no human symbol is without negative as well as positive connotations. One only needs to think of the Mediterranean correlate of chief: *kyrios* or Lord, with its imperial overtones.

Kabasélé continues with reflections on two other images, Christ as ancestor and Christ as elder brother. He is keenly aware of the controversies that have surrounded calling Christ ancestor or proto-ancestor. Many of these are generated by the varying ways that ancestors are related to by the living in different parts of Africa. But the debate is also fueled by the relative position of ancestors between God, the spirits, and the living human community. Thus generalizations are nearly impossible; to speak of Christ as ancestor requires careful description of the cultural settings in which the image is used. In that light Kabasélé suggests the image of Christ as elder brother to function complementarily with the ancestor image.

Cécé Kolié gives a careful analysis of one of the most widespread namings of the face of Jesus in Africa, Jesus the healer. An important aspect of this naming is how it has reintroduced reflections on Jesus the healer into the study of the Gospel stories, especially as exegeted by scholars living in secularized cultures. That Jesus was a healer is something that cannot be ignored, even though his modes of healing do not suit or conform to the therapeutic imagery of the secularized West. Kolié develops African understandings of healing and shows the commensurability of Jesus' activity with that of Africa, going on to recount the clash between Western and African medical traditions. But a haunting note is raised in the course of the presentation: how can we preach Christ the healer to the starving in the Sahel, the victims of injustice and corruption, those plagued with parasitic diseases in the tropical forests and equatorial areas?

Kolié's question echoes in the two closing essays of this book, dealing with suffering and liberation from suffering. Laurenti Magesa traces the problems that beset Africa today and from which Africans need liberation. He notes the disappointments of dreams unrealized since independence, caused both by North-South economic imbalances and the often sorry situation of African domestic politics. He calls for the development of a liberating christology that will take up the aspirations of Africa's youth and its rural masses in which Jesus appears in utter solidarity with the people.

John Waliggo's contribution was already referred to in some detail above. He sets out in a masterful fashion the problems that Africa must face and some of the root issues that must be addressed if those problems are to be overcome. Foremost among them is rejection: rejection of Africa by the powerful North Atlantic states, and the cultural self-rejection that colonialism has inculcated into Africans themselves. He portrays a Jesus who underwent rejection (echoing here especially the Suffering Servant hymn) and who therefore knows the problems with which contemporary Africans struggle.

All in all, these eleven essays present some of the faces of Jesus and how Africans today are responding to the Christ who encounters their cultures. Some of the struggles will look familiar to persons from other cultures: the struggle for integrating Christian and local identity, the exploration of local images to give intelligible form to Christian confession, the struggle to find the images of solidarity with those who suffer. But these African theologies give us more. They ask whether death always has to be identified with punishment and cannot be seen as a necessary step on the way to human fullness. In so doing, they raise questions about the models of salvation that have dominated Western European theology. Must we think in terms of Christ's saving us only as atonement? Might we not retrieve Paul's image of redemption as freeing from slavery and inclusion — a model of access and inclusion rather than substitutionary atonement? Has the secularized West been too casual in its dismissal of the spirit world? And what role should healing play in contemporary Christianity? More questions could be adduced. But these represent some of the most formidable challenges that African theology is presenting to the world church today. As it struggles to find the Christ active in its midst — Christ the African — it mirrors in a dramatic way a whole range of issues that touches the lives of Christian communities around the world. It is hoped that this volume of essays by African theologians will provide some entry for the rest of us into that vibrant and exciting network of churches today.

PART ONE

SURVEYING AFRICAN CHRISTOLOGIES

1

African Christologies Today

CHARLES NYAMITI

There is no doubt that christology is the subject which has been most developed in today's African theology. This is so true that already at the present moment an adequate survey of that subject would need a much broader essay than is possible within the confines of this paper. This essay, then, gives a brief schematic presentation.

There is already a variety of African christologies in the making. This variety corresponds to the schools of contemporary African theology, namely those of inculturation and liberation theology.

AFRICAN CHRISTOLOGIES OF INCULTURATION

There are two main types of African theology today. The first of these is that of inculturation; namely, the one in which an effort is made to incarnate the Gospel message in the African cultures on the theological level. By far this is the most common and most developed theological school in black Africa. Most of the current African christologies belong to this school; only a few writers of these christologies will be mentioned here.

A careful examination of the procedures undertaken by African christologists reveals two ways of approaching the subject. There are those who attempt to construct an African christology by starting from the biblical teaching about Christ and strive afterwards to find from the African cultural situation the relevant christological themes. Secondly, there are those who take the African cultural background as their point of departure for christological elaboration.

FROM THE BIBLE TO AFRICAN REALITY

John S. Mbiti has two major concerns: to find out the christological subjects which have particular interest for the African and to confront the

3

New Testament teaching about Christ with the African traditional world-view.[1]

With regard to the first, Mbiti discovers that the idea of *Christus Victor* (miracle worker and risen Lord) is particularly relevant, for this Christ is the conqueror of those evil powers (spirits, magic, disease, death) feared by the African and is guarantor of immortality. Other subjects which Mbiti sees as meaningful to the African are Christ's birth, baptism, and death, since they correspond to the life crises ritually stressed by the African.

In confronting the New Testament teaching on Christ with the African worldview, Mbiti uses the comparative method by trying to discover similarities and differences between the two types of teaching. In his effort to inculturate the Christian teaching, he stresses the biblical themes parallel to African traditional cultural items—*son of God* (an idea which is found in some African tribes, such as Shona, Ndebele, Shilluk, and Dogon), *Servant of God* (found in some African societies), as well as *Redeemer, Conqueror, Lord*, and Christ's *birth, baptism, death* and *resurrection*—which correspond to the African's life crises and are found in African initiation rituals.

However, Mbiti is careful to stress the christological elements whose parallels are not found in African tradition but are nevertheless important for Christian life, for example, the *Last Supper*.

Kofi Appiah-Kubi employs a similar method as Mbiti and stresses Jesus as Mediator or Intermediary; Saviour, Redeemer, and Power; Liberator; Healer.[2]

FROM AFRICAN REALITY TO CHRISTOLOGY

In this approach the author examines the mystery of Christ from either the perspective of the African worldview, or from the angle of some particular theme taken from the African worldview or culture. This second type of theologising (which can aptly be called the "thematic approach") is the one is most frequently used.

Christologies in the Light of the African Worldview. The basis of E. J. Pénoukou's christology is the spiritual and historical vision of the world (cosmotheandric vision of the world in which God, men, and the world are united symbiotically) and the conceptual ritual attitude of life and death among the Ewe-Mina tribe of Togo to which he belongs.[3] Life is seen beyond death, and death is understood as a necessary passage to life. The global reality is conceived as a living organism in the process of perpetual regeneration through successive phases of birth, death, and rebirth. These phases are moments of the accomplishment of what he calls "the being-there-with" others (with God, spirits, fellow human beings, and the cosmos). One sees here a kind of ontological process whereby the human subject is accomplished within a cosmotheandric relation implying a necessary relationship between the Supreme Being and the socio-cosmic universe.

With this Ewe-Mina worldview in mind Pénoukou reflects on the mystery of the Christ-Event and comes to various conclusions. The Christ-Event is a passage, a way of accomplishment of a project of being. Having existed before all and having emptied himself by becoming like us, Christ underwent death as a necessary passage to a new kind of life. Christ is the mediator ("organic Medium") between God the Father and the whole of creation. Since everything was created through and for Christ, the incarnation is the supreme expression of the cosmotheandric relationship. Through incarnation, death, and resurrection, Christ is at the centre of all history and is the accomplishment of the cosmotheandric relationship in the universe. The Ewe-Mina Christian who needs to be liberated from fear of evil spirits will find in Christ incarnate the God who is ontologically in solidarity with human destiny. Indeed, through his death and resurrection, Christ has vanquished evil and death in the world and has given them a new meaning. Christ's ontological solidarity demands total and global engagement on the part of human beings to share actively in creation. Finally, Christ is *Jete*-Ancestor (an ancestor who is the source of life). An ancestor is, according to the Ewe-Mina, co-fecundator of birth and is capable of providing to many newly born children the necessary vital energy for his apparition in them. Christ as *Jete*-Ancestor means that he is the Ancestor who is the source of life and the fulfilment of the cosmotheandric relationship in the world.

A similar christological approach is found in Charles Nyamiti.[4] Previous anthropological research reveals that in many African societies personality is conceived in vitalistic terms in the sense that true personality consists in fullness of life or vital maturity. Such vital plenitude comprises *fecundity* both on procreative and non-procreative levels, *practical wisdom* (implying knowledge of the ancestral traditions), *magico-religious sacred powers, responsibilities* and *rights, fulfilled openness* or relationality to the Supreme Being and other spirits, to human community (both of the living and the dead) and to the cosmos, together with *liberty*—not only as emancipation from all kinds of oppression but also in the sense of conciousness or awareness of giving oneself to the other(s) and of being accepted by that (those) other(s).

The elements in the African understanding of person are, in fact, coextensive with the elements found in the African traditional worldview. It is from such a vitalistic point of departure that it is possible to elaborate an African theology of the mystery of incarnation.

Incarnation is the highest fulfillment of personality as understood by the African. For the African, to achieve personality is to become truly human and, in a sense, authentically Black; hence, the incarnate Logos is the Black Person par excellence. There is therefore, no genuine blackness or negritude outside him.[5] As an instance of the fulfillment of personality in the

African sense the incarnation is directly linked with the mysteries of the Trinity, grace, the paschal mystery, pentecost, Parousia, and ecclesiology. Equally relevant are the events of Christ's circumcision and time of puberty. The vitalistic approach leads to a holistic interpretation as well as to a new African personalistic understanding of the incarnation and the mysteries with which it is immediately linked. African identity is best realized by self-identification with Christ, the Black Person par excellence. Christian spirituality is the practical actualization of such identity in today's African social and cultural situation. Christ's personality in the African sense implies also his initiation into the community of God, other spirits, and fellow human beings. In this connection his age of puberty has particular significance for the growth of his incarnation and for the life of the adolescent at the pubertal age. Indeed, Jesus—who was human like us in everything, and "has been tempted in every way we are, though he is without sin" (Hebrews 4:15; and 2:18) —must have acquired that age and experienced its particular difficulties. He triumphed over them most victoriously. As such, Christ is the best model for the African or any other adolescent at that age.

Thematic Approach to Christology. H. Sawyerr begins by denying the applicability of the term *chief* to Jesus Christ for a number of reasons.[6] Chiefs have lost their positive power and influence. Chiefship per se does not imply unquestioned supreme rule. Chiefs have never been readily accessible to the ordinary man: they had to be approached through the middlemen. Chiefs generally live in walled settlements and are therefore not exposed to the ordinary contacts of their subjects.

Sawyerr therefore suggests calling Christ *the elder Brother*, "the firstborn among many brethren who with Him form the Church" in which there is no distinction of race, sex, colour, or social condition. For him "to present Jesus Christ as the first-born among many brethren who with Him together form the Church is in true keeping with African notions. For Christians, an effort must be made to bring home the mystical relation between Christ and the Christian which St. Paul talks of in Gal. 2:19ff."

From this insight Sawyerr draws various practical implications, among which is the truth that Christ is the founder of the Great Family, the church, which embraces everyone irrespective of colour, sex, or nation. This engenders a new kind of relationship which "provides the means of overcoming the deeply ingrained feeling of insecurity which creates acute social and psychological problems among even African Christians" and helps us to refrain from "idolatrous escapisms."

J. S. Pobee pleads for a functional christology as fit for the mentality of the Akan, a Ghanaian people to which he belongs.[7] In his theological reflections he starts with the credo: *Christ is true God and true man.* He then attempts to express this credo in Akan thought forms by interpreting Christ's divinity and humanity according to the Akan understanding.

According to the Akan, man fully realizes himself in society. From this fact Pobee asserts that Akan christology demands stress on Christ's kinship, circumcision, and baptism as rites of incorporation into a group. Humanity is further shown by dread of death and finitude in knowledge. Both are found in Christ: his attitude in Gethsemane manifested the fear of his approaching death, and the Synoptic Gospels clearly inform us of the limits of his knowledge. Another human characteristic, according to the Akan, is dependence on superior power. Pobee sees this characteristic in Jesus in his frequent prayers to his Father. Pobee concludes that the Akan and biblical ways of expressing humanity are very similar.

Sinlessness is one of the divine qualities according to the Akan. Pobee sees Christ's sinlessness as a true sign of his divinity. Christ committed no sin but fought against sin by his conduct of love towards others and by his concern for those oppressed in any way or form and his efforts to relieve their pain and suffering. For, according to the Akan, sin is an antisocial fact. In Akan society the divinity is also shown in authority and power, in the capacity to heal and to create. By performing miracles and cures, Christ manifested his divine status. However, Pobee is careful to stress the Christian belief that Christ is the preexistent agent of creation. According to Pobee, this is the distinctively Christian claim which has no parallel in Akan religion.

Among the Akan a chief is expected to be the judge, legislator, religious leader, head of the community, fire extinguisher (fire being the symbol of pain and disaster), one who does not break his oath, and one who saves in battle. Pobee believes that Christ possessed all these qualities. However, he notes the differences between Christ's chiefship and that of the Akan. Christ is a prince of peace; this is a new idea not found in the Akan understanding of chief. Pobee concludes that *royal-priestly christology* (as one among many) is fit for the Akan. Christ's chiefship demands effective engagement on our part, including sharing in the struggles for liberation. Pobee warns us against "the dangers of the chief analogy." It leads to a *theologia gloriae* which lacks a *theologia crucis.* "In other words, the Chief analogy denotes authority and power derived from other ways than the way of suffering and humanity (Luke 24:46ff.)."

According to Pobee Christ is the great ancestor (*Nana* in Akan language). As such he has power and authority to judge, reward, and punish. But as God-man he is superior to all ancestors and all spiritual beings. What is the practical relevance of this ancestral christology? Pobee answers: "To say Jesus is *Nana* is to let his standards reign supreme in personal orientation, in the structures of society, in the economic processes, and in political forces. It means in practical terms personal and social justice and re-creation."

Kwesi A. Dickson attempts to present an *African theology of the cross.*[8] He begins by criticizing Western theology in which "the cross gets to be overshadowed in significance, it becomes a *disaster,* a *regrettable* prelude to

Easter." That is why their theology of the cross is rather negative and pessimistic.

Kwesi maintains that this may be due to the fact that "with the growing complexity of life in the West, death is fast ceasing to be a public event, an event which involves community as a whole." Hence death is seen as "an embarrassment to be passed over as quickly as possible . . ." He then points out various elements connected with the African traditional understanding of death. Death is caused by evil: it is always purposefully caused by someone. Death does not end life, nor does it sever the bond between the living and the dead. Death is an occasion for seeking life: "The dead are believed to be in a position to grant boons, to have superhuman powers." Death does not negate self-expression. Hence, death rituals are sometimes accompanied by "discreet feasting and circumspect conviviality," implying the belief that life must go on. Death affects the whole community by affecting a much wider social group than the deceased's immediate family.

In the light of the above and the New Testament teaching on the cross, the author presents a theology of the cross in keeping with the African understanding of death. The cross should be presented in "glorious affirmation of it as that which is the *basis of Christian hope*"; namely, "the cross demonstrates human degradation and evil, but it also *demonstrates triumph*." Stress should be put on the fact that eating and drinking at the Lord's table is sharing Christ's death on the cross and also *sharing life with one another*. In Africa, death is the door to beneficial ancestral status; likewise, by his death Christ "merits to be looked upon as Ancestor, the greatest of ancestors, who never ceases to be of the 'living dead.' " Just as for the African, death does not negate natural self-expression (one's own identity), so also is the theology of the cross not basically opposed to its interpretation in African cultural terms.

Jesus as Head and Master of initiation is the basic theme of A. T. Sanon's christology.[9] He begins with a somewhat detailed explanation of African initiation rituals. Initiation accompanies various stages of life: birth, growth, puberty, and marriage. Initiation (especially pubertal initiation) involves two main elements: passage from a lower condition to a higher status with new rights and responsibilities and introduction into community membership (family, tribe, particular society). Initiation involves various rites and other conditions such as separation from one's own community to a separate locality, various instructions (usually accompanied by initiatic secrecy), ordeals, prayers, and rituals (of purification, sacrifice), imposition of a new name, use of symbols, death and resurrection (symbolically manifested).

After an anthropological description, Sanon applies the African initiatic items to the understanding of the mystery of Christ. With the New Testament teaching (especially the letters to the Hebrews and the Philippians and the Synoptic Gospels), he interprets the various stages in Christ's life in the light of the African sense of initiation. He discovers in Christ's life a gradual movement towards a goal, perfection (Hebrews 2:10; 7:28; 5:9). He also notes that Jesus was initiated according to Jewish tradition at birth, when he was circumcised, when he received his name, and when he was presented in the temple—so as to enter ritually into his Jewish family and community.

Jesus' remaining in the temple when he was twelve years old is interpreted in terms of initiation as involving separation from his family, receiving instructions from Jewish rabbis, and instructing his father and mother (initiates are to instruct others). Likewise, the washing of Jesus' disciples at the Last Supper is seen as an initiatic gesture: Jesus, the Master of his disciples, instructs them to follow in his footsteps (love, pardon).

But Sanon sees the climax of Christ's initiation in his death and resurrection. These events comprise the initiatic ordeals and transformation to higher status. He points out that these two events are also familiar themes in African initiation rites.

Sanon indicates other initiatory elements linked with the life of Jesus: his messianic secret (Mark 1:44; 3:12), his use of symbols and signs (parables), solidarity (Christ's initiation involved us), cross (initiatic tree), church (place of initiation), time of initiation (time of grace), global act of initiation (sacraments).

From this ancestral christology Sanon draws several conclusions. As one who was initiated, Christ is the Head (chief) and master of our initiation: having been made perfect, he becomes chief (Head) of those who obey him (Hebrews 5:9). Sharing in his initiation involves following his initiatic steps to the cross for motives of charity. Through baptism we share in Christ's initiation by sharing in his initiatic death and resurrection. Christ is the unique Master of Christian initiation. He was initiated once and for all and thus created a new initiatic community whose tradition is that of Christ himself. Thus through his initiation he introduced in all initiatic traditions a radical newness which will never expire.

"Healing" is the theme which Aylward Shorter takes as the perspective for his christology.[10] Shorter sees healing as a central feature of the life and ministry of Christ. For this reason he believes that the African traditional interest in healing requires a christology based on Christ's healing function.[11]

Shorter then compares the Galilean healers (whose techniques were adopted by Jesus) with the African traditional medicine men. He discovers similarities between them in that both traditions practiced a holistic form of healing on the physical, psycho-emotional, moral-spiritual, social, and environmental levels. According to him both traditions tend to confuse these levels of wholeness or sickness, for example through the common belief that sickness was direct punishment for personal sin.

Belief in sorcery was common in the Mediterranean world of Christ's time, as it is in the African world today. Jesus employed traditional techniques of healing, but he relativized them and tried to warn his followers away from magical attitudes. Not only did he take an integral approach to healing, but he also taught about definite healing of the sickness of the world and that suffering has a salvific power, as manifested through his death on the cross. That is why Shorter calls Christ a "wounded healer" and "victim." This quality of being a wounded healer persists in his glorified condition. "He continues to show his wounds to the Father and to draw inestimable good from them for mankind." The believer is called to be a wounded healer with Christ. All healing is directed towards eternal life and wholeness. In the church this is realized through the sacraments, especially the Eucharist, which is the renewal of the mystery of Christ's cross and resurrection. The sacraments are the works of the divine Spirit, whom Shorter calls "medicine of life" since he continues Christ's healing mission. Besides, "the final wholeness to which all of this healing activity contributes is God becoming 'all in all'—the healing *pleroma.*"

Shorter further describes the implications of this healing christology. The human being is understood as "flesh of the flesh in the world." Healing becomes a possibility to establish and maintain harmony with the natural environment. Environmental wholeness is fundamental to human well-being. Social factors are important in the healing process. The subconscious (for example in dreams) has power to inspire, to affirm, and to heal.

Finally, Shorter believes that the African approach to healing "can produce a corrective for western scientific medicine which has become so effective at the physical level that it encourages an unfounded belief in its infallibility and leads to extremes of despair in terminal cases."

Bénézet Bujo starts his christological reflection from African ancestral beliefs and practices.[12] According to him, in Africa the *gesta* of ancestors are constantly re-enacted through ritual. This enables the African to recall these *gesta* and to conform his conduct to them. Hence such rituals become a life-and-death rule of conduct, guarantors of salvation, and a testament for posterity. In other words, this kind of ritual becomes a "commemorative narrative soteriology" which assures unity of the past, present, and future community, including the dead.

From this background Bujo reflects on the mystery of Christ. He sees him as *proto-ancestor*—the unique ancestor, the source of life and highest model of ancestorship. Through the incarnation Christ assumed the whole of human history, including the legitimate aspirations of our ancestors. This assumption of the future which the ancestors sought to guarantee is assured because our ancestors' experiences have been made efficacious in Jesus, crucified and risen. Thus the incarnation enables Christ to be the unique and privileged locus of total encounter with our ancestors and allows them to be the locus where we encounter the God of salvation.

Bujo holds that the idea of Christ as Ancestor is more meaningful to the African than the terms *Logos* or *Kyrios.* It also enables the African anthropocentrism (prominent in ancestral thinking) to be the source for incarnating Christianity. This, according to Bujo, demands a christology from below.

Moreover, Christ as proto-ancestor is, for Bujo, the foundation of a narrative ethic affirming that Christ is the proto-Source of life and accomplishment and the model of human conduct through the experience of his paschal mystery. Bujo believes that this christocentric ethic confirms the positive elements in African anthropocentrism such as hospitality, family spirit, solicitude for parents. At the same time it corrects and completes African traditional and modern customs.

As Bujo, I base my christological reflections on the African understanding of "ancestor," although I develop the subject along different lines.[13] The starting point is the beliefs and practices found in many (though not all) African traditional societies. According to these beliefs ancestral relationship (between the living and the dead, and sometimes between the Supreme Being and humanity on earth) comprises the following elements:

- *Kinship* (consanguineous or non-consanguineous) between the dead and the living kin. In many cases the ancestor also has to be the *source of life* for the earthly relatives.
- *Superhuman* status (usually acquired through death) comprising nearness to God, sacred powers, and other superhuman qualities.
- *Meditation* (not indispensable) between God and the earthly kin.
- *Exemplarity* of behavior in community.
- *Right or title to frequent sacred communication* with the living kin through prayers and ritual offerings (oblations).

With an understanding of ancestral relationship it is possible to examine the inner life of God (Trinity) and discover that there is an ancestral kinship among the divine persons: the Father is the Ancestor of the Son, the Son is the Descendant of the Father. These two persons live their ancestral kinship through the Spirit whom they mutually communicate to as their ancestral Oblation and Eucharist. The Spirit is reciprocally donated not only in token of their mutual love as *Gift* but also on behalf of the homage to their reciprocal holiness (as *Oblation*) and gratitude to their beneficence to each other (as *Eucharist*, from the Greek: *eucharistein* "to thank").

Several inferences can be drawn from these insights. In God there is a true doxological and eucharistic ritual. This trinitarian ritual or ceremony is the ultimate basis and model of all other rituals. The ultimate goal of this trinitarian ceremony is the intimate unification of the Father (Ancestor) and the Son (Descendant) in the Holy Spirit (pneumatic *perichoresis*). In God the terms *Ancestor* and *Descendant* are essentially doxological, eucharistic, pneumatic (inseparably linked with the Holy Spirit), and ritual categories.

The mystery of Christ from the African ancestral angle and the relationship which his ancestral kinship with us bears to the Trinity also leads

to several conclusions. Because of his divine-human status and redemptive
function, Christ is our Brother-Ancestor *par excellence.* Christ's ancestorship
to us is rooted in the Trinity. In fact, it is the economization of his eternal
descendancy in God for our salvation: it is, indeed, his redeeming descendancy as Logos incarnate. The incarnation and Christ's redemptive ministry, culminating in the paschal mystery, are the extensions of the trinitarian
ancestral communication to the man Jesus and, through him, to the rest of
creation. Christ functions ancestrally towards us through the Holy Spirit by
virtue of the salvific mission he received from the Father. Through Christ,
God the Father has become our Ancestor. Through Jesus' redemptive activity his ancestorship gradually grows and will reach its maturity at the Parousia. The Mass is a true ancestral ritual, and the tabernacle is the Christian
shrine in which Christ the Ancestor is daily present for ancestral communication with us. Likewise, our bodies are sacred living shrines inhabited
by our divine Ancestors (God the Father and Christ in the divine Spirit).

   The theology of the ancestorship of the Son of God is incomplete without
theological considerations of its link with us; for indeed, Christ the Head
is incomplete without his Body, the church, of which we, and the saints in
the other world, are members. This has led to an examination of the relevance of Christ's ancestorship to the heavenly saints and those of purgatory.

   Reflection on the relationship between Jesus and the saints shows that
the saints in heaven and purgatory are, in different degrees, our ancestors
in Christ, that is, they are ancestrally related to us by virtue of their participation in the ancestral status of the Redeemer. Among these saints are
the African ancestors who died in friendship with God. In addition to being
our consanguineous kin, they are our ancestors in Christ. This "Christian
ancestorship" of the saints is qualitatively different from that of the traditional African and surpasses all racial or any other natural distinctions.

   What are the implications of this ancestral christology? There is need
for the insistence on the central importance of the life of the grace of the
Spirit (traditionally known as sanctifying grace) in order to live our ancestral relationship with Christ and the saints, fully and authentically. Such
authentic ancestral relationship is impossible without frequent prayer,
devout reception of the sacraments (especially the Eucharist), together with
special devotion to the saints. Any racial or other discrimination is dia-
metrically opposed to ancestral kinship in Christ. Ancestral kinship with
Jesus is authentically lived by sincerely and perseveringly following Christ
the Ancestor in his universal love of God and humanity shown especially
by his ministry of evangelization (through words and deeds) and other forms
of service in the church, together with active engagement in the struggles
for peace, justice, and integral liberation, in view of the Kingdom of God.

AFRICAN CHRISTOLOGIES OF LIBERATION

   Christologies of liberation in Africa[14] correspond to the current trends
in African liberation theology. There are two kinds of such theology. The

first is generally known as *South African Black theology*, and is centred chiefly on the racial or colour factor (apartheid). It is linked with the North American Black theology, although it is gradually being influenced by Latin American theology of liberation. The second kind is simply called *African liberation theology*, found especially in independent sub-Saharan Africa. Its theological approach is broader than the one of South African Black theology, for it endeavours to integrate the theme of liberation into the rest of the African cultural background and is more affiliated to Latin American liberation theology. It is to this trend that African feminist theology (centred on the emancipation of women) chiefly belongs.

Generally speaking, South African Black christology and the christology of liberation in the rest of Africa have various features in common. In both cases the christology is from below, namely, the starting point is the man Jesus of Nazareth. Stress is put on the historical background and biblical texts concerning Him: Jesus lived in a society which was oppressed and exploited by the Romans. He was poor because of Roman exploitation and oppression. Hence, he was "black." It was his mission to fight against this poverty, oppression, and lack of freedom. Hence, texts such as Luke 4:18 are interpreted in this sense. Jesus died in this fight against oppression. But by raising him, God has shown that he was for him and with him in his struggle against oppression.

The Christians who fight against their oppression participate in Jesus' fight: they carry on his work of liberation and thus identify themselves with the "black Messiah" and with God's will. Just as he was with Jesus, God is also on the side of these oppressed Christians fighting for their liberation.

Black christology has many parallels with North American Black theology but differs from it in various aspects. Whereas North American Black theology is based chiefly on the *Black Power Movement*, South African theology starts from *Black Consciousness*. It affirms the positive value of blackness and denounces the christology of the traditional churches for their silence on the problem of apartheid and their presentation of a white Christ in favor of white oppressors. The American Black power movement is fundamentally secular in character, but South African Black consciousness is basically religious, grounded as it is on African traditional religiosity. However, it must be admitted that some Afro-American writers attempt to found their christology on the past religious experience of the American Blacks.[15] In many cases American black theology is one of revolution; South African theology is usually opposed to the use of violent means. In recent years some South African Black theologians tend more and more to integrate African traditional items in their theology, but North American Black theology can hardly do this.

Compared to South African Black christology, the liberation christology in independent sub-Saharan Africa is less developed and even less original. Yet, because of its broader perspective, it has a more promising future — all the more so now that women theologians pleading for a christology of emancipation for women have started raising their voices in this part of the continent.[16]

FINAL OBSERVATIONS

ASSESSMENT OF AFRICAN CHRISTOLOGIES

A careful comparative analysis reveals that just as the inculturation trend in theology is more frequent and better developed on the Black continent so also the African christologies of inculturation are, on the whole, more numerous and in many cases relatively more profound. Despite the positive results already achieved there still remains much to be done in order to ameliorate and affect African communities. There are strengths and weakness in these christologies. Some christological models have a future and their positive insights should be integrated into the life of African churches.

Strengths. To the sincere and unbiased reader many of the African christologies written so far must appear, in different degrees, as genuine creative contributions to African Christian theology, and not mere *prolegomena* to it. One has only to compare the contents of the symposium, *Les prêtres noirs s'interrogent* published in 1956 with the book *Chemins de la christologie africaine* written thirty years later.[17] In the first case French-speaking African theologians are speaking about the *possibility* of and *need* for African theology; in the latter case, they are actually building it.

Various factors are indicative of the originality of these christologies. Perhaps for the first time in the history of sub-Saharan Africa new African categories are systematically employed to express and expound upon the mystery of our Saviour: think of expressions such as "Christ the *integral healer, chief, elder-brother, master of initiation, ancestor, black messiah* (liberator), *plenitude of human maturity.*" It should be stressed that in order to better perceive the originality of these titles as applied to Christ one should take them in their African senses and should see them from the perspective of the African social cultural background from which they are taken.

All this is brought about by the new African points of departure from which the various writers envisage Christ's mystery. This is what conduces them to accentuate, in their own specific way, the different christological teachings implicit in the Bible, for example, Christ as victor, or as ancestral mediator, the cross as a mystery which inspires "discreet feasting and circumspect conviviality" and so forth. We are inevitably led to new theological problems and insights. Think of what is implied, for instance, in the affirmations that the Holy Spirit is the ancestral ritual Offer (Oblation) and Eucharist between the Father and the Son in the Trinity.

If one takes into account the teaching that all the Christian mysteries are organically interconnected (*nexus mysteriorum*) in such a way that it is possible to gain a deeper understanding of one particular mystery (in itself and its relevance for us) in the light of others,[18] then one must admit that the present African christologies have already opened the way not only to deeper African christologies and theologies in general, but also to an authentically African Christianity in all sectors of church life. An African christological statement such as "Christ is our Ancestor or Healer" (in the African sense) must have implications for our understanding of any other Christian mystery, including church life at all levels. In the measure that these christologies are truly Christian and African, they have something positive to contribute not only to African churches, but to the world church too.

Weaknesses. It is sometimes stated that in Africa there have been no christological studies comparable to those of Sobrino, Segundo, or Boff. One could rightly question the validity of this statement, especially when it is taken without qualification. It might be true with regard to liberation christologies, but there has been no Latin American inculturation christology that could claim to be better than its African counterparts. As with other theologies, today's African christologies stand in need of improvement. In many cases the approach to the sociocultural and theological elements involved is too narrow and superficial.

Several points need to be mentioned in connection with theological elaboration. The principle of interconnection of Christian mysteries whereby one or several mysteries can be interpreted in the light of the other(s) has already been alluded to. Few African writers make extensive use of this theologically fecund principle. Although any mystery can, in principle, be associated with any other revealed truth and be interpreted in terms of it, there are nonetheless two theological themes which should always be linked with any African christological elaboration. These are the Trinity and ecclesiology.

There are various reasons for the importance of trinitology for any christology. The first one is the primary importance of the *person* of Jesus Christ and the consequent *relevance* he has for us. Obviously, an African christologist must ask the question: Who is Christ for the African? But this question cannot be properly answered unless one knows first who Christ is *in himself.* For, the relevance and importance of a Christ who is both true God and true man is radically and essentially different from that of a Jesus who is a mere man, however perfect a man he might be. According to Scripture, Christ is, by definition, the only-begotten of the Father, who was sent by this same Father to save us in the power of the divine Spirit. To ignore or disregard any of these facts is to falsify the true picture of Jesus' personality and the consequent relevance he bears towards us. But such understanding of Christ plunges us immediately into the theology of the Trinity. Those who pretend to have interest in Christ but not in the Trinity are in fact interested in a false Christ, a Jesus who is not of the Bible — a mere Galilean villager or political revolutionary. But in such cases one could rightly ask: If Christ were a mere man, what is the foundation of his absolute claim for his message above all prophets and religious leaders?

Another reason for the significance of the Trinity for African christology is the centrality of the trinitarian mystery in Christian life and Gospel message. It is idle to give theological proofs for the truth that the central message and objective of Christian revelation is God's self-communication to us. What is meant by this is that the purpose of God's self-revelation is to make us sharers of his inner life, to make us partakers of his divine nature (2 Peter 1:4) by making us his true sons and daughters in his Son, through the power of the divine Spirit. Christian life is nothing but the living of the intrinsic claims of our quality as sons and daughters of *the Father*, and true brothers and sisters of *the Son* in *the Holy Spirit*. All truly profound theology must therefore be ultimately rooted in the Trinity—so much so that without this grounding it is bound to be radically superficial. Without the Trinity, Christ himself (and hence, christology) would lose his personality and *raison d'être*, for he is nothing but the revealer and communicator of his Father in the Spirit. Consequently, to ignore the Trinity is to manifest a radical misunderstanding of Christian life and Gospel message. It is useful to stress this issue since some African christologists explicitly affirm the nonrelevance of the Trinity for African christology. This is one of the great weaknesses of such christologies.[19]

Ecclesiology is another subject which should be inseparable from African christology. There are anthropological, theological, and pastoral reasons for this contention. To begin with, social or cultural anthropologists often tell us that community life is basically significant in African traditional societies; and the African categories (chief, elder-brother, initiator, healer, ancestor, liberator) ascribed to Christ by African writers are, for the African, unthinkable without their close relationship to human society. Hence, a christology which seeks to be in line with the African way of thinking must associate the Redeemer with the human community, that is, the church and humanity at large.

Furthermore, we know from theology that Christ the Head is incomplete without his Body, the church. This latter is even said to be the continuation of his incarnation in history. It follows from this that although a christology of Christ alone, a "christology of the Head without members"[20] is legitimate, it is nonetheless inadequate and is, to that extent, somehow deficient. Indeed, a "head without members" is an organism in its anomalous condition!

There are pastoral reasons to support the affirmation that ecclesiology should always be linked with African christology. In fact, unless our theology is going to affect positively the life of our church communities, our work is in vain. But it cannot affect them positively unless it is really relevant for their spiritual and bodily needs. There is no better way of constructing such relevant theology than by associating it directly with the theology of the church.

Inculturation christologies are more frequent and more developed than those of liberation in sub-Saharan Africa. This state of affairs might be an indication of lack of serious interest in the very actual and relevant problem of socio-economic and political subjugation on the part of many African writers, especially those belonging to the independent part of the continent. On the other hand, the relative inferiority of liberation christology to that of inculturation may be due, at least partly, to the narrower perspective from which it is elaborated. In both cases there is an obvious shortcoming to overcome—either through closer dialogue between the writers of the two trends, or through some kind of integration of the counter approach into one's own theology. In fact, all true and integral inculturation chris-tology must also be one of liberation, and vice versa.

Of all the African christologies there is none which has been constructed for didactic purposes in African seminaries or similar theological institutes. This is an important demand and should not be dismissed as irrelevant since "the age of using theological manuals is over . . ." Such christology raises special problems not yet solved, one of which is the presentation of *the whole of christology* found in the faith of the church from an African point of view.[21] Even if one is not convinced of the utility of christological textbooks today, one can hardly support arguments against the advantages of reflecting upon the entire christology from the perspective of African needs and mentality.

FUTURE CHRISTOLOGICAL MODELS

It is difficult to predict which christological models will remain and for how long in the future. It depends on unforeseen reasons and circum-stances, and such foretelling is more wish than prediction. The existing christological models in Africa are not exhaustive. In fact, the number of potential models is practically indefinite, and more are expected in the future.

The permanence of such theological models depends on several factors. The African element upon which a christological model is built must also be permanent. A theology which is founded on outdated or extinct cultural elements has no future. It is important to distinguish between universal permanent value underlying a cultural item and the outward manifestation of such value. Thus, healing practice has universal and lasting utility, but the manner of exercising such a function will always differ according to time and place. Likewise, it would be wrong to conclude that ancestral veneration has totally vanished in some given locality for the mere reason that it is no longer practiced in the same way as it was done before in that locality. The value behind a cultural trait is no guarantee of its future permanence, for experience shows that human societies have often lost and even rejected authentic human values.

The permanence of such cultural goods also depends on active commit-ment to maintain them in the community. Another condition for the per-manence of a theological model is the quality of the theology behind such a model. It is certain that a christology which is directly opposed to the solemnly defined teaching of the church has no future in the Roman Catholic Church. Similarly, a theology which has little or no originality and is irrelevant to the needs and mentality of the people cannot have a future.

In view of these observations one may say that, although one or several models will be stressed more than others in different times and places, all the christological models described previously are potentially permanent (depending, of course, on how the conditions given above are going to be fulfilled in each case). Such models as "Christ as Chief" or "Initiator" have a perpetual future, for although chiefship might no longer exist in some localities in its traditional form, human society will always need some kind of leadership from certain individuals. Moreover, Christ's Kingship, to which African chiefship is analogous, has everlasting permanence and will always require socio-cultural models for its theological expression. The same must be said with regard to the initiatic model. As M. Eliade has pointed out, initiation forms an integral part of human life and will always be present in one way or another. This is confirmed by the fact that initiatic motives are found in various ways even in the modern secular world which at first seems to be foreign to the notion of the sacred.[22]

The permanence or non-permanence of African christological models depends on the fulfillment of particular relevant tasks, such as: maintenance of the human and religious values underlying the African socio-cultural phenomena; integration of these values in today's African way of life; creation of christologies which are doctrinally sound, truly original, and genuinely relevant for the African needs and thought-forms.

AFRICAN CHRISTOLOGIES IN AFRICAN CHURCHES

With the exception, perhaps, of Black christology in South Africa, none of the existing African christologies has had any appreciable influence in the life of the African churches. There are various reasons for this lacuna. Many of these christologies are still unknown to the majority; and even where they are known they are seldom taken seriously. White theology still dominates in Africa, and in most seminaries and other theological institutes African christologies are either unknown or simply ignored. When known they are at best treated as an appendix—in summary form— to christologies from abroad. This may also be because many African christologies are still rudimentary; none of them could be taken as sufficiently profound and comprehensive to answer to the needs for christological teaching in seminaries. But the same might be said with regard to many of the christologies from abroad—which are, nonetheless, usually taken more seriously.

The channels through which African christologies could penetrate the churches have not yet been utilized. This is especially so with regard to catechesis, liturgy, theological institutes, and bishops' conferences.

All the christologies described previously can be said to be systematic or academic: they are the result of a critical and systematic reflection on the mystery of Christ in the light of African realities. But there are other ways of looking at African theology, and most probably there are more African christologies in churches than is generally acknowledged. Indeed, if African theology is the understanding and presentation of the Christ-event in accordance with African needs and mentality, then African christologies must have existed since the beginning of evangelization on the Black continent (although mainly in a latent, oral, and unsystematic form). Despite their predominantly Western way of theologizing, missionaries were often induced to present Christ's mystery to answer to the problems and ways of thinking of the African people. The people received that message in its Western form according to which it was delivered and also in accordance with their African experience. Therefore, serious scientific research of this subject in African Christian communities would reveal various authentically African christologies from which all could profit in many ways. The existence of similar christologies in today's African Independent churches confirms this hypothesis.[23]

African christologies can be gathered from African Christian communities by researchers living among such communities in close and sympathetic collaboration with them, so as to discover their understanding of Christ and his relevance to their current problems and aspirations. This method is regularly employed by some Latin American and other writers, with whom the African theologian could have profitable dialogue.[24] It would, however, be shortsighted to consider this theology from the grassroots as the only valuable type to the exclusion of systematic or academic theological discourse. Both have their specific strengths and limitations and, as such, need each other for useful mutual complementarity.

There are various channels through which the existing African christologies could be introduced into African churches. Among such channels, catechesis, liturgy, theological institutes, and bishops' conferences or synods are among the most appropriate. In this connection, therefore, there is urgent need for new African catechisms and liturgies into which the theology of African christologies should be inserted. These christologies should be taken more seriously and be regularly taught in seminaries and other theological colleges. This is all the more urgent because seminarians and other theology students are the future propagators of the Christian faith in the African communities. In order to better achieve this goal it is necessary to develop African christologies to a higher and more comprehensive level.

The most decisive step towards the acceptance of these christologies in churches will be reached when they are allowed to enter into the magisterial teaching of the Church. Hence, efforts should be made to allow them to influence, as far as possible, the doctrinal formulations of African bishops' conferences and synods. In this regard, the prospective African Synod has unique importance.

NOTES

1. J. Mbiti, "Afrikanische Beiträge zur Christologie," in P. Beyerhaus et al. (eds), *Theologische Stimmen aus Asien, Afrika und Lateinamerika*, vol. 3, Munich, 1968, pp. 72-85.

2. Kofi Appiah-Kubi, "Jesus Christ: Some christological aspects from African perspectives," in J. Mbiti (ed.), *African and Asian Contributions to Contemporary Theology* (report of a consultation held at the Ecumenical Institute, Bossey, 8-14 June, 1976), Geneva, 1977.

3. E. J. Pénoukou, "Realité africaine et salut en Jésus Christ," *Spiritus*, vol. 23, no. 88, December, 1982, pp. 374ff.; Pénoukou, "Christologie au village," in F. Kabasélé et al. (eds.), *Chemins de la christologie africaine* (Paris: Desclée, 1986), pp. 69-106.

4. Charles Nyamiti, "The Incarnation in the light of African understanding of personality," in *Christology from some African perspectives* (mimeo), CHIEA (Nairobi, 1984), pp. 138-253.

5. Notice that the expression "Christ is black" is used here in a different sense from that in Black theology of liberation, where it is taken to signify Christ as the oppressed.

6. H. Sawyerr, *Creative Evangelism: Toward a New Christian Encounter with Africa* (London, 1968), p. 72ff.

7. J. S. Pobee, *Toward an African Theology* (Nashville: Abingdon, 1979), pp. 81-98.

8. Kwesi A. Dickson, *Theology in Africa* (Maryknoll, N.Y.: Orbis, 1984), pp. 185-99.

9. A. T. Sanon, "Jésus, Maître d'initiation," in F. Kabasélé et al. (eds.) *Chemins de la christologie africaine*, pp. 143-166; *Enraciner l'évangile: initiations africaines et pedagogie de la foi* (Paris, 1982).

10. Aylward Shorter, *Jesus and the Witchdoctor. An approach to healing and wholeness* (London, N.Y., 1985); "Christian healing and traditional medicine in Africa," *Kerygma*, 20 (1986), pp. 51-58.

11. Previous to *Jesus and the Witchdoctor*, Shorter published an article in which he pleaded for a functional christology of two types:

(a) Liturgical: presenting Christ as Lord of life in the Eucharist, which is the feast of life and through which the life of the Spirit is continually imparted to the community.

(b) Christ as *Nganga* (doctor-diviner, healer, medicine-man). Such stress is confirmed by some modern African literature and tendencies of "folk Christianity" and independent churches in which such christology appears. See "Folk Christianity and Functional Christology," *AFER* (June 1982), pp. 133ff.

12. B. Bujo, "Pour une éthique africano-christocentrique," *Bulletin de la théologie africaine*, vol. 3, no. 5 (January-June), Kinshasa, 1981, pp. 41-52; "A Christocentric ethic for black Africa," *Theology Digest*, vol. 30, no. 2 (1982), pp. 143-46; *Afrikanische Theologie: in ihrem gesellschaftlichen Kontext* (*Theologie Interkulturell*, vol. 1) (Düsseldorf, 1986), pp. 79-137.

13. C. Nyamiti, *Christ as Our Ancestor: Christology from an African perspective* (Gweru, Zimbabwe, 1984); "Ancestral Kinship in the Trinity: an African theology of the Trinity," in *Inculturation: working papers on living faith and cultures* (effective

inculturation and ethnic identity, vol. IX) (Rome, 1987), pp. 29-48; "The Mass as divine and ancestral encounter between the living and the dead," in *African Christian Studies*, CHIEA, Nairobi (August 1985), pp. 28-48; "Uganda Martyrs: ancestors of mankind," ibid. (July 1986), pp. 41-66; "African tradition and the Christian God," *Spearhead*, no. 49, Gaba Publications, Eldoret, Kenya, 1977.

More writers than those mentioned here have written on ancestral christology. Among these the following may be mentioned: F. Kabasélé, "Le Christ comme Ancêtre et Aîné" in F. Kabasélé et al. (eds.), *Chemins de la christologie africaine*, pp. 127-41; H. Rücker, *Afrikanische Theologie Darstellung und Dialog* (Innsbruck-Vienna, 1985), pp. 171-72; J. Mutiso-Mbinda, "Anthropology and the paschal mystery," *Spearhead*, no. 59, p. 52; E. Sambou, "Rencontre et altérité: enjeu d'un christianisme en milieu Joola," *Bulletin de litterature écclesiastique*, 85/3 (July-September, 1984), Toulouse, France, pp. 220-49 (summary of doctoral diss.); M. Ntetem, *Die Negro-Afrikanische Stammesinitiation* (Münsterschwarzach, 1983), pp. 272ff; A. T. Sanon, *Tierce Eglise, ma mère ou la conversion d'une communaté païenne au Christ* (mimeo: doctoral diss.) (Paris, 1970), pp. 170-72.

14. T. Sundermeier (ed.), *Christus der schwarze Befreier* (Erlangen, 1973); *Zwischen Kultur und Politik* (Hamburg, 1978); B. Chenu, *Theologies chrétiennes des tiers mondes. Théologies latino-americaine, noire americaine, noire sur-africaine, asiatique* (Paris, 1987), pp. 91-121; J. U. Young, *Black and African Theologies: Siblings or Distant Cousins?* (Maryknoll, N.Y.: Orbis, 1986), pp. 62ff.; B. Kabongo, "Jesus dans les théologies sud-africaines," in F. Kabasélé et al. (eds.), *Chemins de la christologie africaine*, pp. 299-311; T. A. Mofokeng, *The Crucified Among the Crossbearers: Towards a Black Christology* (doctoral diss.) (Kampen, Holland, 1983); B. Moore (ed.), *Black Theology. The South African Voice* (London, 1973); A. A. Boesak, *Farewell to Innocence* (Kampen, Holland, 1976); H. J. Becken, *Relevant Theology for Africa* (Durban, 1973); S. Biko, *Black Viewpoint* (Durban, 1972); M. Mothlabi (ed.), *Essays on Black Theology* (Johannesburg, 1972); M. Buthelezi, "Violence and the Cross in South Africa," *Journal of Theology for Southern Africa* (December 1979); R. Vander Gucht, "Théologie engagée et lutte des noirs en Afrique du sud," *Telema*, Kinshasa (July-December 1988), pp. 59-72; G. H. Muzorewa, *The Origins and Development of African Theology* (Maryknoll, N. Y.: Orbis, 1985), pp. 101-13; V. Salvodi and R. K. Sesana, Africa: *The Gospel Belongs to Us* (Ndola, Zambia, 1986).

15. See J. U. Young, *Black and African Theologies: Siblings or Distant Cousins?*, pp. 31ff.

16. Virginia Fabella and Mercy Amba Oduyoye, *With Passion and Compassion: Third World Women Doing Theology* (Maryknoll, N. Y.: Orbis, 1988), especially pp. 3-65; Mercy Amba Oduyoye, *Hearing and Knowing: Theological Reflections on Christianity in Africa* (Maryknoll, N. Y.: Orbis, 1986). Recently some South African women have also raised their voices in the same sense (cf. R. Vander Gucht, "Théologie engagée et lutte der noirs en Afrique du sud," pp. 69f.); see also Constance Baratang Thetele, "Women in South Africa: The WAAICC," in K. Appiah-Kubi and S. Torres (eds.), *African Theology en Route* (Maryknoll, N. Y.: Orbis, 1979), pp. 150-54.

17. Other African christological writings include: R. Moloney, "African Christology," *Theological Studies*, 48 (1987), pp. 505-15; B. Chenu, *Theologies chrétiennes des tiers mondes*, pp. 151-59; P. Stadler, "Christological Approaches in Africa," *Theology Digest*, 31, no. 3, (1984), pp. 219–22; J. Parrat, *A Reader in African Christian*

Theology (London, 1987), pp. 69-79, 106-7, 156-58, and passim; R. Dain and J. V. Diepen, *Luke's Gospel for Africa Today* (Dar es Salaam-Lusaka-Addis Ababa, 1975); C. Nyamiti, "Christ's resurrection in the light of African tribal initiation ritual," in *RAT* vol. 3, no. 6, Kinshasa (1979), pp. 171-84, "Christ's ministry in the light of African tribal initiation ritual," *African Christian Studies*, CHIEA, Nairobi (March 1987), pp. 65-87; "The naming ceremony in the Trinity," ibid. (March 1988), pp. 41-73, and November 1988, pp. 55-83; E. M. Metogo, "La personne du Christ dans l'oeuvre de Mongo Beti," *Chemins de christologie africaine*, pp. 43-67; C. Kolié. "Jésus Guerisseur?," ibid., pp. 167-99; F. Kabasélé, "Jésus au-delà des modèles," ibid., pp. 203-28; "Christ dans l'actualité de nos communautés," ibid., pp. 273-72; A. V. Mbadu Kwalu, "Dieu connu en Jésus-Christ: une approche paulinienne d'après l'epître aux Romains," ibid., pp. 229-46; J. Hitimana, "Evangile et liberation: la pensée de Jean-Marc Ela," ibid., pp. 249-61; A. Quattara, "Les jeunes parlent de Jésus," ibid., pp. 273-87; B. Goba, "Jésus Christ mort pour nos péchés ressuscité pour notre vie" *Spiritus*, vol. 24, no. 90 (February 1983), pp. 55ff; P. N. Wachege, "Christ Our Elder: A christological study from the Kikuyu concept of elder," mimeographed thesis, CHIEA, Nairobi, 1986; G. W. Lumbasi; "Christ's Role in Christian Marriage: With reference to marriage customs among the Babukusu of Western Kenya," mimeographed thesis, CHIEA, Nairobi, 1986; S. Ssekmanda, "Christ our 'Kabaka': A christology from the Ganda perspective," mimeographed thesis, CHIEA, Nairobi, 1988.

18. DS 3016; Vatican II: *Optatam totius*, p. 16, 19.

19. See J. Bukasa Kabongo, "Jésus dans les théologies sud-africaines," p. 308. In his own way B. Bujo minimizes the central importance of the Trinity in the ancestral christology which he develops in an original, though still rudimentary, manner. This is first shown by his rejection of the application of the term *Ancestor* to God (cf. his book, *Afrikanische Theologie . . .*, p. 91, fn. 25) — a rejection which is not only incompatible with anthropological data (cf. among many others, H. Gravrand, *Meeting the African Religions* [Rome, 1968], p. 28), but is also unacceptable in the face of systematic theological reasoning (see Nyamiti "Ancestral Kinship in the Trinity," p. 31ff.), to which the author gives no direct answer. One would, moreover, wish a more developed trinitarian theology than the one he presents in his book in connection with his ancestral christology (ibid., pp. 91-93, 101-2).

It is also astonishing that Bujo rejects the application of the term *ancestor* to the saints (ibid.) without any direct counterevidence to the arguments, which are proposed to support such application (see Nyamiti, *Christ as Our Ancestor*, pp. 103f., and passim). Indeed, if Christ's divine Sonship can be shared with us, why not his Ancestorship? And if the saints participate in his Ancestorship (or ancestral mediation), why can they not be called our ancestors (or ancestral mediators) in Christ? What theological status does Bujo attribute to the African traditional ancestors? Is their status not linked in any way with that of Christ, the "proto-Ancestor"? Is Christ's Ancestorship not intimately linked with the church, of which the saints (including the African "saintly" ancestors) are members? Bujo gives no answer to these questions which are, nevertheless, very relevant for his subject.

20. Nyamiti, *Christ as our Ancestor*, p. 82.

21. For more details on this issue the reader is referred to Nyamiti, *The Scope of African Theology*, Gaba Publications, no. 30 (Eldoret, Kenya, 1973), pp. 33-38.

22. M. Eliade, "L'initiation et le monde moderne," *Initiation* (*Studies in the History of Religions*) vol. 10 (Leiden, Brill, 1965), pp. 1-14.

23. See also V. Salvoldi and R. K. Sesana, *Africa: The Gospel Belongs to Us*, pp. 114ff.

24. In this connection it is useful to note that after accepting the existence of the theology of inculturation, Black theology, and liberation theology in sub-Saharan Africa, V. Salvodi and R. K. Sesana add another kind of African theology which they call the *theology of community development*. It is, according to them,

the theology which provides the theoretical basis for pastoral action in the basic communities and the conscientization of development. The most important representatives of this current line of thought are figures similar to patristic times, that is they are bishops directly involved in pastoral work and their theology is a response to the problems they meet in their everyday life as pastors.

Among such pastors the authors mention bishops Sarpong, Sanon, Malula, Mwoleka, Kalilombe, and others. They also point out that the AMECEA Pastoral Institute with its famous publications and the South African Lumko Pastoral Institute are two important sources for this type of theology, ibid., pp. 119-20.

2

Christology in the Village

EFOÉ JULIEN PÉNOUKOU

PRELIMINARY CONSIDERATIONS

THE CHRIST OF MY UNCLE

I had returned to my native village, to prepare this essay in christology in contact with Christian friends of mine, people of the land. One morning, as I was just sitting down to put a semblance of order into my notes, I received an unexpected visit from a maternal great-uncle, seventy-five years of age, a convert to Christianity, baptized a half-century ago and "practicing" ever since. Long did I listen to his explanation of the object of his visit; then I mentioned that I was about to "do a white person's paper" (read: write a paper), and that he could certainly help me. He had scarcely recovered from his astonishment when I asked him the following question: "Uncle, you are a Christian. Who is Jesus for you?" Here is an extract of his brief, spontaneous reply, which I took care to record on tape, literally translated from the Mina.

> Jesus
> is really someone [an identifiable person]
> for me,
> savior (*hlwengan*)
> in solidarity and savior of the world,
> come to tell us that God, who has created us,
> has sent him for us.
> We had once been on the road
> to perdition,
> in the devil's hands.
> He showed us the whole road to follow

to be saved.
We are sure of this;
we have placed our faith in it;
we have learned and understood it
in this way.
He came to witness to truth here,
and not the lie
as the devil does.
He is the person of truth.

A christological profession, if ever there was one. Without anything like "scholarly" research behind it, of course, and therefore authorizing no immediate conclusion. Nevertheless, Uncle's reply suggests a number of remarks.

Let us begin with an observation. In Uncle's statement, the initial christological datum bears less on the being of Jesus Christ as such (sometimes called his "nature" or his "person") than on the kind of relationship that his coming establishes with the human being for the "destiny" of that human being. In this perspective, we are dealing not with titles, but rather with a type of relation, of function, of activity of Jesus Christ . Here let us notice the expressions, "Jesus is truly someone for me," "savior," "in solidarity," "come to tell us," "has shown us the way to follow," "come to witness to truth here," and so on.

In Ewe-Mina society, which will concern us a great deal in this study, being is not thought of primarily in terms of essence, substance, nature, and idea, nor so much in terms of history and time as happens more in the West since Heidegger, but basically in terms of a relationship of community and solidarity. In other words, being is not so much contemplated as a speculative mystery, but is unveiled in its "to be there with," in an encounter which allows for wonder, the unthinkable, the unexpected, mystery.

Once we have been willing to posit the christological question in a perspective of relation, it will no longer be reducible simply to the identity or entity of Jesus Christ. Now it will have to be defined as relationship with others, as a mode of being-in-relation in the overall dynamics of salvation history. Thus, Jesus Christ is important not only by reason of his function, or what he has done "for us men and for our salvation," but also for his position in the mystery of the trinitarian, communitarian God. Here let us note Uncle's observation, "God, who has created us, sent him for us." As we know, an African will readily speak of an essentially relational God, a God in solidarity, rather than of a solitary one. Christology above all, then, will be primarily trinitarian and ecclesial.

The problem of the diversity of theological language, naturally, is a problem first and foremost for the christological fact. Even the Gospel traditions, while they are from the same cultural milieu, each present their own christology. Furthermore, even with one and the same author, the apostle Paul, christological reflection develops and changes, from the early letters to the post-Pauline tradition. How much more, then, will a variety of individual mentalities and cultural sensibilities not only entail a christological pluralism, but contribute new elements and explanations, calculated to enhance one's grasp of the person of Christ. For the Christian communities of Africa, this is a basic question. After all, a christological faith can acquire authenticity and maturity only to the extent that it takes root in the depths of a particular cultural development, thereupon to be re-expressed in an original language.

IDENTIFYING THE OBJECT OF BELIEF

My uncle's profession of faith is, as we see, a classical one. It is very orthodox. We find the same basic profession among many African Christians. The fact remains, however, that there are still many among us who do not succeed in expressing for themselves just what Jesus Christ is for them, what his genuine position is in the mysterious world of the spirits— how to name him, not with a name common to the spirits, but in his particularity, in his primacy over all other powers, visible and invisible (cf. Col. 1:16). We are dealing with a drama of faith—with the interior torment of these hearts seized by Christ and seeking in vain to grasp him in turn (Phil. 3:12-13). But the African case, overall, is not primarily (although it is this ultimately) a problem of "spiritual progress," of deeper faith. Primarily it presents the basic question of identification or authentification of the object "believed."

Indeed, what poses a problem for us in Africa is not so much faith in Christ as Jesus Christ himself, in his proper being, his unique, singular character (cf. 1 Tim. 2:6). Are we saying that Africans, described by some as "incurably religious," would be inclined to believe in anything at all in any way they please, so that in the case at hand it would be indifferent to them in what Christ they believe? Surely not, unless we mean to elevate a psychologizing subjectivism into the determining criterion of truth to be believed. We are only saying that a person who claims to believe in Christ, yet has recourse to other spiritual, cosmic, or metacosmic forces, has not yet succeeded in identifying who Jesus Christ is, that he or she may profess him radically. This is why, for so many baptized Africans, the data of faith will have to be freed not only from the formulations or categories—however legitimate—of other cultures, but also from certain traditional religious conceptions of our own—from anything that sterilizes the maturation of the life of faith among us.

The christological question is vast and complex. But precisely for this reason, it offers various methodological opportunities. It presents, as we say in the village, several heads and several mouths—that is, one does not quite know where to grasp it.

We could begin with the New Testament, and its list of christological titles, and supply a more or less original commentary as we pass them in review.[1] Or our method might consist in researching the underlying schemata of these same christological titles.[2] Another approach, the historico-kerygmatic, would trace the christology of the New Testament through the various stages of its development.[3] And so on. All of these approaches offer their manifest advantages, if only that of helping us to discern the basic christological data. But precisely by reason of the particular experiences upon which they are based, as also in view of the identity of the respective addressees of the various christologies of the New Testament, these data could be concretely pertinent to us Africans only upon our attainment and incorporation of our own experience of faith in Christ.

On the level of the *history of dogmas,* we could begin with the dogmatic syntheses of the great christological councils. Here again, perhaps we would construct a lengthy commentary on the christology of the patristic churches, issuing in an attempt to take a position within the parameters of a flawless orthodox christology. The attempt would be a laudable, comforting one, surely, but one that, in and of itself, would not necessarily open new perspectives calculated to further the maturation, *hic et nunc,* of the faith of us Africans in Christ.

A final approach might be by way of *current christological perspectives,* with their various tendencies or schools, as reported, for example, by the Pontifical Biblical Commission in an official document.[4] Here we would review the contemporary studies of Jesus Christ—theological treatments constituting various attempts to reread, in function of the signs of the times, the basic christological data. The methodological originality and quality of this undertaking would be of interest to us in that they would confirm, should such confirmation still be needed, the importance of our treating the christological question in function of the signs of the African times—that is, in function of the expectations and demands of our cultures.

Therefore, the christological treatment proposed here will take its point of departure in a basic anthropological datum, proper to a number of African societies, that perceives and conceives comprehensive reality as a continuous passage from life to death and from death to life. Our next task will be to see how such an anthropological datum is open to an articulation with the event of the death-and-resurrection of Jesus. This theological confrontation should be a help in the development of models calculated to package the identity of Christ in a language proper to African Christians.

But then why begin precisely with this African anthropological fact, which perceives existence as a whole as life/death/life, and with the event of Jesus' death-and-resurrection, to construct our theological discourse? Far from being arbitrary, this twofold resource contacts basic data on both sides. As we shall presently explain, in black Africa, death and life represent the determining poles about which all cultural and religious elaborations revolve in concert; and as we know, on our continent the life of the dead appears at all important steps of human existence. For that matter, the foundation of Christian faith is none other than the resurrection of the Crucified One.[5] And the oldest professions of faith are often limited to the twin fact of the Crucified and the Risen One, constituted by God as Lord and Christ. It is understandable, then, that Paul, in a very early passage, written around Easter of the year 57, should unequivocally assert: "If Christ is not risen, then is our preaching vain, and vain too our faith" (1 Cor. 15:14). Could there be a more appropriate christological undertaking than this, that from a starting point in the anthropological fact of life/death/life, we effect a confrontation with the event of the death-and-resurrection of Jesus Christ?

UTTERING THE SAME FAITH DIFFERENTLY

Precisely at this level of preliminary considerations, I should like to make three brief remarks that I hope will preclude possible mistaken notions regarding my enterprise and perspectives, and thereby reassure certain theologians who might otherwise have misgivings as to the same.

Our proposition to begin from the anthropological phenomenon, with a view to an original encounter with the Jesus Christ event, in no way implies that the latter is to be determined by the former. In other words, we know full well that the object to be believed is not to be gauged by the yardstick of anthropological data, or of any other cultural elaboration. Our proposition is to attempt to discover and articulate the interrogations and aspirations imbedded in a precise anthropological datum with a view to investing them in the salvation project of the Crucified Risen One. The goal of a like undertaking is not, then, to reduce the content of faith in Christ to human questions, but rather to begin with the latter in a concrete enterprise of conversion, of actual questioning, of these human questions. Our intent is an undertaking ultimately opening out upon the infinite Hope of the Risen One. That is to say, here as elsewhere, the decisive criterion of judgment is not our cultural legacy, but the Word made flesh.

The christological questions sketched here make no pretense to any radical originality, such as might be awaited by those who, with eagerness or annoyance, always expect an African theological project to display its novelty and its particularity. (We have already had the occasion to remark, in this regard, that "many viewpoints presented as African are actually European imports, and maintain with authentic African traditions far more slender ties than with classic Christian tradition. . . ."[6]) Such an unfortunate judgment remains to be verified in a particular case. But it may of itself incline its subject to a double contempt. It may lead one to think, on the one hand, that African theologizing ought necessarily to issue in the unprecedented and unheard of; and on the other, that, in the space of a quarter century, theological thought in Africa ought to have reached the maturity of that of the two-thousand-year-old churches of the Greco-Latin cultures. African theology is in the midst of its birthpangs; and it seeks to utter nothing other than what God, in the Son to whom God bequeaths all, has definitively uttered to the whole of humanity (cf. Heb. 1:2).

Finally, while one can no longer speak of "Africans" in general, or of "African tradition" in a pure state (despite its evident diversity and complexity, and in the face of profound current mutations), black Africa does exhibit certain constant data and represents a more and more precise cultural and historical entity. As the well-known historian J. Ki-Zerbo would say, put the Serer and the Lobi with Lubas and Zulus, and you may see a mixed group; but put that group side by side with Swedes or Greeks and you will see at once how akin they are. In the name of a like observation, while we shall occasionally speak of "Africans" or "African values" in this study, we shall do so with all of the reserves of usage implied in such an "unscientific" generalization.

THE INSTANCES OF FULFILLMENT OF BEING-THERE-WITH: LIFE/DEATH/LIFE

In a consumer civilization, life is regarded as bereft of an eschatological future, for the simple reason that it is inexorably condemned to death, and hence to absurdity and nothingness. Elsewhere the case is different—in Africa, for example. Here life is perceived as extending beyond death, and death is conceived as a sure passage to life. Nor are we dealing with a simple belief—some vague, ludicrous phantasm or other. No, this is a profound conviction, that structures the vision of things—of the universe, of human persons, and of spiritual beings. Thus, comprehensive reality generally makes its appearance, here and there, as a living organism, in the pangs of perpetual birthgiving, and this by way of the successive phases of birth, degeneration, and regeneration. I qualify these phases of life/death/life (for reasons that will be made explicit in the course of this study) as instances of fulfillment of being-there-with. In the present case, I see a kind of ontological connector or crucible in which the human being unfolds, feeds, and matures, within the cosmotheandric relationship.[7]

I should like to begin with the Ewe-Mina ethnosocial group of the South of Togo (and, of the South of Benin, in part) and systematize such a basic anthropological datum in order to see how, in its assertion of the ultimate primacy of life over death, it might point us toward a more or less particular christological language.

THE MYTH OF BOMYNEN: OF THE CIRCULATION OF BEING

Is not the best way to speak of a basic anthropological datum to refer to the foundation of all word, that of the first beginnings, that of the primordial time upon which myth bears? For the topic concerning us here, the Ewe-Mina have, among other myths, one on the original process of accomplishment of being-there-with: the myth of Bomynen.

Bomynen, the resident (ne) of a prenatal universe (Bomy), is a spiritual personage to whom the creator of all things (Mawu) has entrusted the task of introducing into the earthly world the "human being's little ones." The latter already exist in this prenatal universe (Bomy), waiting to be "released" upon the orbit of existential history. In order to release one, Bomynen introduces a miniature human being (Agbe-te) into the belly of woman (nyenu b'adeny). But human beings are sent here below for a limited time; they must one day return to the country of their origin, passing through the belly of the earth (e la to anyigban my).

One is struck at once, in the structure of this extraordinarily suggestive myth, that it presents three persons in three spaces, and that it establishes the very prototype of relation that has sometimes been called cosmotheandric.

The Supreme Being (Mawu), the spiritual being (Bomynen), and the human being (Agbete) represent the three personages, while Bomy is the womb of Woman and Earth is constituted by the three spaces. Here we have a system, essentially African, of relation by interposition, which always establishes, between two distant instances, an organic Medium. Here, Bomynen is the intermediary between Mawu and Agbete. As for the womb of Woman, it mediates Bomy and Earth.

The medium in question is organic in the sense that it belongs to both spheres of the instances that it interlinks. Bomynen is perceived as "divinity," that is, as being close to the Supreme Being, which it now renders close to the human being. Woman belongs to the same sphere as Bomy, inasmuch as she represents a locus of fecundation and procreation by Mawu (the Supreme Being), who, the Fons of the South of Benin say, is the engenderment of the theogamic couple Mawu-Lissa. But we also know that several African myths identify Woman with the nourishing Mother Earth.[8] We already surmise a conception of *mediation in solidarity,* which develops here within a cosmotheandric relation: it is the Supreme Being, Mawu, who conceives and unleashes upon the world of spirits the process of the creation of the human being. This human being is obviously at the center of the mythic account. Everything develops around and for the human being, who ranges from end to end in an all-encompassing socio-cosmic universe including Bomy (of the world of spirits), the earth (of the world of things), and Woman (of the world of humans).

These are general considerations, rather too hasty, owing to the restricted framework of this study, but capable of leading us to the discovery of a series of three basic data. To be *credible,* the latter must be verified at other levels of the Ewe-Mina cultural space. More precisely, we shall have to apply here the principle of coherence, or constancy of meaning and show that the data observed in the myth are found elsewhere, in the same cultural area—find the same segments of sense at some anthropological level or other, which will then justify an adequate theological confrontation. The three basic data that emerge from this myth bear on the human being as a being in course of fulfillment; this being's ontological dependence; and finally, this being's eschatological dimension.

THE HUMAN BEING, A BEING ON THE WAY TO COMPLETION

First, we must recall that the myth of Bomynen is primarily a thanatogenic myth—an attempt at a genetic and topological reading of the fact of death. Death is perceived here as a normal passage of human existence, a natural, organic fact, constitutive of human destiny. Through a like vision of death, not only does an outline of the notion of life appear, but a conception of the human being, as well. It is the human being, called to life but prey to death, who is the ultimate object of this myth. This human being is presented here as a project of being, in course of ontological development. Created by Mawu, the human being is immediately invested in a process of hominization, marked by passages, existential leaps, factors of ontological maturation. So true is this interpretation of the myth of Bomynen that a naive, immature person (the incomplete, uncompleted person) is referred to colloquially as a Bomycite—someone who has remained in Bomy, the prenatal universe, and who on this account has not achieved a certain maturity of being.

In other words, in order to become a completed human (unsu), one must pass from Bomy to the world of humans by the belly of Woman, then from the world of humans to the world of the Ancestors (completed human beings par excellence) through the belly of Earth. The womb of Woman and the womb of Earth here represent death passages—in which, nevertheless, life is fertilized.[9] These successive deaths introduce being-human into successively higher degrees of completion. The human being is completed only in passing from life to death, for a better life.

We are dealing with a fundamental conviction that permeates various elaborations of Ewe-Mina sociocultural space. First, in the face of death itself, the rites and the various literary sources (hymns, mythic accounts, funeral stories and legends) all intimate how a "good death" (ku nywyn), especially in the case of the aged, leads human beings to their true dwelling. As a familiar proverb has it: "We are only here on business; we hail from the land of the dead." Indeed, a number of funeral ceremonies, being "weddings of death," obviously indicate that we are dealing with an inevitable passage to life, to a finished, fulfilled life. That protection, health, success, and prosperity in all things, and so on, are besought of the Ancestors, that certain Ancestors are even exalted into "Vodus,"[10] which confers on them a superior status to that of ordinary mortals—these are all acts of faith not only in human beings' immortality, but also in their ontological completion beyond death.

The same notion, once more, prevails in the rites of passage, or initiatory integration of the individual. For example, in the Ewe-Mina country of Togo, and in several regions of the South of Benin, the initiation, performed in Vodu convents, to the worship of a particular Vodu is conferred and experienced as a passage from the life of a noninitiate (ahe) to that, deemed better, of an initiate, one consecrated to the Vodu (Vodusi). To this purpose, the initiation process comports a series of interruptions, seen as deaths to the old profane life — passages to the new status that constitutes the *Vodusi.*

First comes a monastic seclusion, which, elsewhere, can be in the furthest part of a sacred wood, and signifies a breach with the social group. This is followed by other breaches introducing radical changes. For example, at the term of his course of initiation, the candidate will have definitively changed his name (one's name being a factor of one's identification and being-there-with), will temporarily speak a dialect of the initiated, and will be marked for all time with tatoos indicating that he belongs to this particular Vodu, to whom he will have been taught, by dint of ascetic trials, to offer adequate worship. Never again will the candidate be or live as before. This death to the old human being, and rebirth as a new one, is occasionally expressed by a rite simulating death, symbolically marking the passage of the candidate to another type of vital relationship. Change of life, in this case the maturation of the religious life, is effected by way of a passage through death, which, here as elsewhere, appears as a factor of reparturition. L. V. Thomas writes:

> Initiation always involves a putting to death, followed by a resurrection, ritually played out and represented collectively. As G. Balandier emphasizes, initiation presents itself as an institution that allows a symbolic dying with a view to rebirth, or rather, rebirth to a kind of fullness.[11]

This entire anthropological datum can lead to a tentative twofold conclusion:

First, being-human is not a static datum, but a historical becoming, and takes the form of a dynamic project. This project of being places the human subject in a state of striving for an increase in life. Several religious developments, for example a number of rites of appropriation of spiritual and cosmic forces, or of participation in their dynamism, represent attempts on the part of the Ewe-Mina human being to become mature, to become full and complete.

Second, both life and the death that assaults it represent, however differently, precise instances of ontological completion. They are not fortuitous or gratuitous phenomena, but constitutive data of the maturity of being.

ONTOLOGICAL DEPENDENCE OF THE HUMAN BEING

The myth unequivocally indicates that human beings are first of all dependent on Mawu, the Supreme Being who has created them and entrusted them to Bomynen. It is the creator who has taken the initiative of calling them to life, of causing their being to be born, of conferring upon them an existence. The myth of Bomynen thus evokes a profound conviction anchored in African mentalities, as we may say without risk of abusive generalization. Everywhere in so-called traditional Africa, the sense of the existence of a Supreme Being—the orderer of all things, as the Ewe-Mina say awu (Mye do enu wo kpata)—always goes hand in hand with an awareness of one's total dependence on that being. That human beings owe their existence to the Master of Destiny (Sê) has become a commonplace, as has the familiar tendency to call on the Supreme Being in all circumstances, to form theophoric names, and so on—all of these expressions representing attitudes of the human being's profound recognition of dependency on the Supreme Being.

But we must go beyond these banal propositions, radical though they may be, and attempt to formulate more precisely the meaning of this awareness of ontological dependency, that first foundation of the celebrated African religiousness. Let us return, then, to the myth of Bomynen, this pointillistic discourse which, like all mythic language, is the image of the semantics of a reality, and of a comprehensive conduct. The structure of the account indicates from the outset that the Supreme Being simultaneously proposes and disposes the becoming of the human being within a network of constitutive relations. Simultaneously, the ontological dependence of which there is question here is defined first and foremost in terms of fundamental relationships.

This means two things. First, not only do human beings owe their being to the Supreme Being, but also, and especially, they can fulfill themselves only by entering into a dynamics of relations with their Creator, only in becoming and remaining a *being-there-with the Supreme Being*. The second thing that the myth explicitly suggests bears on the intermediate relationships that are necessary if human beings are to realize this historical becoming of theirs which has been projected, cast forth, by their creator. In other words, the human being can become complete only in becoming a *being-there-with others*.

The first intermediate relationship in question is of a spiritual order here. Nor is this fortuitous. We are dealing with a relation already binding the "human being's little one" to Bomynen—that is, to the world of spirits. A twin conviction surfaces here. First is the indispensable intermediary role of spiritual beings. Next, especially, is the conviction that these spiritual beings have been constituted and instituted as intermediaries precisely by the Supreme Being. Here, as we might well imagine, we have the ideological foundation of various Ewe-Mina, or even African, elaborations. But a like conception of the spirits' role and relations with the world does not, as we shall see below, always represent an intrinsic value for a more radical faith in Christ—although the notion of intermediary, and hence of mediation, can be put to good use in a christological reflection that would lay claim to some degree of originality.

The myth of Bomynen also underscores the human being's dependence on the *world of human beings and the world of things* — a dependency on the belly of Woman and the belly of Earth. We have already noted the analogical relationship between Woman and Earth. That the life of the human being enters history by the intermediary of Woman, and that this human being cannot nourish that life without Earth, scarcely constitutes an object of debate. The profound meaning of this assertion bears rather on a mode of relation here — a community of destiny, which promotes comprehensive reality to the status of a harmonious system. At this level, we can speak more of a reciprocal dependency — or better, a solidarity in the same historical becoming. Here we touch on the dominant notion of a number of foundational accounts: the organic order of all things at the beginning of time, their disharmonious disturbance by the arrival of evil, and subsequently the attempts of worship and rites to rediscover the original balance.

Becoming a completed human being does not commence with a preliminary decision on individuals' part, but on an initial project ever anticipating them and unceasingly constituting them in the historical unfolding of their being. The Ewe-Mina are aware that the truth of human beings, of their origin and their destiny, always come to them from without. The bustle of their dealings, often in such anxiety, with fortune-tellers and soothsayers of all kinds indicate the extent of the conviction that human beings do not build their own truth.

Just so, becoming a complete human being could never be the deed of a single individual. It must consist in the conformity of the individual's being-human to the project of being established by the Supreme Being, which is a basically communitarian project of being. Here as elsewhere in Africa, becoming a "person," that is, a responsible, complete subject, is not an individualistic act, but a common project, the relationship of a commitment of solidarity in being-in-history to those who share the same becoming. By conforming to the laws and customs of the group, by consciously interiorizing the group's religious, moral, and human values, individuals ensure the coherence and cohesion of a society that will now assist them to assume their particular destinies — destinies whose eschatological dimension we must now ponder.

ESCHATOLOGICAL DIMENSION OF PERSON AND HISTORY

It is often uncomfortable to qualify a datum before having delineated its content, especially when one is obliged to express that content in a foreign tongue. This is the case with what we shall refer to as the "eschatological dimension" in the Ewe-Mina culture.

In all etymological rigor, "eschatology" denotes a discourse or doctrine on the last things. But the Greek *eschatos* as used in the Bible does not seem always to have rendered the exact sense of the Hebrew or Aramaic expressions vis-à-vis future perspectives.[12] To my view, it would be poor method to begin with an attempt to define the content of the biblical and Greek eschatologies, before posing the problem in African terms. We ought rather to begin with an inquiry into the ultimate becoming of human beings and their universe according to the Ewe-Mina view of history, and only then address the question whether such a view can be a locus of christological reflection.

To this purpose, let us turn once more to the myth of Bomynen. There, from the outset, we have the proposition of a kind of prenatal universe (Bomy), inhabited by spiritual personages in immediate rapport with the Supreme Being. This prenatal universe is thereupon perceived as the place of the birth and transmission of human life. Then the myth speaks of a "here below," where human beings merely sojourn, having one day to return to a "beyond" that is specified as their "country of origin."

The interpretation of this myth has led us—in considering the human being as a being in course of development—to speak of the Ancestors (those who have led a good life, and completed the passage of a good death) as fulfilled human beings par excellence. A like ontological fulfillment is marked not simply by the life/death/life passage, but especially by a harmonious integration in the beyond, the country of origin of human beings. There follows a type of particular relationships between the living and the living dead, whence, as we shall see, emerges a certain view of human destiny. Indeed, to assert, as the myth has done, that the human being cannot be fulfilled apart from the project-of-being settled upon him by the Supreme Being, is once more to indicate the importance, in this human being's ultimate becoming, of a decisive supraterrestrial dimension.

As we see, the myth of Bomynen poses the problem of human destiny from the very outset. But it seems to conceive that destiny less as a "last end" than as an event reserved for the end of time. The myth points to human destiny rather in terms of the forward march of a project of being that promises total fulfillment. In order to comprehend a like perspective, and grasp its particularity, it will be appropriate to begin with the unitary, comprehensive view of history proper to the Ewe-Mina culture, along with other African societies.[13] One fundamental characteristic of such a view is its establishment of a correlative, interactive relationship between space and time, past and future, beyond and below, the living and the living dead, the world of spirits, human beings, and things—a firm rapport implying a view of history not simply under the aspect of a particular, transitory historicity, but always as comprehensive history, at once past, present, and future.[14]

Translated into *eschatological* language, this means: what human beings are and will *definitively* be is *already* given them at the outset (as their destiny) by the Creator; but at the same time, they will *really be in the beyond* what they will have made of their destiny *here below*, in relationship with their socio-cosmic universe. The Ewe-Mina conception of the status of the dead is suggestive on this point: those who will have lived badly on earth, scorning customs and the other orders of the *Vodus,* will remain forever on their knees before the Ancestors in the land of the dead; while righteous, honest persons will abide forever in the Ancestors' company. Thus, eschatology appears as a comprehensive movement, within which is realized the existential project established by the Creator from the beginning. Eschatology constantly determines the deployment of history, just as history is caught up in ultimate destiny. In Africa, the dead are not dead: they live once more, to the full, in the beyond, the intrafililial and ethnosocial relationships that they have constructed around their existential projects here below.

Thus far we have mentioned certain features basic to the Ewe-Mina cultures and cult. They suggest several conclusions. First, in the perspective of a unitary view of history—or more precisely, of the cosmotheandric relation—*time* and *space* now no longer appear as temporary moment and transitory space; now they are viewed as the undefined framework of an all-encompassing history and continuous expansion and unfolding. It is understandable, then, that the past time of the Ancestors should continue to determine the present and the future, just as their living space ceaselessly penetrates that of their descendants living on the earth. Thus, Ewe-Mina space represents not so much the *place* as the permanent *milieu* in which the undefined time of history is played out—a space by no means anonymous and individualistic, but *personal* and *communitary,* the origin and witness of the creative hope that animates the awareness of history. This space, like time, therefore envelops the below and the beyond, the now and the always. Each is defined as an eschatological datum.

Second, the content of eschatological destiny is neither a ludicrous fantasy nor a pure voluntaristic leap, but rather what we have been calling a project of being, or destiny—a message traversing space and time, inspired by the *Vodus,* transmitted by the Founding Ancestors, and everlastingly reinterpreted by the soothsayers, as a factor of ontological fulfillment.

Third, the Supreme Being is at the heart of the destiny of human beings and history; we have already seen what a mighty grip it has on all creatures. The African God is a *transcendently intimate God*—a God who, without being identified with history, rules and wields the universe by creating and ordaining act.

Such, in broad strokes, are some of the anthropological considerations suggested by the Ewe-Mina view of human existence and destiny as a passage from life to death and death to life, which we have defined in terms of completion and being-there-with. Now we shall attempt to sketch a christological treatment of this same view, by investing in it not only the profound mutations actually affecting these traditional data, but also the anguish and the aspirations of the African Christian today. First of all, a decisive question arises here, which can be formulated thus: Can the event of the death-and-resurrection of Jesus, as a message that traverses space and time, be transferred to a like anthropological perspective, in terms of Ewe-Mina thought as a factor of the completion/fulfillment of being-there-with?

PATHWAYS OF CHRISTOLOGY

The spiritual torment—or to put it positively, the profound hope—of Christians of Africa in our day recalls Jesus' challenge to his disciples: "And you—who do you say that I am?" The episode, reported by all three Synoptics (Mark 8:27-30, Matt. 16:13-20, Luke 9:18-21), is staged in a strongly suggestive double context. First, the *place and milieu* of the event—that of the region of Caesarea Phillipi, as Mark and Matthew explicitly indicate— is a region of traditional religion, where the God Pan (the ancient Phineas) is still worshiped, in a sanctuary hewn in the rock overlooking the source of the Jordan.[15] Is it a coincidence that both evangelists have made a point of citing this land of traditional belief as the place where Jesus will pose precisely the question of the identity and truth of his person?

The context is also that of the *time and moment* at which Jesus poses his question. The event occurs midway through the disciples' messianic experience. Jesus questions them not at the very outset of their commitment to follow him, as if they would of course had to know who he was before answering his call. Rather, he challenges them only after they have made their irrevocable decision to follow him, but before they have had any understanding whatsoever of what this decision entails. First they have been chosen to believe, and now they are invited to make the acquaintance of Jesus in interiority and depth. True knowledge of Jesus, of his presence of love and his promise of salvation occurs only within a relationship of love with his person, in a life of faith without the antecedent guarantee or surety of human reason. First and always, it is Jesus who gives to know himself first, allowing human beings to abandon themselves to his gift of love.

This is why the decisive, visceral acknowledgment of Jesus Christ can never flow from anthropological presuppositions, or be reduced to the sole criterion of cultural values, however certain such values may seem to be.

This recognition is the reward of a genuine spiritual maturity, and hence occurs only as a development, an unfolding, in the twin context of cultural milieu and antecedent experience of faith. We shall constantly have to reread or evaluate our intuitions and eleborations regarding the data revealed by the Son of God, in order to better know ourselves in him and to better recognize him in ourselves. What appear here are paths of christology, paths to an ever deepening reappropriation of our faith in Christ, for a new outlook on the spiritual and human expectations of the African.

CHRIST IN HIS LIFE/DEATH/LIFE PASSAGE

The Ewe-Mina believing epistemology, which conceives comprehensive reality in terms of a life/death/life process, immediately perceives the Jesus

Christ event as a passage, as a pathway to the completion and fulfillment of a project of being. Preexisting all things, stripping himself of every divine prerogative and becoming a human being like all others, Jesus traverses death as a necessary passage to a new life.

Christ Is First of All the One Who Preexists All That Exists. If we turn to the wisdom tradition of the Old Testament, which so often founds its theology on a contemplation of creation, we observe, for example in the Book of Proverbs, that Wisdom—synonymous with Word or Logos (Prov. 8:1-2)—is established before the earth is formed, is presented at the moment of the installation of the heavens, thus standing as the bond of an "organic medium" (in the sense defined above) between God and the universe (cf. Prov. 8:27-35).

Paul, as we know, will exploit this sapiential tradition in his christological reflections, although his cosmic formulae will not always be that of the Old Testament vocabulary (cf. Col. 1:15-16). Need we become entangled in the controversies of the exegetes in order to discern here the notion of the preexistence of Christ, his universal sovereignty?

But let us return for a moment to the Ewe-Mina intuition of the existence of a prenatal universe of the human being, and of a procreative spirit (Bomynen), as indicated by the myth analyzed above. It is evident—and this is a fact of mutation—that no intellectual or "developed" African can believe today in the literal content of such mythic language. But a goodly number generally accept—and is this not ultimately what the myth inculcates?—that human beings come from elsewhere, from a *vital elsewhere* ever preceding them, giving them birth and being. This belief in a vital elsewhere, a source of human existence, is confirmed by two other cultural data. First we have the engendering ancestor, the Jete, as concentration of the life and vital energy necessary for the birth of each member of the lineage. The engendering ancestor is said to be the one to present the Supreme Being with the soil of which the latter fashions the infant. The second datum is the awareness that the Ewe-Mina has of being the vessel of a particular destiny, preestablished by the Creator (Bieva) as the sense (meaning and orientation) of his or her existence.

In a like perspective, the tendency would be to make of Christ at once the procreative spirit (Bomynen), the ancestor Jete, and the holder of all destinies. There are those who would characterize this tendency out of hand as concordistic. Still, an Ewe-Mina christological reflection will necessarily have to take into account the essential signification of such data and the conviction that they express, namely, the ontological dependence of the human being on a vital elsewhere. Human beings do not create themselves: they are the fruit of a free act of willing that precedes them, and that determines them in their very freedom and destiny.

At this precise level, Christ's preexistence and sovereignty, which St. Paul professes from a point of departure in the soteriological nature of the death-and-resurrection of the Crucified One, now open to the Ewe-Mina certain paths of christological reflection.

First, Christ seems to fit into the Ewe-Mina view of a universe preexisting all things. The revealed datum confirms such an intuition, asserting that life does not begin with the human being—that it comes from a source of life. However, it specifies that Christ not only shares this source of life, but himself constitutes it, in the communion of God the Father (cf. John 1:4, 3:15, 14:6).

In this respect, Christ cannot be perceived as a secondary divine being, but must be recognized as being of the same divine essence as the Supreme Being. Concretely, this means that he could not be one spirit among others, capable of "caprices" to the detriment of human beings, after the fashion of certain *vodus*. All that he says and does is by the will of the Father, of whom he is the perfect image and personal expression (Heb. 1:3): "What I tell, I tell as the Father has told me," Jesus declares (John 12:50).

The relationship of Christ as Source of life with the human being now appears to the Ewe-Mina as that of the vital procreative force of human existence. He is genuinely divinity, in whom being-human is conceived (in both senses of the word) as being-there-with. From all eternity, consequently, Christ has something in common with the human being, as "organic medium" between God the Father and the whole of creation. Here we have arrived at the threshold of the mystery of Emmanuel, *the* Being-there-with, which we shall explicate further.

Jesus Christ, in His Life and in His Death for Life. To say that Christ's being, which is of the same divine essence as that of the Supreme Being, has freely stripped itself of the rank that placed it on an equal level with God in order to become a human being, like in all things to other human beings, is humanly unthinkable. Here is a Christian mystery if ever there was one, now come to disturb not only the Ewe-Minas' notion of the inaccessible transcendence of Mawu the Creator, but also their view of being-human as a being-on-a-visit-to-earth. Thus do all cultural attempts to explain or apprehend the true scope of the incarnation of God the Son in the ludicrous history of human beings seem inadequate from the outset. Even the chosen people, whom all things conspired to prepare for just such an event, preferred to speak of blasphemy (cf. Matt. 26:63-65, John 10:33). What we have here is simply a datum of faith—the revelation and realization of a divine project proposed to our religious awareness.

However in the Ewe-Mina milieu, there would be three possible pre-christological avenues of approach, per se incapable of explaining anything whatsoever, but calculated to assist in the perception of the new perspectives of conversion and relationship broached by the event of Jesus Christ.

The first avenue of approach, less convincing and more applicable to the relationship of sacramental union between Christ and the believer, would involve the positing of an analogy with the *vodu* initiation cited above. The latter generally deals with cases of possession, sometimes going so far as a symbolic putting to death. One then says that the *vodu* becomes incarnate in the candidate and that the latter is identified with the personhood of the *vodu* thought to possess him. This ritualized phenomenon in itself indicates, according to the Ewe-Minas, the possibility of a divinity's taking flesh in a human life. That would mean, perhaps, in prechristological language, that the hominization of God the Son, Christ, could be compared with the schema of the irruption of the tutelary gods into the life of their devotees; or again, and especially, that there is no dichotomy whatever between divinity and humanity. But the *risk* of a comparison between the incarnation of Christ and *vodu* possession should go no further. The ritualized scenario characterizing *vodu* possession, which now exposes it to the rational demands of a world in mutation, scarcely qualifies it for giving an account of the Jesus Christ event as a fact of historical revelation. Furthermore, and contrary to the phenomenon of possession, the incarnate Christ is not confounded with the life of any other person: he is his own distinct person.

This, one might say, is precisely the point, and here might be a second avenue of approach. The Ewe-Mina, like so many other Africans, believes in the personified incarnation of spirits and genies, to which are often attributed human forms of exceptional beauty, or on the contrary, exceptional ugliness. In any case they are perceived as matchless human beings, possessed of exceptional gifts. It is said that one encounters them by chance, when least expected, in waters and forests, on mountains and in valleys, and so forth. It is evident that, here again, any comparison with the incarnate Christ appears specious and dangerous. Jesus of Nazareth was never a bizarre person, or a ghost (*nukpekpe;* cf. Matt. 14:26, Luke 24:37), but the carpenter, Mary's son, with brothers and sisters everyone knew (Mark 6:3). Surely his was a matchless wisdom, and surely he performed miracles. Still, as a human being he lived the joys and trials of human beings, and this to death on a cross.

The operative notion, however, for our purposes, in this belief in the incarnation of spiritual beings, derives from the fact that they are perceived as manifesting a genuine interest in the world of human beings. Indeed, people are convinced that the tutelary gods intervene in the lives of their subjects, to hold sway from within their history. This conviction surely indicates a developed religious sense, even if it sometimes flirts with superstition. In this perspective, in an approach to such a religious intuition with a view to conversion, the Jesus Christ event could appear as God's direct intervention in the life of all societies, in order to lead them to definitive happiness. Better, Christ becomes a human being in order to lead the human being to share in the fullness of the very life of God (2 Pet. 1:4). In other words, human beings are not condemned to a fate of woe or of fear of spiritual powers, but are promised a project of love, and of intimate union with their Creator.

This christological language, classic as it is, nevertheless arouses a particular faith-echo in the Ewe-Mina. It subsumes their own vision of a necessary relationship between the world of the gods and the world of human beings. *It confirms and matures the originality of such a view, which as a matter of course assigns to every spiritual being a necessarily anthropological dimension.*

This brings us to the third possible prechristological avenue of approach, the one which could be seriously represented by the Ewe-Mina concept of "organic medium." The latter—that, for example, of Bomynen—discharges a function of mediation, since it belongs to each sphere of instances that it interlinks. This has led us to conclude that Christ, the "organic medium" between God the Father and the whole of creation, has had, from all eternity, something in common with the human being.

In this sense, for the Ewe-Mina, the incarnation of God the Son would signify far more than a punctual historical act, and something far better than a physiological taking-flesh. It would fall rather within the dynamics of the community of life that has always linked Christ to the human being and to cosmic creation. Having given birth and being to the human being and to the cosmos, Christ, in whom and by whom all things have been created, has from all time been a partner of creation, a being in solidarity with creation. *The fact of the incarnation thus appears as the supreme expression of the cosmotheandric relation.*

This christological perspective is interesting for the faith of Ewe-Mina Christians. It suggests, with regard to Jesus Christ in his life and his death for life, several observations.

First, the coming of Christ, as a human being with a life and a death, is not an unusual event, or anything contrary to the being of God. It belongs to the very being of God the Son, in whose image everything has been created, to be from all time in the image of his creation. The incarnation is primarily a consequence or proof of this ontological solidarity linking being-human and being-divine in a communion of life. In other words, God is not in solidarity with human beings by virtue of having become a human being; it has always pertained to the being of God to be in solidarity with the human being.

Second, is it possible to hold the exclusively *soteriological* interpretation of the Jesus Christ event? Has Christ become a human being first and foremost to deliver human beings from the sin of Adam? Or rather, *in the radicality of his love-in-solidarity,* which has willed to love to the end by becoming a human being unto victory over death, does Christ not *also* deliver the human being from all that prevents the latter from *becoming complete* in such a Love? We shall return to this question later. Meanwhile, we may draw the following conclusion, that Ewe-Mina Christians, so in need of ridding themselves of all their obsessive fear of evil and of the spirits of woe, discover in the incarnate Christ the God who is in ontological solidarity with their human destiny. They establish a rapport with him not out of fear of sin or of hell, but in abandonment to a divine Love that is committed to the human being's very existence.

Finally, inasmuch as it belongs to the very being of God the Son to be in solidarity with the being of the human being, the active presence of Christ and his Spirit in creation cannot be reduced to the historical fact of his incarnation. This means, for example, that our African cultural and religious elaborations represent constitutive theological loci of any African christological approach. It also means that the tendency to establish an opposition between human nature and divine nature, or even to speak of a "christology from above" and a "christology from below" is not necessarily pertinent. Indeed, what is meant by "nature"? For what christological category does it actually account?

CHRIST, THE "TO-BE-THERE-WITH"

As the reader will surely have remarked, our anthropologico-christological journey has led us from the ontological dependence of the human being to the ontological solidarity of God the Son with humanity. For the Ewe-Mina, we say, the human being is at once a to-be-there-with-the-Supreme-Being and a to-be-there-with-others—this because the Creator has settled that human being in a dynamics of relations that are constitutive of his or her becoming. Indeed, this status of the human being is articulated primarily upon that of the "organic medium" Bomynen, the procreator who mediates all relationship of being between Creator and creature. We have now seen what perspectives a like consideration opens to christological reflection. The status of "organic medium" as applied to Christ here means that Christ has always been the first to-be-there-with-the-Supreme-Being and the first to-be-there-with-others; but it also means that he is all of this in dependence upon the Supreme Being, even though he is of the same divine essence, and that he is in solidarity with all creatures, which, being created in him, can be dependent only on him.

Christ, Who Is "Being-There-with-the-Supreme-Being." There is scarcely any need here to belabor the classic data, viewed as being beyond dispute, of the trinitarian discourse proper to the West, or to loll in abstract considerations that befog rather than shed light on the ineffable mystery of the Holy Trinity. Our task will rather be to lay out the anthropological data that we have now cited, in such a way that it will be capable of receiving, *in faith,* this mystery, and so to interpret the latter in a way that will be pertinent to the Ewe-Mina Christian.

To speak of the capacity of an anthropological datum to receive a Christian mystery in no way implies that such a datum is itself adequate to create this mystery, or to render it comprehensible. It only means that this mystery does not contradict, still less annihilate, the structure or content of the anthropological datum, and can be appropriated as a locus of encounter with and conversion of the human being.

By way of example, let us take the Ewe-Mina view of being, which is conceived in terms of a necessarily interdependent and communitary relationship—a view that the concept of organic medium applies to the Supreme Being itself. In this perspective, the mystery of the Holy Trinity— a datum of faith defined as perfect community or communion of divine Persons—appears primarily as an *intratrinitarian structure of communitary being.* This is the relationship that determines the parenthood of God the Father, the filiation of God the Son, and the procession of God the Spirit. Thus, for the Ewe-Mina, the datum of trinitarian faith is not perceived primarily at the level of a common divine essence, but principally as a *type of inner relation proper to such an essence.*

We cannot apprehend this divine essence in itself, whatever the theological rigor of our considerations on the immanent Trinity. Actually what we think to perceive of God is actually not so much what God is *in se* as what God condescends to communicate to us *de se* in the divine relationship with us. Faith in the trinitarian God, then, is acknowledgment (1) of a God who lives an inner life, and (2)—on that account, vis-à-vis all that emanates from the divine being—of a dynamics of relations in which that divinity is eternally made complete. Thereupon, Christ obviously represents the perfect organic medium through which our relationship with the trinitarian God, and consequently our knowledge of what that God is for us, develops. In other words, our only knowledge of the trinitarian God is in the knowledge given by the relationship of faith in Jesus Christ. Thus, Christ himself declares at Philippi: "Do you not *believe* that I am in the Father and that the Father is in me? Who has seen me, has seen the Father" (John 14:9-10). And further on: "When the Paraclete comes, whom I shall send you from the Father, the Spirit who comes from the Father will bear witness to me" (John 15:26).

This suggests three reflections. With regard to Ewe-Mina anthropology, the mystery of the trinitarian God is perceived as that of a *God who is a to-be-there-with.* God is not a solitude *in se,* but community and solidarity. What defines God in the divine Trinity is not so much the substance of the divine essence as the internal necessity that such an essence be a to-be-relation, a to-be-in-self, and a to-be-there-with. Is this not what the apostle John means when he states simply: "God is Love" (1 John 4:16)? The fundamental revelation of the Jesus Christ event to human beings is that God is *in se* and *propter se* Love. Creation, like redemption in Christ, finds its content and its finality in the dynamics of this relation of intratrinitarian love. In other words, God creates and saves in the divine image—in accordance with the internal structure of a to-be-communion-of-love.

This basic faith-datum, second, goes to the heart of the Ewe-Mina anthropology, which perceives and accepts, in its conception of being as necessary relation, the necessity that the Supreme Being be *in se* a relation of perfect love. True knowledge of the trinitarian God by the human being emerges less from rational categories than from a form of relation that strives to be in the image of the intratrinitarian relation itself. Here we are on the threshold of the eschatological communion that moved Saint Augustine to say: "When we shall have reached you, there will be an end of the words we multiply without reaching you."[16]

Finally, to know themselves to be loved by God as God loves the divine self *in se* is for the Ewe-Mina a revelation that liberates and enlightens their consciousness and sense of God. It discovers to them that the Sovereign of Destiny (Sy), the Supreme Being, confers upon the human being no other destiny than that by which it gives its own life to be shared. According to faith in the trinitarian God, then, there is no reprobation or predestination. The destiny preestablished by the Creator (Bieva) is that of a God-who-is-Love who has created the human being in the divine image of love. That destiny is accordingly the project and promise of a life of love which it belongs to the human being freely to assume or not in a relation of love with the Creator. This is the ontological solidarity proper to the trinitarian God, revealed and realized for the human being by the event of Jesus Christ.

Christ, the To-Be-There-With the Human Being and the Cosmos. With regard to the considerations that we have just entertained, the unfathomable mystery of the advent of Christ into the history of human beings and the created universe ultimately appears as a radical, necessary (in the sense of "proper to one's being") consequence of God's inner ontological solidarity. In this perspective, the creative and redemptive act can only be the deployment of the structure of intratrinitarian being, defined as a relation of reciprocal love. In creation as in redemption, God determines to establish, in Christ, with each product of the divine creation, the kind of differential love proper to the very divinity, the trinitarian life being a perfect communion of differences, a perfect oneness in diversity. Thus, Christ's rapport with the human being and the universe is determined by his personal relation with the other divine Persons. It is in function and by virtue of his rapport with the Father and the Spirit, then, and of their respective rapport with creation, that God the Son deploys and effects salvation history.

For the Ewe-Mina anthropology, this datum of trinitarian christology presents particularly suggestive elements of confrontation. We shall cite only two of them here, articulating them upon the twofold concept of organic medium and to-be-there-with.

Christ assumes ontological dependency as a relation of filial love. Christ's rapport to the human being and the universe, we have said, is determined by his specific relation to the other divine persons. How may this proposition be understood in the perspective of the Ewe-Mina anthropology?

The concept of organic medium, as we have noted above, implies an ontological solidarity with the instances that it interlinks. Or again, the organic medium, in that which characterizes its to-be-there-with, contains something ontologically common with the beings that it mediates. This is the case, as we have said, with the organic medium Bomynen, perceived as divinity—that is, as akin to the Supreme Being that renders him simultaneously akin to the human being.

In applying this concept of organic medium to Christ, we are evidently going further than the Ewe-Mina acceptation, for the twofold reason that Christ is not simply *perceived* as divinity but is of the divine essence itself, and that he is not only *akin* to the human being but really *is* a human being. For example, what Christ has in common with God the Father, he expresses in terms of *communion of being* but in a *relation of filiation:* "That they may be one, as you, Father, in me and I in you" (John 17:11,21); and earlier, "Father, glorify your Son, that your Son may glorify you . . ." (John 17:1; cf. Matt. 17:5; John 5:21, 10:36). Furthermore, what Christ has in common with the human being is also expressed in terms of *communion of being,* but in a relation of a *union of siblingship:* "That they too may be one in us, . . . as we are one, I in them as you in me . . ." (John 17:21-23); cf. John 6:56, 15:4). And: "Whoever does the will of my Father is a brother to me . . ." (cf. Mark 3:32-35).[17] Or again: "I no longer call you servants, . . . I call you friends . . ." (John 15:15). It is this communion that is experienced and confirmed through the sacraments.

In this sense, the designation of Christ as organic medium between God the Father and the human creature, indicates not only that he belongs integrally to the two mediated instances, but also that these two instances have *from all time* enjoyed a communion of being (cf. 2 Tim. 1:9-10). God the Son, however, in a relationship of eternal filial love with the Father, can assume humanity only in this particular rapport with God the Father. We are children in the Son (cf. Gal. 3:26).[18]

Thus, Christ becomes the predicate of attribution of the Ewe-Minas' consciousness of an ontological dependence of the human being and the universe vis-à-vis the Supreme Being. Or better: Christ now enables the Ewe-Mina to express and experience this dependence as a relation of filial love. In Christ, the God-there-with the human being and the created universe, the Supreme Being manifests and realizes the divine parental love.

Christ, the Universal To-Be-There-With. The view of the human being, the world, and history maintained by the societies of Africa is frequently faulted for its restriction to the horizon of clan and tribe, its want of any openness to comprehensive, global reality. Some go as far as to fear that a theology of inculturation would, for this reason, entrap the universality of the gospel message in a ruinous particularism. The fear is a legitimate one. Nor has it always failed to materialize. Even today, theologies and institutions developed within historical categories of thought and forms of development proper to certain cultures sometimes continue to be posited as a datum of universal faith.

For its part, the Ewe-Mina anthropology offers opportunities to expand the so-called tribal purview, and to receive Christ, the organic medium, as the universal to-be-there-with.

Indeed, the problematic of the myth of Bomynen, like that of any foundational mythic discourse, bears on the fundamental sense of a comprehensive reality. Here, then, it proposes a conception of the human being in general, whose origin it represents, and which it characterizes, by its ontological dependence and its project of fulfillment. That is, the organic medium Bomynen is not that of particular Ewe-Mina social groups only, but is rather the universal symbol of a type of relation obtaining between every human being and that being's Creator.

The organic medium Christ thus appears—vis-à-vis such an anthropology—as he whose ontological solidarity affects all things created by him. In Christ is constituted anthropological solidarity, that which binds human being to human being, and the human being to the cosmos. My sibling or partner is the one with whom I share the same blood, that of humanity, or the same project, our destiny.

In the hospitable lands of Africa, everyone is always another's brother or sister, son or daughter, uncle or aunt, father or mother. This sense of anthropological *convivium,* invested in the dynamics of the love of Christ, is eminently calculated to open horizons of siblingship still hidden by certain current tendencies and practices. Thus, we might arrive at two concrete conclusions.

First, every person, and every social group, irrespective of age, race, values or nonvalues, scientific, technological, or economic development or backwardness, is a partner in humanity. Thus, these persons and groups ought to be respected and helped as such partners. Their planned domination by way of shutting them up in a system of anthropological impoverishment is inhuman and antihuman. Far more than any subject whose dignity is made sport of, it is the dominating person who is thereby deprived of true human dignity.

Second, to be a partner (on a basis of equality) of Christ himself means that all peoples, baptized in the same Spirit, and celebrating with their spiritual leaders the same faith in the trinitarian God, bear the charism of truth-to-be-believed. No local church community, therefore, is better situated than another to interpret the common good of faith. A cultural monopoly on the word of God is a negation of the universal ontological solidarity revealed and realized in Christ.

CHRIST, FULFILLMENT OF THE HUMAN BEING AND THE UNIVERSE

The anthropologico-christological treatment sketched thus far naturally leads to a perception of Christ as an organic medium capable of completing human beings and their universe. We have identified this project of fulfillment among the Ewe-Mina as that of a life/death/life process of personal, responsible, and eschatological maturation of to-be-there-with. The content of such a project bears *hic et nunc* on facts and situations constituting a series of challenges to any current christological reflection.

Outlook on Human Problems. The names and faces are those of men, women, youth, and children. They are the hopes, the anguish, and the sufferings that, in an Ewe-Mina milieu as elsewhere in Africa, cry out for the promise of salvation in Christ. Let us list the most important of these longings and strivings. The quest for identity, and of the meaning not of a quaint, archaic past, but of history, of human, social, economic, moral, and religious values—things that still determine the life of the African everywhere.

The search for ways and means, offered by such cultures, and by encounters with other cultures, to a fulfillment of legitimate aspirations such as:

To eat when hungry

To drink when thirsty

To be cared for in sickness

To save for the future

To fight drought and bad weather of all kinds

Freely to chose one's political leader and regime

To succeed in life and society without being threatened by or threatening others with poisoning or malevolent forces

To be delivered from fears and delusions

Not to be condemned to mimicking the errors of other civilizations

To be enriched by these civilizations' wealth without being enslaved by any services they might render to their siblings

To enrich their other siblings without being plundered by them

To utter and celebrate God with all that God has created in the divine image, in the traditions of the Ancestors

For the Christian of the churches of Africa it is a question of need, first, to deliver Christ from Christianity—that is, from institutions, practices, theological currents, and so forth, based on cultural monolithism, which always render him unrecognizable in other cultures. Even today, many African Christians continue to think that the West has delivered Christ to them bound hand and foot.

Second, we should recognize Christ as being in radical solidarity with all human situations, as Savior of all human beings, the most derelict as well as the most secure. Is Christ truly at the side of those who suffer—the innocent, helpless victims of misery, of the arbitrary, of the sinister drama of a raped ecology? How may we believe this, live this, and transmit this?

Thirdly, to cling to Christ as Africans, capable of confronting, in the name of this faith, the challenges of the ancestral traditions, the mutations of intercultural infiltration, and the various forms of religious life in Africa today. And so on.

These are some of the aspects, as urgent as they are hastily sketched here, of the human problems confronting any christological reflection in Africa today. Do the Ewe-Mina anthropological data treated up to this point demonstrate how the Jesus Christ event can subsume these facts and aspirations?

From Ontological Solidarity to Anthropological Fulfillment. The sure assertion of Christ's ontological solidarity with the human being and the created universe is possible only in the faith inspired by his incarnation, death, and resurrection. This solidarity, surmised in Ewe-Mina anthropology as an organic mediation of to-be-there-with, is fully revealed and realized in Christ as a relation of radical love. It could not but go all the way: it could be authentic and credible only in setting human beings on the path to living in their Creator the communion of being to which the latter has destined them from all time.

Thus, the Jesus Christ event is set within the radical fidelity of God's love for the human being and for the whole of creation. It indicates the extent to which creation has forever been called to be completed in Christ (cf. Rom. 8:22), the extent to which the finality of Christ's solidarity is to fulfill human beings — to fill them up in their aspirations to be more human. In living a human life of human anguish and hope, in being willing to die to vanquish death, in rising to the fullness of life, Jesus Christ traverses the life/death/life sequence as locus of accomplishment of human salvation. In other words, Jesus integrates himself into human life, dies a human death, and enters into a transformed life, not for himself, but for the human being. Thus, as Pope John Paul II has said, he penetrates the mystery of the human being in a unique and absolutely singular way.[19] He invests with his divine being the depths of being-human.

The finality of Christ's ontological solidarity is the anthropological fulfillment of all creation, then, that God may be all in all (cf. 1 Cor. 15:28). Confronted with the Ewe-Mina anthropological perspective, and with the current challenges of human problems, the Jesus Christ event suggests a number of elements for reflection.

The human being and the universe can be fulfilled only in a life/death/life process. Life, as it has been given by the Creator and received by creatures, is a project of being. This project can be taken up by the human being only in a total life-commitment to it. Christ has revealed the content of this project and has carried it out in obedience to God the Father. Conversion of heart, renunciation of the evil that slays life, transcendence of self—these are the death trials that prepare the human being for definitive fulfillment in God.

Christ's ontological solidarity, whose purpose is to lead the whole of creation to its fulfillment, implies a total, comprehensive taking-charge on the part of human beings. No individual, no social group is beyond the pale of this relation of love, whose universal character we have just cited. As we know, St. Paul demonstrates and deduces the universality of this phenomenon from the Adamic typology.[20] In other words, the ever more determined will of African Christians to invest their traditional values in the life of Christ itself constitutes an act of basic christological faith. In the name of this faith, they have understood that, as they are created in the image of God, they must render an account of that fact. Thus they attain Christ in his ontological solidarity, which has for its foundation the pluralism of the trinitarian God.

This ontological solidarity extends to all human problems, inasmuch as, in becoming a human being, Christ has lived in every way as a human being of his time. By his life, his teaching, his miracles, by his death and his resurrection, he reaches human beings at the crossroads of their anguish, their suffering, and their aspirations. But the attitude of Christ toward human problems is fundamentally determined by God the Father's will to love. For the Ewe-Mina, this means that the human being is really and actually fulfilled according to the intention of the Creator: as we have said, the Ewe-Mina are convinced that all human beings bear within themselves a destiny assigned by the Creator, a destiny comprehensively perceived in Christ as ontological solidarity and relation of love. To put it another way, this means that human beings cannot be realized from a human point of departure: they will ever be the deed of their Creator. It is only in this wise that any human act of fulfillment will find and realize its ultimate sense. That is to say, the fulfillment of the human being is not, when all is said and done, a question of human (ideological, political, economic, or the like) means. First and last, the fulfillment of the human being is a question of faith, of conversion, and of communion of being with the Source of all being.

Christ has shown that this communion of to-be-there-with the Supreme Being is not only a spiritual attitude, or a post-mortem objective reserved for the eschatological consummation. Ewe-Mina eschatology, as defined above, presents a *totally human* Christ, at once spiritual and temporal, notwithstanding the dualistic or monistic threats of certain theologies of Greco-Latin culture. The African is right to ask of Christ health, success, prosperity, and so on. These are all things that, according to many traditional beliefs, are obtained only if one is honest and upright of heart, only if one is without hatred or wickedness. But here, the Cross of Christ, God the Son himself, rises up as a scandalous challenge. Actually it is a sign of contradiction only because it is a sign of hope in a resurrection. Is that Cross, that Son, not the supreme response to all of our human problems?

We have been unwilling, in this rapid, narrowly focused study, tailored to the restricted dimensions of the present collection, to approach christology along the secure pathways of the classic methods of approach. Nor have we sought to regard all the aspects, even the essential aspects, of faith in Christ, or to exploit all of the anthropological conclusions we have cited. Rather we have sought to compose a modest monograph from a point of departure in a precise anthropological datum, with a view to sketching certain reflections on the God-for-the-human-being who has been revealed in Christ. We have purposely avoided entering into the great christological debates, to meditate with serenity on the Jesus Christ event in its foundations.

We have rediscovered, in the name of our faith and in terms of the Ewe-Mina vision of the human being and history, Christ as an organic medium, as the to-be-there-with who realizes the whole ontological solidarity of the Creator with creatures as a radical relation. We have caught a glimpse of Christ's capacity for really and totally assuming all of the religious aspirations and cultural elaborations proper to our societies in Africa—not by way of adapting to them (that unfortunate term!), but by going to the depths of their meaning, thereupon to lead them to maturity in the love of the triune God. Is that not the hope that dwells in more than one African Christian heart? This by itself justifies the assertion that the love of Christ is worthy of African faith.

NOTES

1. The "christological titles method" is used, for example, by Oscar Cullmann, *Christologie du Nouveau Testament* (Paris: Delachaux et Niestlé, 1958; English translation, *Christology of the New Testament* [Philadelphia: Westminster, 1959]); W. Kraemer, *Christos, Kyrios, Gottessohn* (Zürich: Zwingli, 1963).

2. See, for example, the works of R. H. Fuller, such as *The Foundations of New Testament Christology* (London, 1965); F. Hahn, *Christologische Hochheitstitel: Ihre Geschichte im frühen Christentum* (Göttingen, 1963).

3. See R. Schnackenburg, "La christologie du Nouveau Testament," in *Mysterium Salutis*, vol. 10 (Paris: Cerf, 1974), pp. 13-234.

4. Joseph A. Fitzmyer, S.J., "The Biblical Commission and Christology," *Theological Studies* 46 (1985) 407-43.

5. See Schnackenburg, "Christologie du Nouveau Testament," pp. 17-41.

6. See *Documentation Catholique*, no. 1895 (May 5, 1985), pp. 508-9.

7. The cosmotheandric relation, proper to the conceptual structure of more than one African society, defines reality in general, and human existence in particular, in terms of a necessary rapport between the human being with the Supreme Being and the socio-cosmic universe.

8. For general information on this point see Mircea Eliade, *Patterns in Comparative Religion* (New York: Sheed and Ward, 1958). See pp. 331-66, "Agriculture and Fertility Cults."

9. Let us observe in passing that death and the seed to be sown in the earth—which must die in order to sprout—are designated in Ewe-Mina by the same verbonominal radical, *ku*.

10. See B. Adoukonou, *Jalons pour une théologie africaine* (Paris: Lethielleux, 1980), 2:21-30.

11. L. V. Thomas, *Anthropologie de la mort* (Paris: Payot, 1975), p. 176, where the author also indicates that "Serer initiation [Senegal] clearly reproduces the death-resurrection schema." See A. T. Sanon and R. Luneau, *Enraciner l'Evangile* (Paris: Cerf, 1982), pp. 63-129.

12. See, for example, J. Carmignac, "Les dangers de l'eschatologie," *NTS* 17 (1970-71):366-67. Refer also to P. Grelot, "Histoire et eschatologie dans le livre de Daniel," in *Apocalypses et théologie de l'espérance* (Paris: Cerf, 1977), pp. 63-109.

13. For more details, see E. J. Pénoukou, "Eschatologie en terre africaine," *Lumière et vie*, no. 159 (September-October 1982), pp. 75-88.

14. For the theoretical basis of such a view of history, see "Religion et foi chrétienne comme sources de relations interpersonnelles d'intégration et de trans-formation," in *L'expérience religieuse africaine et les relations interpersonnelles: Colloque d'Abidjan 16-20 sept. 1980* (Institut Catholique de l'Afrique de l'Ouest), pp. 453-88.

15. See G. Dalmann, *Orte und Wege Jesu,* 3rd ed. (Gütersloh, 1924), p. 217, n. 1.

16. St. Augustine, concluding prayer of his *De Trinitate,* XV, 28, 51.

17. See *Traduction Oecuménique de la Bible,* note *f* on Mark 3:32.

18. "The Father's love eternally engendering the Son becomes creative love. It calls to life creatures constituted to the image of the Son, who, in community with the Son, return the Father his love. Creation proceeds from the Father's love for the eternal Son. It is destined to join itself to the obedience of the Son and to his love returned to the Father, and thus to become the Father's happiness" (Jürgen Moltmann, *The Trinity and the Kingdom* [San Francisco: Harper and Row, 1981], p. 212).

19. John Paul II, *Redemptor Hominis,* no. 8.

20. Cf. 1 Cor. 15:20-22, Rom. 5:12-21. See Cullmann, *Christologie du Nouveau Testament,* p. 150.

3

Who Is Jesus Christ
for Africans Today?
Prophet, Priest, Potentate

DOUGLAS W. WARUTA

Several years ago, an evangelical church was built on a strategic road in Nairobi with a big neon-light sign that read, "CHRIST IS THE ANSWER." As a young theological student I remember my reaction to the sign: But what is the question? In the Gospel of Mark (8:27-32), which is believed to be the earliest Gospel or story about Jesus Christ, Jesus confronted his disciples not with an answer but with a question which is still pertinent to all those everywhere who claim to be his disciples. Jesus repeated his question. The first time he wanted to know what the disciples knew others to say about who Jesus was. And he got some answers. Some say this, others that, and so on. Then Jesus went straight to the point and asked them, "And what do you say that I am?" Peter, who often assumed the role of their spokesman, responded without hesitation: "You are the Christ. You are the promised Messiah!"

Other people may say a thousand things as to who Jesus is; it will never suffice, however, for the disciples of Christ to mimic the confessions of others, no matter how valid. Ever since the coming of Western missionary Christianity to Africa, African Christians have more or less been content to embrace the answers supplied to them by the "mother" church. Quite often these answers have been defended with the arguments that they are orthodox, faithful to the faith handed down from the apostles. Such arguments have stifled every attempt by indigenous Christians to find their own questions so that they may give their own answers.

An attempt to answer the question Who is Jesus Christ? is an attempt

52

to develop a christology; an interpretation as to who Jesus really is in every context and situation. It is not merely to provide a catechetical answer or a pious evangelical slogan. In this paper, I contend that Africans have every right to formulate their own christology, their own response to who Jesus is to them. Such a response should reflect their consciousness as to who this Messiah really is. I also contend that Africans understand Jesus Christ in the context of their own religious consciousness. They are looking for a Christ who will play the mediating role between humanity and divinity. In African religious tradition, meditation between humanity and divinity; between the natural and the supernatural; between the world of man and the world of spirit was accomplished through three main religious specialists—the prophet, the priest and the sacred king ruler, chief-elder or the accepted potentate. In this paper, the mediating Christ will be outlined as prophet, priest, and potentate.

When Peter confessed Jesus as the Christ, he was expressing a confession that was very much in the minds and hearts of his Jewish contemporaries. The Jews were an oppressed and colonized people. They lived as strangers and were dominated by strangers in their own land. Peter, as all other Jews, knew and expected a day when the promised Messiah would come to restore not only the glorious Kingdom of their ancestor David (Micah 5:2) but also their dignity and freedom (Isaiah 61). The strength of Peter's confession was not that it was original or new; rather, it was because it expressed his genuine desire, prayers, and hopes and these were not only his but also those of the other disciples, fellow Jews and the entire humanity, particularly the oppressed peoples everywhere. With this confession, Jesus knew that "the Kingdom of God" had dawned among men, the fulfillment of God's promises to his people had been inaugurated and nothing would stop it from reaching God's people in every place and in every age. Aware of the misunderstanding such a confession would cause to those with the mistaken notions of a narrow, nativistic political Messiah, Jesus admonished his disciples to keep such a revolutionary confession to themselves, at least temporarily (Mark 8:30).

The recognition that Jesus Christ is to be understood in the threefold office of prophet, priest, and king is not uniquely African. Belief in Jesus as Prophet, Priest, and King may be traced back to Eusebius of Caesarea who in the fourth century said:

> And it has come down to us that some also of the same prophets have by anointing become typically Christs, so they may be referred to as the Same Christ the divine Heavenly word, who is the only High Priest of the Universe, the only King of Creation, and the only supreme Prophet among His Father's prophets.[1]

By the time of the Reformation in the sixteenth century, the church had fully recognized the threefold office of Christ, although various sections of

Christianity emphasized a particular office sometimes at the expense of others. Sometimes the office of the prophet was combined with that of the priest, especially when emphases were on understanding Jesus as the "Revealer of God."[2]

It is not in the scope of this paper to dwell at length on the development of the "threefold office" doctrine throughout the history of the church. It suffices to mention that the church has taken this path throughout the centuries. However, the Western wing of the church, while acknowledging the threefold office has also tended to dwell too much on the person of Christ rather than the work of Christ. Even the Protestant theologian, Emil Brunner, in his very relevant statement on christology (*The Mediator*) emphasizes the person rather than the work of Christ. The Roman Catholic christologies lean heavily toward the person of Christ also. Nevertheless, attempts to understand Christ from what he does rather than who he is have become dominant in recent years, particularly with the emergence of the theologies of liberation. In our attempt to understand Christ as Prophet, Priest, and King as key to an African christology, the work of Christ rather than his person will have priority.

JESUS THE PROPHET

During the New Testament period, it was the Messianic consciousness which was dominant among the people to whom Jesus came. They were looking for the coming of a Messiah. However, the Gospels present an unmistakable Prophetic consciousness represented by the disciples' answer to Jesus' question, "What do men say that I am?" Without any hesitation the disciples were quick to answer, "some say that you are John the Baptist; others say that you are Elijah, while others say that you are one of the prophets" (Mark 8:28). The disciples of Jesus saw in him a prophet in the line of Moses, Elijah, Amos, and the other pre-exilic prophets (Matthew 1:14, Luke 7:16, 39, 24:19, John 9:17). Even Jesus gave the impression that he viewed himself as the prophet (Matthew 13:57, Luke 4:24, John 4:44).

One of the basic qualifications of a prophet was that he was sent from God. The Gospels clearly indicate that Jesus was sent from God. As Moses was sent from God in the Old Testament, so was Jesus in the New Testament.[3] The Gospel of Matthew (5:17-48) compares and contrasts Jesus with Moses, pointing out that Moses received the Torah but Jesus gave the New Torah. Jesus is not only compared to Moses but also to other prophets of the Old Testament. Many of the parables, pronouncements, denunciations, and "signs" Jesus made conformed well to the prophetic tradition of his day. This does not mean that Jesus was no more than a prophet; it does mean that he was also no less than a prophet. Jesus the man and Jesus the prophet cannot be separated. Jesus understood himself and was also understood by others to be not just a prophet but also the prophet from God.

This prophetic office of Jesus could be one important aspect in the development of an African christology.

JESUS THE PRIEST

The Gospel story does not portray Jesus as a Messiah and a prophet only but also as a priest. One cannot understand the work of a priest without the ideas of suffering and sacrifice. In the Gospels, Jesus is not only presented as the "suffering servant" of Isaiah 53:11ff. but also as the sacrificial victim offered through his death on the cross (Mark 15:37, Matthew 27:46). Jesus, as the German theologian Jürgen Moltmann says, died a "God-forsaken death for a God-forsaken people."[4] The use of sacrificial language in Paul's writings and the presentation of Christ as the High Priest in Hebrews conform to one of the most basic aspects of the early church's understanding of Jesus. Paul states this priestly ministry of Jesus in the famous statement, "God was in Christ reconciling the world to Himself" (I Cor. 5:19). As a priest, Jesus stands in between human beings and God to provide the essential link between man and God. The priestly office of Jesus Christ which is the central theme of Hebrews, chapters 1-7, and the first epistle of Peter show the relationship his priestly office has with his office as king (Hebrews 2: 8f.) and as the leader of his people (2:10-13) and as High Priest (2:14-18). Jesus, however, offers a better priesthood (Hebrews 8-10) because he leads his people into the City of God (Hebrews 11-13).

In the New Testament, Jesus appears in the presence of God as a priest on behalf of believers. He is not, however, presented only as the priest at the altar but also as the sacrificial victim on the altar. This is the dual role in the priestly work of Christ.

JESUS THE POTENTATE

In 1 Timothy 6:15, Jesus is referred to as "the blessed and only Potentate, the King of Kings and the Lord of Lords" (AV). The word *Potentate* is translated in the other versions as *Sovereign* (RSV) and *Ruler* (TEV). Jesus is presented as the potentate in many expressions in the New Testament. He is the eschatological "Son of David" (Mark 10:46-52, Matthew 20:29-34) who is destined to come and establish the glorious reign of David over God's people Israel (Psalm 2:7). He is the eschatological "Son of Man" of Daniel 7:13f. signifying the authority of historical Jesus with the authority not only over Sabbath but also the authority to forgive sins (Mark 2:10, 28). Mark combines Psalm 110:1 and Daniel 7:13 to answer the chief priest Caiaphas (Mark 14:62) where Jesus is reported to have answered the Chief Priest's question: "Are you the Messiah, the son of the Blessed God?" (14:16) with the statement: "I am, and you will see the Son of Man seated on the right hand of the Almighty and coming with clouds of heaven" (14:62).

The risen Christ becomes the "King of Kings and the Lord of Lords" (Rev. 19:16) and is the culmination in the development of a theology which identifies Jesus with the rule of God in the world. Jesus is the Kyrios, the reigning Lord (Acts 2:36) upon whom apostolic Christianity based its proclamation. God has entrusted to Jesus his eternal rule on earth (Acts 11:20, 14:30).

In Jesus of Nazareth, God speaks to his people as Prophet, relates to them as Priest, and establishes his rule not only in the world to come but in this present world also. A christology which revolves around the three offices of Christ as Prophet, Priest, and Potentate is not only soundly biblical but will be the most comprehensible to African Christians.

THE QUEST FOR A RELEVANT AFRICAN CHRISTOLOGY

In spite of the fact that Jesus Christ is taken very seriously and followed by a large segment of the African population, very little effort has been made by Africans to define and establish who Jesus Christ is to them. However, as John S. Mbiti observes, some special interest is growing among many African scholars to develop an African christology.[5] And this is quite in order because without a very clear concept of who Jesus is to African Christians, the church in Africa may be standing on quicksand.

WHO DO AFRICANS SAY THAT JESUS CHRIST IS?

If Peter understood Jesus as the Christ, the Messiah of his contemporary Jewish thought, the African response to the above question must reflect African consciousness. The efforts by forces of colonialism to exterminate and suppress the African religious consciousness have not succeeded, and today African people are asserting their own experience of God and their own reflection of how that God relates to them. In African religious tradition, God relates to people in concrete, experiential, and practical terms rather than in a mystical and spiritualistic manner. As Mbiti observes:

> Traditional religions and philosophy are concerned with man in past and present time. God comes into the picture as an explanation of man's contact with time. There is no messianic hope or apocalyptic vision with God stopping in at some future moment to bring about a radical reversal of man's normal life. God is not pictured in an ethical/ spiritual relationship with man. Man's acts of worship and turning to God are pragmatic and utilitarian rather than spiritual or mystical.[6]

The nature of the quest for African christology is to translate Jesus Christ to the tongue, style, genius, character, and cultures of African people. If African peoples, as Mbiti observes, are more conscious of a relationship with God based on living contacts, in concrete situations and experiences, it is easy to appreciate the importance of the religious authorities who in some very real way symbolize God's presence among the people. In African religion, faith is not expressed through credal formulations or theological statements but in day-to-day encounter with the challenges of life. Every encounter is understood in its temporal or material sense as well as its religious or supernatural sense. The African, as Mbiti has observed, "lives in a religious universe so that natural phenomena and objects are intimately associated with God."[7] The religious specialists, whom Mbiti calls medicine men, rainmakers, kings, and priests (he combines priests and prophets), mediate between the world of man and the spiritual or sacred reality even if in many cases this is only in a symbolic manner. Mbiti says:

> "Specialists" are in effect the repositories in knowledge, practice and symbolically, of the religious life of their communities. They are the ones who make history of African traditional societies both sacred and religious. "Specialists" are the symbolic points of contact between the historical and spiritual worlds. In them are the continuity and essence of African religious thought and life.[8]

A religion without a creed, definite structure, or definite organizational forms finds its expression and impact on its visible symbols such as its rituals and religious personages. The prophet, priest, and king in African religious tradition is at the very centre of the religious life of the African people. No ritual observance would make any sense without them.

THE PROPHET IN AFRICAN RELIGIOUS TRADITION

The prophet in Africa is known by several names. He (or she) is the diviner, seer, revealer of secrets, possessor of the spirit, or just the man of God.[9] Prophets are special persons in that they are the leaders of their communities in matters both political and religious. Sometimes the role of diviner or seer is considered more religious than that of the prophet who functions as an intermediary within the community. But as Benjamin Ray observes, the difference is insignificant:

> African prophets go directly to the people and inspire religious and political movements. Diviners and prophets alike are the mediators of the divine, but prophets speak forth the divine word directly without reading it off a symbolic medium. For this reason, prophets are often sources of creative religious change. . . . Under certain circumstance, diviners and priests may develop prophetic powers and become leaders of religious and social change.[10]

As we saw earlier, the social, political, economic, and religious life of African people was seen as one and the same. The role of the prophet was not restricted to the religious aspects of the community but also involved its social and political dimensions. The prophet was therefore the socio-political as well as the spiritual leader of his people. While in most cases the priest was a male, the prophet in African religion could be a man or a woman. In fact, female prophets are numerous in African society. In African religion, prophets as "possessors of the spirit" surprised everybody at times when they were manifested in persons of lower rank in the community. At such times the community did not see the person but the "power" which he or she possessed.

During crises, particularly in times of war, the prophets were the spokes-persons of the people, advising the community on the proper steps to be taken in order to overcome the crises. The prophets also expressed the aspirations and ideals of their communities. In times of epidemics or polit-ical upheaval, African communities looked up to them for guidance.

Prophecy in its African sense has been a primary aspect of African Christian independency. Most founders of the African Independent churches were seen as prophetic leaders. Leaders such as Simon Kimbangu from the very beginning presented himself as a messenger or prophet (ngunza) of God and healed in the name of Jesus.[11] Simon Kimbangu of Zaïre is the best example of the most popular form of Christian independ-ency which revolted against the brand of Christianity represented by the missionary-founded churches from the West. Benjamin Ray observes:

> These prophet-led sects represent a radical indigenization of Chris-tianity in Africa. Often called "Zionist," "Prayer," "Spiritual," "Prophet," these churches have created a thorough synthesis of Chris-tian and African ritual forms. They emphasize revelation from the Holy Spirit, through prophets and a practical, this-worldly notion of salvation in which healing is prominent. They stress communal soli-darity in terms of the Old Testament ideal of prophet-led community based in a Holy City.[12]

In general, the independent churches have done quite well in making the Christian faith relevant in the daily life of African people. They have also demonstrated the potency of the African religious heritage by addressing the issues affecting African societies, be they political or religious. Many of the independent prophet-leaders have led religious rebellions and com-bined religious and political revolt. Whether it is the Kinjikitile of the Maji Maji revolt against the Germans in Tanganyika, the Mau Mau movement in Kenya, or the recent "Holy Spirit Movement" led by self-declared proph-etess Alice Lakwena in Uganda, the essential elements remain the same — the quest for spiritual/physical liberation from external domination. For the followers of these independent churches, the prophet is their spiritual and political leader and liberator. While the prophet may resist identifications or designations as the Messiah, his followers do not see much of a difference, and such a prophet often gets the kind of reverence and status accorded to Jesus.

Prophecy in African Independent churches is also associated with dreams, visions, and trances as means of interpreting the existential events of life. The prophecy of Joel quoted in the book of Acts 2:16–18 is extremely pertinent:

> This is what I will do in the last days, says God,
>   I will pour out my spirit on everyone,
> your sons and your daughters will proclaim my message;
>   your young men will see visions,
>   and your old men will have dreams.
> Yes, even my servants, both men and women,
>   I will pour out my spirit in those days,
>   and they will proclaim my message . . .

Prophecies like this are the basic leitmotif in independent Christianity and are extremely potent in the life of the believing community symbolized in those who are believed to be the prophets or the "possessors of the Spirit." As Peter proclaimed to the people of Jerusalem, "Jesus of Nazareth was a man whose divine authority was clearly proven to you by all the miracles and wonders which God performed through Him" (Acts 2:22). This Jesus is still doing wonders through his own servants. In other words, Jesus is real in what he continues to do even at the present time. He pours his spirit, heals the sick, and leads his people from their spiritual and physical bondage. This is evidenced through the special people through whom he works in the life and faith of the community of faith. In this aspect, Christianity and African religion blend well.

THE PRIEST IN AFRICAN RELIGION

One of the important points to underline is that the prophet in African religion would also be the priest. But at times, the priestly role will be separated from that of the prophet. As Benjamin Ray observes, "it is sometimes misleading to distinguish sharply between 'priest' and 'prophet,' the distinctive mark of a priest is his ritual and symbolic authority."[13]

The priest in African religion is seen as the medium through which the life-giving power of God comes to man. The priest contains within himself the "life force" which he mediates to his people. In the community the priest presided over religious rituals, led the people in worship, and solemnized the Rites of Passage ceremonies. The priests are masters of traditional wisdom, rituals, and ceremonial practices. More than anything else, they are the living symbols of religious life of the African community. People go to them with the hope of allaying their fears and sufferings. They lead in the communal sacrifice where God's intervention to meet the needs of the community is sought. It is through the priest that divine power is employed for the purpose of changing the human condition for the better. As Ray observes, "ritual sacrifices thus had a basic threefold structure: consecration, invocation-immolation, communion-purification."[14] The priest officiates these rituals in order to establish the bond between the people and the divinity and between the people themselves. The sacrificial animal provides the link between the people and divinity through the symbolic actions and words of the priest.

THE KING IN AFRICAN RELIGION

He may be called the King, Ruler, Chief Elder, Leader, or any other term which marks the person who symbolizes the identity of an African people and their unity. This position may be acquired through hereditary means or through special recognition. In the former case, the power of the position is passed on through a rigid ancestral lineage, and in the latter case quite often through ritual action. The king or ruler plays a priestly role on behalf of his people on the basis of the fact that he stands as the intermediary between them and the divinity. "African Kings perform priestly functions, for they are often the focal points of their Kingdoms."[15] Among the Swazi, the king is both the ritual and political head of his people, and the annual Ncwala ceremony signified the religious and political dimensions of the Swazi society.[16] Until recently, the Kabaka of Buganda was the symbol of Buganda's national and religious heritage. Even his deposition from Uganda has not diminished his symbolic significance.

In African society, leadership was never purely political or mere civil authority. It always carried with it a religious aspect in which the leader of the people exerted ritual and religious authority as well. Through these leaders, Aylward Shorter observes:

> traditional religion received its visible expression. Authority in traditional Africa was basically political-religious and professional priesthoods and other cultic offices or forms of religious dedication represented partial approaches or specializations within the religious system taken as a whole. At the universal or territorial level it was the hierarchy of family heads, clan-leaders and chiefs who presided over religious rituals, led the people in worship and took initiative in creating and manipulating religious institutions such as oracles or rites of initiation.[17]

The sacred element in African society guaranteed not only the identity and a sense of belonging to each person in the community but also his sense of security and just protection. Traditional rulers were not tyrants to their people, for their leadership was a sacred trust with codes and procedures religiously sanctioned and for which individual rulers could not betray or change according to their own whims. Leadership also was not threatened with deposition from the inside; the danger always lay from outside, from foreign invaders. Such an invasion, however, was to the entire community, and the loss was to all, not to the king alone. The defence of the king was the defence of the community as a whole.

Mbiti has observed that in independent churches, individuals of great religious fame "emerge and become the focus for corporate or communal expression of faith among members of the particular group."[18] Africans still tend to link leadership with the sort of sacredness it was identified with in the traditional religion. The leader was the visible expression of the religious life of his people. While the office of the leader was not always similar—some were monarchial, others chieftainships, while yet others were clan elders and leaders—the office or the recognition bestowed in leadership was never without religious connotations.

JESUS AS PROPHET, PRIEST AND POTENTATE IN AFRICAN CHRISTOLOGY

Ever since the first consultation of African Theologies held at Ibadan in 1965, African Christians have been struggling hard to establish and develop a truly African Christology. During that consultation, the quest for an African christology was inaugurated with these words: "We recognize the radical quality of God's self-revelation in Jesus Christ, and yet it is because of this revelation that we can discern what is truly of God in our pre-Christian heritage. This knowledge of God is not discontinuous with our people's previous traditional knowledge of Him."[19]

As the disciples of Jesus Christ, the African Christians will definitely view Jesus Christ from their own religious consciousness. If Jesus is to mean something to Africans, he will certainly be the answer to their aspirations and expectations. The majority of the African people are black, and blackness has been conspicuously associated with an oppressed, exploited, and humiliated segment of the human race. How can African Christians discern Jesus? One thing that is very evident in African Christianity is that Africans have understood Jesus as Prophet, Priest, and King. Any observer of African Christians, particularly of the independent church groups, will quickly notice that certain persons symbolize their faith in Jesus Christ whom these religious leaders claim to serve. Individuals of great faith and spiritual gifts are central in the evolution of a genuinely African Christianity. It is persons and not ideas or doctrinal tenets who captivate the masses of African people and bring them to faith. Prophet William Wade Harris, who shook the western African zone with his prophetic message, is perhaps one of the perfect examples of early African Christianity:

[He was] ... an imposing figure ... out of the Old Testament. His
long white robe, his white turban and white beard identified him as
a prophetic figure; the black bands crossed over his chest and the tall
cross of cane which he carried in his hand suggested that he was a
Christian. He was followed through the streets of Axim (Ghana 1914)
by a crowd of people, some of whom fell into convulsions before
him, some of whom trembled with the emotions his presence
unleashed ...[20]

African peoples have always known and taken very seriously the role of
their spiritual leaders. The community in Africa has always approached the
divinity through its religious personages. These personages are necessary
in bridging the gap between ordinary persons and the divine world. This
does not mean Africans did not pray to God directly. Indeed, they often
did so, particularly with informal prayers and invocations.[21]

The Christian doctrine of incarnation provides an excellent base for the
development of an African christology. In Jesus God is not a mysterious
hidden reality but one who comes down to the people through his servant
Jesus. Kofi Appia-Kubi very well describes the way an African christology
has evolved:

the concept[s] of Christology of such traditional African Christians
are practical, dynamic, living and basically based on real-life experience, and a comprehensive African notion of religion and of God
taking off faithfully from the Gospel message and African culture and
notion of man. ... Their concepts of Christology revolve around
geneaology, rites of passage—birth, baptism, eucharist, and death;
kinship and community aspects; such titles as Mediators, Redeemer,
Saviour, Liberator and Healer are pregnant with meaning for these
indigenous African Christians.[22]

The Jesus who deals with Africans and their existential situation in a
real and dynamic way will be extremely comprehensible to the African
people. Africans are not interested in suffering through their problems now
while waiting for the bliss of heaven. This is the type of Christianity evan-
gelistic missionary Christianity to a large extent communicated to the African people. Africans want a leader who shows them the way to liberation
now—liberation from disease, oppression, hunger, fear, and death. This
type of Jesus is the one presented in the Gospels. Africans identify very
much with him. He is the prophet who exhorts them to a better and more
hopeful living. He is a priest who mediates between them and the external
powers of the living God. He is the King who leads his people to victory
over the overwhelming threats of life. In the one Jesus, the threefold office
is seen in its unity. Jesus is Prophet, Priest, and Potentate, all rolled into

one. This is the way the New Testament sees him. Africans would like to see him so.

There are some dangers in contemporary African Christianity regarding the threefold symbols of Christianity. While ordinary African Christians genuinely want to maintain a deep respect for their religious symbols (prophets, priests, and bishops), this respect has often been exploited by the African Christian leaders where excesses leading almost to hero worship and personality cults have emerged. Some priests and bishops have definitely exploited this African cultural heritage of reverence to their spiritual leaders for their own personal glory and enrichment. Even in political circles, leaders tend toward personality cult which they know will easily develop in the context of the African cultural respect for their leaders. This tendency may explain why in African church and state, people in authority do not easily relinquish power. Authority in Africa is held as a sacred rather than as a public trust. The tendency is to take authority as sacred and permanent (till death terminates it). Taken by fallen human beings, the African reverence for authority can become a source of great abuses and sufferings.

Nevertheless, Jesus as Prophet, Priest, and Potentate does provide for the African people the most perfect model for them. Jesus is not the man after self-glory and personal enrichment. Jesus is the "man for others" who gave his life for the most wretched people of the earth. He is referred to in Acts 3:15 as the *Archegos*, the one who leads his people into life. Jesus means life, and never death. The Western models of Christian leadership—whether bishops, priests, or moderators in church leadership—have been grossly tainted by their authoritarianism, pomposity, and lack of a servant spirit, none of which were demonstrated by Jesus. Many Africans fail to see the real Jesus because of such unworthy models of Christianity. Jesus must be Prophet, Priest, and King because, as Paul writes in Philippians 2:5-11, he first humbled himself and accepted the role of servant. Have Africans lost him in the jungle of the two thousand years of Christian history? Where can they find him? How can they know him? Who is he to them? He is still the Jesus of Nazareth, very close to the African people as Prophet, Priest, and Potentate. When seen in the Gospels, he is easily known—by the scars on his hands and body from being crucified. His true servants will bear these scars too—the cross before the crown (Gal. 6:17). Africans know how to look for these scars. Jesus supplied them in plenty. Many African women and men have exemplified the true Christ to the extent that many African Christians are able to say: "Jesus we know, and we know His disciple Paul; but you, who are you?" (Acts 19:15). Sons of Sceva beware!

NOTES

1. H. E. I. 8, "The Creed of Caesarea" in Henry Bettenson, *Documents of the Christian Church*, 2nd Edition (New York: Oxford University Press, 1967).

2. H. R. Mackintosh and A. B. Macaulay, *The Christian Doctrine of Justification and Reconciliation*, 2nd Edition (Edinburgh, 1902), pp. 442-52.

3. H. A. Guy, *New Testament Prophecy* (London: Epworth Press, 1947), pp. 24, 83-85.

4. Jürgen Moltmann, *The Crucified God* (Philadelphia: Westminster Press, 1974), pp. 142-43.

5. John S. Mbiti, *Bible and Theology in African Christianity* (Nairobi: Oxford University Press, 1986), pp. 50-51.

6. John S. Mbiti, *African Religions and Philosophy* (London: Heinemann, 1969), p. 5.

7. Ibid., p. 48.

8. Ibid., p. 193.

9. Benjamin Ray, *African Religions* (Englewood Cliffs, New Jersey: Prentice Hall, 1976), pp. 103-15.

10. Ibid., p. 111.

11. Ibid., p. 196.

12. Ibid., p. 194.

13. Ibid., p. 116.

14. Ibid., p. 79.

15. Ibid., p. 119.

16. Ibid., p. 122.

17. Aylward Shorter, *African Christian Theology—Adaptation or Incarnation?* (Maryknoll, N.Y.: Orbis Books, 1977), p. 12.

18. Mbiti, 1986, p. 120.

19. Kwesi Dickson and Paul Ellingworth, *Biblical Revelation and African Beliefs* (London: Lutterworth Press, 1969).

20. Mbiti, 1986, p. 120.

21. John S. Mbiti, *Prayers of African Religion* (London, SPCK: 1975), p. 178ff.

22. Kofi Appia-Kubi and S. Torres, eds., *African Theology en Route* (Maryknoll, N.Y.: Orbis Books, 1979), pp. 83-84.

4

Christ as Seen by an African:
A Christological Quest

ZABLON NTHAMBURI

The early church believed that one encountered the image of God in the proclamation and ministry of Jesus. In the somewhat radical demand characteristic of his ministry, Jesus declared the will of God the creator. For Jesus, sacrificial death on the cross was the ultimate proof that he had fulfilled his work and ministry in obedience to God's will. The reference to the resurrection was, in fact, the basis for the faith of the primitive church. The Messiahship of Jesus acquired great importance in the early church and became identified with his sacrificial act on the cross. Within the rapidly growing church, among the Gentiles, the term *Messiah* did not have the same central importance, and the equivalent term *Christos* became the proper name: Jesus Christ.[1]

The New Testament expanded this high christology even further by declaring the preexistence of Christ and his participation in God's creation. Paul describes this preexistent Christ as the One who empties himself (*Kenosis*) and takes the form of a servant (Phil. 2); hence, he is identified with the suffering servant. In the Gospel of John he is described as the Word (*Logos*), a formulation which is usually used in reference to Jewish wisdom literature.[2] This Word which was with God and which was God functioning at creation became flesh, incarnate in Jesus Christ. The essence of the church's faith in Christ was that Christ had come from God and had returned to him and that it was God himself who in Christ reconciled the world to himself. The christological confession had its origin in the Easter event. At Easter the community of the crucified Christ, born after Easter, considered itself an eschatological congregation of salvation. The entire New Testament bears witness to this new faith in Christ. The kernel of the message is that God was in Christ reconciling the world to himself. He lived in our midst and was able to reveal to us who God really is. We are reminded that without faith in Christ, our knowledge of Jesus will not only be incomplete but uninspiring. Our faith in Christ helps us to grasp and comprehend Jesus' proclamation and the sovereignty of his word in our own situation.[3]

Judaism seemed to be threatened by the preaching of Jesus as the Christ because this would have been interpreted to mean that they had been responsible for the death of the Messiah. It has been argued that the usual way of understanding Christ, particularly his incarnation, is to start from the top downwards. This view starts from the divinity of Christ and takes into account what may be said about his humanity in his endeavour to effect our salvation. It is based on the understanding that the second person of the Trinity became human. This way of understanding Christ is called "theocentric christology." The problem with this approach to christology is that Christ's humanity is sacrificed at the altar of his divinity. By emphasizing Christ's divinity at the expense of humanity, we give the impression that the human side of Christ is peripheral. This distorted approach to christology tends to turn Christians away from the world, pretending to be in heaven while in fact they are still on earth. The result is that we have Christians who are less concerned with their socio-economic and political issues and too preoccupied with their "spiritual" welfare. In the end, we create a schizophrenic community.

The second approach, which is normally called "anthropocentric christology" moves from the historical Jesus to the divinity. It has been argued by the proponents of this view that while we hold to the concept of divinity, we should not superimpose our own ideas of God upon the image and character of Jesus. Rather, we should allow the life and ministry of Jesus to change our image about God. The source of Jesus' divinity should be Jesus' ministry and teaching rather than our own preconceived notions about God. While objections to this type of christology have been raised, it should be borne in mind that we are called upon to speak about Jesus' divinity in terms of his humanity. In other words, Christ's humanity is meant to limit his divinity in such a way that we can easily identify with him since we have a kinship with whoever shares our humanity.[4] My contention is that African christology employs this approach in understanding the salvific work of Christ. This view concentrates on the functions of Christ rather than on his person. Both his divinity and humanity are seen in the light of his concern with saving humankind. What is important is not the person of Christ as such but his role in the salvation of the world.

ATTEMPTS TO EXPLAIN CHRISTOLOGY IN AFRICAN IMAGES

A number of African theologians have endeavoured to explain christology in African images. John Pobee, for instance, focuses on the Akan concept of ancestorship to depict how Christ is the great ancestor. He explains that the Akan *Nana* (ancestor) is full of power and authority over his human counterpart. The ancestor can judge, reward, or even punish human beings at will. Each individual person has a *Kra* (soul) that unites him with God. Since the Kra returns to God after death, the person retains this individuality even after death. Pobee maintains that Jesus has a heavy Kra which links him to God. The superiority of the ancestorship of Christ is demonstrated by the fact that since Christ has authority over all cosmic powers he has authority over other ancestors as well.[5]

J. Mutiso-Mbinda argues from the point of view of African ancestors as being mediators and intermediaries. The ancestors are important for the preservation of stability and progress of a community of the living and the living dead. From this, Mutiso-Mbinda concludes that Christ, being our ancestor par excellence, becomes our mediator who continues to intercede for us. As our ancestor, Christ becomes the new source of human lineage.[6]

Ambrose Moyo gives insight about how people in Africa see Jesus as an intermediary spirit between God and people. He gives a Shona illustration which depicts Jesus as "a supreme universal ancestor spirit." Jesus is called the supreme universal ancestor spirit through whom all other spirits must get access to God. According to Shona traditional religion, God is described either as *Mudzimu Mukuru* (Great Ancestral Spirit) or *Mudzimu Unoyera* (the holy ancestral spirit). By virtue of being a direct offspring of God, Jesus becomes our Mudzimu with powers of intercession. His Jewish ancestry ceases to be important because he becomes *Nyadenga* (heavenly one) who in effect becomes universal. Moyo then concludes that Jesus, being the "heavenly one," his direct offspring can only be a universal spirit which links us with other people.[7]

Nyamiti builds his argument from the premise that African ancestors who died in the state of friendship with God can become Christian ancestors by virtue of the fact that they have participated in Christ's unique ancestorship. Nyamiti goes on to explain that through death a person attains the supernatural status which brings one closer to God. Death is important in making an ancestor, for an ancestor is one who had joined the company of the living dead. Through his death, therefore, Christ becomes our brother-ancestor in fullness. By being linked with Adam, Christ's ancestorship acquires a transcendental quality since he is able to transcend family, clan, tribal, and racial limitations in a way that our own ancestors cannot. This makes it possible for Christ to become the brother-ancestor of all humankind. Nyamiti views Christ's ancestorship on two prongs. On the one prong, Christ's ancestorship is seen as one with the Trinity. On the other prong, his ancestorship is with human beings, this being demonstrated by his redemptive activity.[8]

Let us pause here to ask ourselves the question: What should be the starting point of our christology? Sobrino tells us that a Latin American christology that is relevant cannot start at a confessional point. It cannot start with Jesus Christ. He argues that the historical Jesus must be the key that opens the door to the knowledge of the total Christ, and therefore, God. In order to know Christ well, we must place him within the context of His life and ministry in Palestine during the first century A.D.[9]

Our starting point in the quest for an African christology must be that of the praxis of Jesus of Nazareth which includes his person, ministry, death, resurrection, and ascension. The fact is that the praxis of Jesus of Nazareth was so powerful that his disciples could say that he was indeed the Messiah of God. Their response to the question, "Who do you say that I am?" (Matt. 15:15) was that he was the Christ, Son of the Living God. The impact following the death and resurrection of Jesus was so powerful that it transformed his disciples into people who faced persecution and death with courage. They were determined to proclaim the Saviour they knew through personal encounter.

As we look back at God's revelation, we perceive that there is no way in which God could have revealed himself to us outside history. In his self-disclosure God saw fit to make himself known to us in a historical process, culminating in the history of Jesus who was perceived as the Christ. The incarnation shows us how God acts in the ordinary way. The incarnation is a way of saying that the human becomes divine because in Jesus the divine became human. As soon as we discover that this flesh—frail and weak, tired and hungry, feeling pain, depression, and forsakenness is the flesh of the Logos of God *and* like any other flesh—then we can conclude that the Logos has become flesh in order that we could be transformed and share in God's glory. The act of God becoming flesh removes any dichotomy between humanity and divinity in our own experiences. There is no longer any differentiation between the religious and the secular, sacred and profane. The only difference we can make is between truth and falsity, good and evil, justice and injustice, peace and conflict. Jesus' humanity then becomes the transcendent depths of his humanity.[10]

Our christology in Africa will be meaningful when we translate it to our contextual situation in daily life. Christ must be seen to identify with humanity's suffering, weakness, and pain. What does it mean to tell an African that God was made flesh and dwelt among Africans in the midst of hunger, oppression, loss of dignity, suffering, and pain? Do we associate Christ with the powerful, the rich, the affluent, oppressors and exploiters? Is Christ seen in our midst to be a friend of the upper classes? This is what Christ denounced and rejected in his earthly life. He was known to be the friend of sinners and outcasts. He identified himself with the underprivileged and the scum of society. He befriended the despised.

For Jesus there is no question of neutrality or compromise in relation to evil and injustices. There can be no neutrality in the face of injustices and oppression, domination and exploitation. We can collaborate with the forces of evil through silence. We are reminded that in Africa there is always a struggle between good and evil, justice and injustice, righteousness and unrighteousness. How does our christology help us to be true witnesses in our situation? We cannot tell victims of injustice and inhumanity that God is only concerned about their spiritual lives. If Christ is not concerned about our social, political, economic, and spiritual realism of existence, he will not be relevant in Africa. We need Christ who in his humanity suffers with us, is deprived with us, fights with us, and identifies wholly with our situation.

If this African christology takes as its point of departure Christ's humanity, then it is as it should be. If because of Christ's humanity we tend to identify Christ with our ancestors, then let us state that our concern is not so much with the person of Christ but his function. He becomes our mediator, saviour, redeemer, and hope. We should not forget that the only way in which we can understand Christ is through concrete historical experience of God's action which is always a liberating experience. The major question will always remain: How has our understanding of Christ transformed people in our midst, particularly those who have suffered injustice, poverty and deprivation, physically as well as spiritually?

NOTES

1. Gustaf Aulen, *Jesus in Contemporary Historical Research* (Philadelphia: Fortress Press, 1976), pp. 152-57.

2. Herbert Braun, *Jesus* (Stuttgart: Kreuz, 1969), p. 77.

3. Ferdinand Hahn, Wenzel Lohff, and Günther Bornkamm, eds., *What Can We Know About Jesus?* (Philadelphia: Fortress Press, 1969), pp. 77-79.

4. Albert Nolan, *Jesus before Christianity* (Cape Town: David Philip, 1977), pp. 136-37.

5. John Pobee, *Towards an African Theology* (Nashville: Abingdon, 1979), pp. 81-98.

6. J. Mutiso-Mbinda, "Anthropology and the Paschal Mystery," *Spearhead,* no. 59 (Eldoret, Kenya: Gaba Publications, 1979).

7. Ambrose Mavingire Moyo, "The Quest for African Christian Theology and the Problem of the Relationship between Faith and Culture – The Hermeneutical Perspective," *African Theological Journal,* vol. 12, no. 2 (1983), p. 97.

8. Charles Nyamiti, *Christ as Our Ancestor: Christology from an African Perspective,* Missio-Pastoral series no. 11 (Gwere, Zimbabwe: Mambo Press, 1984).

9. Jon Sobrino, *Christology at the Crossroads* (Maryknoll, N.Y.: Orbis, 1978), p. 4.

10. Edward Schillebeeckx, *Christ: The Experience of Jesus as Lord* (New York: Crossroad, 1981).

5

Christology and an African Woman's Experience

ANNE NASIMIYU-WASIKE

INTRODUCTION

Christology, according to the *Oxford Dictionary of the Christian Church*, is the external expression of God and also the manifestation of God in time. Jesus Christ appeared on earth in history and summed up humanity in himself. Christ is the focus of Christian faith; thus christology is the most understandable symbol of redemption in Christian theology. As Rosemary Radford Ruether says, "Christology is a place where we envision the redemption from all sin and evil. It is a symbol which encompasses our vision of our authentic humanity and the fulfilled hopes of all human persons."[1]

From the beginning of Christianity, critical reflection on christology has occupied many Christian theologians. Unfortunately, most written theology until about twenty-five years ago was written by men and from a male perspective. The female perspective was left unarticulated. The theology on the person of Jesus tended to be much more philosophical and abstract than that of the existential Jesus of the Gospels who calls people as individuals and as a community to authentic human existence. Although Christian women of every century have reflected on the person of Jesus and on their relationship to him, much of their christology remains unwritten. Only a few African women have ventured into writing down their reflection on Christ-Event and their experience of Christ (for example Therese Souga, Luise Tappa, Mercy Oduyoye and Elizabeth Amoah). Therefore, in order for a thorough investigation on christology and the African woman's experience to be carried out, some oral interviews have to be part of the study.

AFRICAN WOMEN'S EXPERIENCE

The ways in which the life experience of women in Africa differ are numerous. On a national level, for example, there are cultural, physical, environmental, political, and economic variations between and within nations.[2] The diversity is even much more pronounced on a personal level, where the lifestyles vary according to poor or rich, single or married, with no children or with ten children, with husband present or absent, participating in domestic or commercial career, traditional or modern, rural or urban, at peace or at war, of social chaos or order, with a family system that is patriarchal or matriarchal, with opportunities for education and self-direction or not. These are some of the differences (and they may seem mind-boggling), but African women together with their African brothers suffer hunger and thirst continuously. Their main struggles are against the forces which rob them of control over their destiny and which do not enable them to fulfil their God-given potential.

African women in communion with their sisters in third-world countries are struggling for the bare necessities. Their lives are full of severe hardships. They work hard carrying heavy burdens such as firewood; fetching water from faraway rivers and wells; planting, weeding, and harvesting crops; caring for children; grinding corn and preparing food. The women in rural sectors, especially those who take on the status of rural educated, tend to work for long hours. Besides fulfilling the duties expected of them as women, they also do eight hours of work in their professional fields (nursing or teaching). They work an average of sixteen hours a day.[3] The main concerns of these women are physical needs: food, water, clothing, shelter, medicine for themselves and their children and education for their children.

There are also some cultural hardships that African women experience. In African ethnic groups, there are taboos which restrict women. For example, a woman should not talk when men are having a conversation. Women are not taken seriously, and at times their intelligence is belittled by men. They are customarily looked upon solely as childbearers and servers and often cruelly oppressed when they have failed in childbearing or when their child dies.[4] Despite their nurturing, maintaining, and serving life for the survival of human communities, women are always marginalized and given an inferior status.

In their oppression, African women have learned tolerance; they fatalistically accept the given conditions. They try to integrate all their experiences so that they appreciate the wholeness of life. The rural pastoralist or agriculturalist woman stands at the centre of the life of the clan. She is the matrix that holds the whole society together. She gives birth to life, maintains it, and continues to nurture it. Her understanding of the universe and her empirical participation in this universe are imbued with religion.

This makes life a profoundly religious phenomenon.[5] This religious background is what shapes the African woman's experience of Christ.

The supernatural is a presence which is felt in every village, and it claims every new life. The African woman believes that there is an indissoluble union between the supernatural and her everyday life, and she seeks to harmonize these elements in her life. For an African woman, Jesus is the person who enables her to combine her authentic inner experience of the divine with her effort to harmonize her life with this divine.

Six women were interviewed about women's experiences in relation to Jesus. Two were from a rural setting, two were religious women, and two were university lecturers. This sampling is very limited and obviously not an exhaustive inquiry. The question put before them was: Who is Jesus Christ in your life? Their answers were:

"Jesus is my strength. He is the one who enables and empowers me to carry on my every day work. He helps me to be able to cope with the hardships I face daily" (P. Nalyanya, 1989).

"Jesus is my saviour. I live in an area where there are so many witches and evil forces that people have had to sell their property and gone in search of safer places. I believe that Jesus is a victorious Lord who conquered all evil spiritual forces and brought them under control. I am confident that Jesus protects me and watches over me so that no evil may come near me and my family. I continue to live here because Jesus' power is over us" (S. Nafula, 1988).

"Jesus Christ is my hope, and He gives me courage to be. He makes everything meaningful when in my everyday living, I try to make my existence original and creative. In my everyday activities I try to enter into communion with all people who are my fellow pilgrims in search of God, God who is the horizon of final meaning and who gives us our true identity. In God we meet Jesus who reveals to us our true identity and empowers us to participate in the on-going process of creation" (A. J. Namwolo, 1989).

"Jesus Christ is my saviour, my model, my helper, my teacher, my everything and my God. His teachings guide my life, and usually I feel very guilty when I fail to follow His example" (A. Kubai, 1989).

"Jesus is my closest friend, who gives me light when everything about me is dark. From the Scriptures I know that He understands me as I am when I am faced with misunderstandings and misjudgments. Jesus accepts all women and men as equals; in Him there is no discrimination. He uplifts me as He does the whole of humanity. He is my everything" (E. Egesa, 1989).

"Jesus is the core of my life; He is my helper, my comforter, my refuge and my closest friend. He is kind and generous and shares in my sorrows when I am in trouble. He teaches me to be tolerant and understanding towards the weakness of others" (L. Wanja, 1989).

In these African women's statements of their acts of faith in Jesus, several factors emerge: first of all, their Christian concepts of Jesus which they have learned from their catechism; second, their holistic view of life, where Jesus affects their whole life; third, their belief in the reality of witches and evil powers from which Jesus has to save them; and finally, their courage to be, to suffer, and to endure hardships with the hope that soon all this will be over and everything will be restored to wholeness in Jesus Christ.

JESUS AND WOMEN IN THE GOSPELS

In order to relate current African women's experience to Jesus Christ, one has to briefly look at the Gospels. In the Gospels Jesus' attitude towards women is very clearly documented. Jesus bears the message of liberation for all, especially for the disadvantaged. In the Jewish society women were given inferior status,[6] but Jesus esteemed them and gave them equal status to men. The original relationship between women and men first established by God at creation was restored in Jesus Christ.

A few examples from Jesus' life will suffice in illustrating his attitude towards women and what he teaches with regard to them. Nowhere in Christ's life do we find him distinguishing between women and men as children of God. There is a startling contrast between Jesus' approach to women and the Jewish and Roman approaches to them during his time. As Sister Magnus McGrath observes: "By the regard he shows to women, by the treatment he gives them in word and act, by the purity and universality of his love and ministry, Jesus Christ erased all lines of superiority and inferiority between men and women and placed all on the same level."[7]

Jesus' attitude towards women is clearly reflected in miracle stories, parables, and discourses. All four Gospels portray Jesus in several incidents as showing concern for women, not just for their well-being but for their being as persons. He gave them their true worth and dignity. Jesus' approach to women was revolutionary. He treated women and men as equals; this was new, given the contemporary cultural view of his time.[8] There is a balanced way in which Jesus used women and men to illustrate his teachings. This approach was new, since the rabbinic parables carefully avoided women.[9] For example, in Matthew 13:31 and 13:33, Jesus compares the Kingdom of God first to a mustard seed which a man took and hid in his field and second, to the yeast a woman took and mixed in with three measures of flour. Woman's daily life experiences and man's daily life experiences are very important to Jesus. Both of them can be used to illustrate the meaning of the kingdom of God which Jesus came to inaugurate. In

Luke 15:4 and 15:8 Jesus describes the love of God for the repentant sinner. First he compares this to a man with a hundred sheep who on losing one would leave the ninety-nine in the wilderness and go after the missing one till he finds it. Second, he compares it to a woman with ten drachmas, who, on losing one would light a lamp and sweep out the house and search thoroughly till she finds it. In Matthew 25:1 and 25:14 Jesus cautions his listeners on the necessity of being vigilant at all times. He compares the fulfillment of the kingdom of heaven to ten bridesmaids who took lamps and went to meet the bridegroom; then, to a man on his way abroad who summoned his servants and entrusted his property to them.

In the Gospels we find Jesus using stories of everyday life experiences of both women and men (ploughing, breadmaking, shepherding, grinding, and house-sweeping). The above examples illustrate God's joy over the salvation of a lost sinner, the need to persevere in prayer, and the necessity to be vigilant. In all these stories Jesus uses two examples in each case. He draws one instance from the women's experience and the other from the men's experience. Thus Jesus portrays that there is equality in the spiritual potential of women and men. Women and men are called to the same spiritual life, and there are no virtues demanded exclusively of women or of men.

In his teachings and relationships, Jesus recognized women as persons in their own right and disapproved of anything that discriminated against women. For example, Jesus explicitly rejected the Jewish law on adultery which penalized women but not men. In Matthew 5:28, Jesus says: "But I say to you that everyone who looks at a woman lustfully has already committed adultery with her in his heart." Again in Mark 10:11, Jesus declares, "The man who divorces his wife and marries another is guilty of adultery (against her)."

In the Jewish worldview, a woman was considered a constant danger to the man. Therefore, women were kept away from the public eye in order to protect men from this danger. It was believed, that if women and men came into social contact, lust was unavoidable.[10] Jesus dismissed this idea and called for recognition of women as persons in their own right and not as objects of men's sexual desire. It is important to recognize the rights and life of women and to accept them as people who can relate to men in other ways than sexually.[11] To affirm this reality, Jesus included women in the group of his disciples.

Adultery in the Jewish law was always a sin against the husband's property rights. But Jesus teaches that adultery could be committed by a man against his wife. This was indeed a new proclamation. It ushered in a recognition of man and woman as equal partners in the marital relationship. The wife is not an object to be dismissed at will but a partner whose rights must be respected. Both husband and wife are responsible in building and maintaining the relationship in marriage. Adultery can be committed against a husband as well as against a wife.[12]

Jesus viewed women as responsible persons who, like men, were sinners standing in need of God's mercy and forgiveness. When the woman caught as an adulterer was brought to Jesus, he challenged the hypocrisy of all those who brought her to him. He recognized the woman as a sinner in need of forgiveness and told her not to sin any more. Jesus charged the woman to be responsible for her life.

The account of the story of Jesus' conversation with the woman of Samaria portrays him as having crossed cultural boundaries. Jesus held conversation with a person who represents two suspect groups of people: first, Samaritans who were enemies of the Jewish people, and second, women who were of inferior status and dangerous to men's chastity according to the Jews. Jesus took the Samaritan woman seriously. He asked her questions and responded to her replies in order to help her understand the theological significance of their conversation.[13]

Jesus brings out two things in the woman of Samaria. First of all, she is a sinner in need of forgiveness and healing. Second, the woman is made to understand that she is responsible for her sins. Jesus recognizes this woman as an individual capable of spiritual discernment and with specific problems to be dealt with.[14] Jesus reveals profound theological truths to her. These truths concern the doctrine of grace, the standards of fitting service to God (John 4:24), and his own mission as Christ the Messiah.[15]

These few examples show how Jesus deeply respected women and inaugurated a startling new equality between women and men. He taught it to the apostles so that they could continue teaching this revolutionary doctrine after he was dead.[16]

If this is the new doctrine that Jesus left for his disciples, why is it that African women feel as if they are second-class disciples in the church? Why do they feel marginalized and not taken seriously? In order to answer these questions one has to briefly examine the tradition of the church which has formulated many declarations in the defence of its faith and which was brought to Africa by the western European missionaries. Early Christianity used the symbol *Logos* or *Word* to define that presence of God which was incarnate in Jesus Christ. The term *Logos* was adapted from the Hellenistic and Jewish traditions. Logos has a creational concept. It means the transcendent God coming forth into the immanence to found and create the world. Thus the Logos is the presence of God, the immanence of God, and the ground of creation. Early Christianity linked the Logos to Christ the Messiah in order to bridge the gap between creation and redemption and counteract the early gnostic beliefs.

The Word of God as revealed in Jesus Christ is the same God who created the world in the beginning. In Jesus Christ, we have the authentic ground of creation manifested in fulfilled form over against the alienation of creation from its true being.[17]

The term *Logos* was also linked to the rational principle of the human soul. Since rationality in Hellenistic and Jewish traditions was presumed to be nominatively male, all the theological references for defining Christ were defined in male-centered or androcentric ways. This reinforced the assumption that God was male; the male metaphors were seen as appropriate for God, and the female metaphors were inappropriate. The term *Logos* was all-inclusive for the divine identity for Christ and pointed the whole of humanity to the true foundation of its being, but the term was shadowed by the patriarchal cultural realities of the time. Therefore, Christ had to be male in order to reveal a male God, and this was taken literally. The male qualities were overemphasized in relation to God. Man was seen as the image of God whereas woman was seen only as an image of man, and it was through man that she was saved. These theological concepts about God and the Christ in relation to woman are the ones which shaped most of the great theologians' thinking throughout Christian history. For example, Thomas Aquinas, in all his sincerity, had this to say: "Woman is an occasional and incomplete being. . . . a misbegotten male. It is unchallengeable that woman is destined to live under man's influence and has no authority from her Lord."[18] Aquinas based his teachings on Aristotle's philosophy regarding woman's physical nature. Aristotle asserted that the female is a male which, for some accidental reason, did not attain its full development.[19] One wonders if this belief is not still being held in the church today. For example, when Pope John Paul II emphasized the ban on women's ordination, he called on the American bishops to support the dignity of women and "every legitimate freedom that is consonant with *their* human nature."[20] The fact that the Pope places *their* before human nature causes one to assume that women's human nature is somehow different from men's human nature.

The African church has inherited the misinterpretation of woman and her relation to God and Jesus from the European church. Therefore, the African woman, in addition to being under her cultural bondage and oppression, also experiences the socio-economic oppression of neo-colonialists in the church. According to missionaries, African women were not to be trusted. It was assumed that people from "hot countries are incapable of continence."[21] In Uganda no woman was allowed near the priest's house after 4:00 P.M.

As we saw at the beginning of this study, most African women spend sixteen to eighteen hours daily working to provide their families with food, shelter, water, clothing, medicine, and education. They have very little time to seriously reflect on their relationship with other people and with God. Nevertheless, these women believe that their lives are lived in union with God; their theology is not one which is written and articulated but one which is lived and practised in everyday activities and experiences. A few African women are awakening to their dignity as human persons. This awakening brings them to the harsh reality that for centuries they have been excluded from the full dignity of human persons by their culture and by the patriarchal church. Their eyes are being opened to their societies' discrimination against women under the pretext of respect for traditions and culture, and their eyes are being opened to the patriarchal structure in the church which hinders the application of equal personhood and equal discipleship to women and men.

CHRISTOLOGY: A WOMAN'S REFLECTION

The African woman's experience calls for a christology that is based on a holistic view of life. She needs the Christ who affects the whole of her life, whose presence is felt in every corner of the village and who participates in everything and everybody's daily life. She needs the Christ who relates to God, the God who can be reached through the spirits and the living dead or through direct intercession. This God, the Christ, is the one who takes on the conditions of the African woman — the conditions of weakness, misery, injustice, and oppression.

In his own lifetime, Jesus rejected the androcentric culture of the Jewish people. His mission was countercultural. He gave special attention to the downtrodden and the marginalized of the society — the prostitutes, beggars, sinners, tax collectors, and ritually unclean. And most of these people were women.

Jesus Christ came to heal a broken humanity. He empowered and enabled the downtrodden of society to realize their dignity and worth as persons. He continues to empower and enable the African woman today so that she passes from unauthentic to authentic human existence, and so that she discovers her true identity of being made in the image and likeness of God.

There are several christological models that emerge, namely the eschatological, anthropological, liberational, and cosmological.[22] In the eschatological model, Christ is sent by God to an alienated world where the presence of God takes the shape of the Crucified One. Why does the One who is perfect and righteous have to suffer and die? This suffering and death was followed by the resurrection promises, which revealed God's ultimate victory over this world's alienating forces and which opened a future for a new humanity. In his suffering Christ took on the conditions of the African woman and conditions of the whole of humanity, and in his resurrection the African woman is called to participate in the restoration of harmony, equality, and inclusiveness in all human relationships in the family, society, and church.

The second christology model is the anthropological one. God calls us in Christ to a lifestyle that is dedicated to the love of neighbor and to a life which puts others first and gives them life. Jesus takes on the qualities of mother. He is a nurturer of life, especially that of the weak. The African woman's primary experience in relation to others is that of mother. This experience or reality is overemphasized to the extent that the African woman's social status depends entirely on it. Although giving birth and nurturing life is very important, women are not merely childbearers. They have other qualities which have for centuries been left untapped and which could help to establish mutual and inclusive human relationships in Africa and the world.

Jesus recognized women as responsible persons in their own right and took them seriously (Luke 11:27-28). Women were among Christ's followers and disciples (Luke 8:1-2). Jesus held theological discourses with women. He encouraged, taught, and held dialogues with them. This was the most revolutionary aspect of Jesus' approach to women, given the cultural context in which he lived.[23] Jesus today recognizes the African woman not just as a nurturer of life but as one who participates fully in the life of the church — as theological teacher, catechist, biblical interpreter, counsellor, and as one called to restore the church and humanity to the initial inclusive, holistic, and mutual relationships between women and men.

The third christological model for the African woman that arises in women's reflection is that of Christ the liberator. Jesus asks the African woman not to accept her hardships and pain fatalistically but to work at eliminating the sufferings and creating a better place for all. In her undertaking against the oppressive structures her struggles become God's struggles. It is then Christ who suffers in her and works in her to give birth to new and better human relationships. For the educated and privileged African woman whose load is lighter, she should identify herself with her disadvantaged sisters. These include petty traders who walk the city streets to find customers for their fruits and vegetables and are often harassed by the police; girls who are forced to drop out of school because their parents cannot afford to pay school fees; women who are forced to enter into polygamous unions because of economic reasons and cultural beliefs; and traditional rural women who are faced with all types of hardships and oppression. These women are always poor and hungry because they have to produce enough food to feed their families and sell the surplus in order to educate their children. In most cases, production remains the same while the number of children increases. In fact, agriculture is the pillar of the Kenyan economy and all national development efforts depend on it. Yet these rural women are hardly recognized. Their subsistence farming is not counted as a great contribution to the development of the nation; yet without it life in Kenya would stop.

Both women and men in rural life are still immersed in traditional beliefs and have fatalistic attitudes towards development. For example, among the Maasai the principles of quality and economic productivity are not the measures used to evaluate the people's wealth; rather, the number of wives and children and the number of cattle a man has constitute his wealth. In both traditional and modern rural life, women and their work are not given recognition despite their fundamental contribution towards national development. The petty traders, housegirls, and women in polygamous unions are a few of the categories of African women who are at the very top of the hierarchical scale of oppression. They are the paradigm of all the oppressed peoples of the world.

Jesus Christ is calling all women and men of good will to work for the liberation of all people. The identification with the poor, the oppressed, and the downtrodden can seem impracticable without the hope and assurance of Jesus Christ's cross and resurrection to affirm that it is God's own undertaking; we are called to fully participate in it.

The fourth christological model is that of Christ the cosmological restorer. In his letter to the Romans, Paul asserts, "We know that the whole creation has been groaning in travail together until now; and not only the creation but we ourselves, who have the first fruits of the spirit, groan inwardly as we wait for the adoption as (children), the redemption of our bodies" (Rom. 8:20-23). Paul affirms that there is no existential reality in this universe outside the influence of the redemption. Christ is the cosmological liberator who reconciles all things to God. The world is liberated because it participates in humankind's sin and redemption and because humanity dominates the world, humanity has united the world with its destiny.

The existential Jesus of the Gospels was sensitive to the harmony and beauty in nature. In Matthew 6:28-29, Jesus calls his disciples' attention to the harmony, form, and beauty found in the lilies which no human splendor could equal, even that of King Solomon. He was aware of the sufferings the people endured at the hostility of nature. He is also aware of and understands the suffering of Africans today. Drought, floods, and famine are harsh realities which have claimed millions of African people. Jesus, who in his time rebuked the winds and ordered harmony and tranquillity to be restored, could today restore peace and harmony to the African continent and to the world.

In Palestine Jesus came face to face with people suffering from various kinds of diseases of natural and spiritual disorders—epilepsy, paralysis, leprosy, haemorrhage, blindness, and demonic possession. Jesus restored those people to wholeness. As Peter says: "[Jesus] went about doing good and healing all who were oppressed by the devil for God was with Him" (Acts 10:38).

This brings us to another christological model which is much closer to the African reality and which speaks to many. That is the model of Christ the healer. Jesus attached great significance to exorcism and healing. In the Gospels, whenever Jesus healed individuals, it was both physical and spiritual, and it was the individual's initial faith which led to the healing. For example, in Jesus' cure of the paralytic, he says: "My son, your sins are forgiven. . . . stand up, take your bed and go home" (Mark 2:5-11). And again in Matthew 9:27-29 Jesus restored the vision of the two blind men after they affirmed that they believed in the power possessed by Jesus. Jesus "touched their eyes, saying, 'According to your faith be it done to you.' "

Jesus inaugurated the restoration of individuals and societies to whole-ness and he invited the disciples to participate in this re-establishment. As Christians and as women who have seen the liberating power of Christ we have two functions to fulfill: first of all to witness to God's love and care for the universe; and second to give testimony to the continued human responsibility of creating a new world.

Jesus, just as African women today, believed in the existence of devils as beings endowed with intelligence and will.[24] Although the natural calam-ities and challenges of illnesses are understood differently today due to scientific advancement, African people still believe in evil spirits and demons as causes for many illnesses. African people are spiritually hungry and will always follow anybody who claims that he or she has the power to restore one to wholeness. We cannot rule out the possibility that today God is using individuals to heal the souls and bodies of those who are ill. One example is Mary Akatsa of Kenya who casts out demons and restores people to good health. This is an exceptional power, but it is a manifestation that humanity is participating in the fulfillment of the world.

CONCLUSION

This reflection is an attempt to give African women's experiences of Christ. Christ meets them in their own cultural, physical, environmental, political, and economic variations. For African women Jesus Christ is the victorious conqueror of all evil spiritual forces; He is the nurturer of life, and a totality of their being. Christ is the liberator of the sufferers, the restorer of all those who are broken, the giver of hope and the courage to be. Despite the threatening hardships encountered in women's daily lives, he is the one who calls all people forth to mutually participate in the creation of a better world for all.

NOTES

1. Rosemary Radford Ruether, "Christology and Feminism," lecture notes, Hiram College, Ohio, 1987.

2. Mary Burke, *Reaching for Justice: The Women's Movement* (Washington D.C.:Center of Concern, 1980), p. 95.

3. Beverly Lindsay, *Comparative Perspectives of Third World Women* (New York: Praeger Special Studies, 1980), p. 78.

4. Burke, p. 95.

5. John S. Mbiti, *African Religions and Philosophy* (New York: Praeger, 1970), p. 262.

6. Therese Souga, "The Christ-Event from the Viewpoint of African Women," in Virginia Fabella and Mercy Amba Oduyoye (eds.), *With Passion and Compassion: Third World Women Doing Theology* (Maryknoll, N.Y.: Orbis Books, 1988), p. 22.

7. Sister Albertus Magnus McGrath, *What a Modern Catholic Believes about Women* (Chicago: Thomas More Press, 1972), p. 17.

8. Mary Evans, *Woman in the Bible* (Exeter: The Paternoster Press, 1983), p. 45.

9. Ibid., p. 48.

10. Ibid., p. 45.

11. Ibid., p. 46.

12. Ibid., p. 47.

13. Evans, p. 52; McGrath, p. 21.

14. Evans, p. 52.

15. McGrath, p. 21.

16. Ibid., p. 20.

17. Ruether, ibid.

18. Thomas Aquinas, *Summa Theologica* I, q. 92, a.1; q. 99, a.2; q. 115, a.3 and 4.

19. Compare Sister Emma Therese Healy, *Woman According to Saint Bonaventure* (New York: Georgian Press, 1956), p. 10.

20. *Origins* 13: 14, 238.

21. Souga, p. 26.

22. Reginald Fuller and Pheme Perkins, 1983, pp. 137-57; Mercy Amba Oduyoye, *Hearing and Knowing* (Maryknoll, N.Y.: Orbis Books, 1986), p. 106.

23. Evans, p. 50.

24. Sebastian Kappen, *Jesus and Freedom* (Maryknoll, N.Y.: Orbis Books, 1977), p. 75.

PART TWO

FACES OF JESUS IN AFRICA

6

Jesus, Master of Initiation

ANSELME T. SANON

But you, do not have yourselves called master,
as you are all brothers,
and you have but one Master, Christ. (Matt. 23:8)

As to Moses before the burning bush, a voice says to me, from deep within a bush, "Approach not: doff your sandals, hide your face, fall to your knees, if you would approach the blessed face of Christ."

What position am I to assume before Christ?

Is it curiosity, or call, or attraction—the attraction to the kind of face that fascinates?

Attraction it surely is, to this face which two thousand years of attempts—not to say temptations!—intellectual and spiritual, theological, artistic and aesthetic, have never ceased to deliver!

In the tradition of a region of my tribe, a new village is always founded on the banks of two currents of water, so that, at their confluence, the root, or place of rooting, of the village is found.

In the new community of Christ, which must be founded on all of the shores of the world, a junction must be struck, under penalty of treason, at a confluence—to drain the rich alluvions of all peoples of all lands to the great river, to the shore of shores, the face of Christ.

It will be the gift of the African tributary (that still spare trickle of a meager stream) to trace its bed, if it is true that, "in most African countries, the prime theological urgency consists in discovering the true face of Jesus Christ, that Christians may have the living experience of that face, in depth and according to their own genius."[1]

My experience had sprung from a meditation I made as a young seminarian. It happened in the years when I went at sacred Scripture with compass and tweezers, striving to pierce both to the meaning of the text and to him whom alone it denoted.

It was the Feast of Christ the King. And Christ appeared, rising up from the gripping presentation of the letter to the Colossians: He is the image of the invisible God, firstborn of all creation (Col. 1:15-29). Let us translate: "He is the image of the invisible God" as *Àà zèba wo Wuro ta bisigi*.[2] The phrase "firstborn of all creation" becomes

> *danfa si pepe na gwere-yi*
> *danfa si pepe na pra-yi*
> *danfa si pepe na fan-yi*
> *a pia danfa si pepe zin.*

One can translate "for in him all things have been created" as *awe laforoma hon, danfa(si) pepe dan(tè)*; "in the heavens and on the earth," *wuro hon ko lo ma*; "visible and invisible" as *zè-dia-ye ko zèbarea-ye*.

I began with a terminology of classification that includes:

image (*eidon*)[3] = *ja, dia*, the double that is clouded or can be clouded.

image (*eikon*) = *bisigi, yeréworo, ven-no*, the re-presentative that renders present, the authentic, the true born of the true, the transparent, which is seen through its very authenticity.

My spiritual life as an African seminarian, then, was reconciled with the religion of my ancestors. It was an unforgettable moment: Jesus Christ, faceless, is the visible, external image (*eidōlon*) of the invisible God, whom he renders visible (*eikon*).

He is: the human being, the visible face/image of the invisible. God, faceless, becomes visible (*eidōlon*) in a human being transparent to the invisible (*eikon*, symbol).

Several times, I attempted to translate the symbols of this letter into my native language (*Madarè*), preserving their dynamism. My first attempt aligned their elements as follows:

> Image ... of the firstborn
> sign ... of the (ancestral) mask[4]
> deed ... of initiation
> person ... of the elder child/sibling
> being ... of the founder.

For purposes of translation, such a quasi-immediate experience will naturally borrow images, expressions, and faces that respect my own culture, and find themselves interposed between Jesus and myself.

Thus the resurrected Christ, the image of the invisible God (Col. 1:15, 2 Cor. 4:4) sheds light on my tradition, which in turn roots him in myself. For, according to a basic text of this ancestral religion: "Until now no one has gone to God to hear or see him. It remains to go see and hear God's messenger."

The Risen One is this messenger, who, come from God, enables me to hear and see God. He confirms or links the biblical tradition (a religion of hearing and seeing), and my own ancestral tradition. Both of these religious traditions are religions of hearing and vision. But in the first, word and vision remain enigmatic. In that of Christ, the Word is unveiled in clear language and with a human face.

God, whom none may see, is rendered visible to our eyes with different faces (Mark 16:12), which we attempt to discern: The human face rendered present by the human, visible Jesus; the transhuman face of Christ at his baptism and transfiguration; the face of the resurrected Christ; the face of the sibling body or sacramental body, the mystical or relational body of Christ which identifies with the poor, becomes African in his members, as Pope John Paul II says—that face of the sibling of a multitude spread throughout the earth. Finally, we see the face of the total, apocalyptic Christ.

Using these images, we dare approach the name and face that such images designate, and to scrutinize through the symbols the mystery they suggest.

TABLE OF CONVERGENCES: CULTURAL IMAGES

One of our young artists, using a kind of spray technique, has fashioned for us a Christ of the redemptive Passion.

Beneath the frightful or frightening face of the mask, we make out a face of Christ carrying his cross, being his cross, being the way of the cross. And the glance that pierces us through his mask-eyes fixes for us the traits of the Suffering Servant.

"He had neither form nor beauty," says Isaiah's poem (Isa. 53:2). We translate, "We knew not how to regard him: He could no longer manage to see us, having lost his face; his regard and ours no longer met, for his face no longer corresponded to the image that we fashioned of him."

A translation of these Servant poems has been made from the Hebrew into our native language—keeping account of our ethnic family traditions, the genealogical accounts that we call *sini*. A comparison of these two traditions seems quite revealing for our purpose here:

In Isaiah	*In the* sini *ethnic family traditions*[5]
Poems, songs, writings:	Oral genealogies (sung, recited)

For Israel, a prophet, the remnant:	For the great families
Historical facts:	Based on historical facts
Images: servant, chosen, suffering intercessor, giving his life for the multitude:	Chief, founder, builder, friend of slaves and the poor

Exalted.

The attempt to translate the Isaian texts from the Hebrew into our native language enables us to effect a transition from the written Suffering Servant texts to the family oral tradition of the genealogies concerning the great tribal families, and an opening of the spirit and genius of these tribal traditions to the biblical spirit.

The reading key is the image of the Servant. He had neither form nor beauty, which is true of Christ, and true as well of the mask as the symbol of the traditional religion known as the religion of the *Do*, the locus of communion with our ancestors.

Taking its point of departure in cultural images, our christology will connect with the fundamental symbols of our ancestral tradition. Before focusing on just one of these cultural symbols, let us continue to make them out.

We shall choose three of these family genealogies. They are related to the image and symbol of "Chief." A synoptic summary yields the following:

The Chief, Vo (*kirevoo, yelevoo, Do-voo*) is designated in each as:

1. *Gwana-bire*	2. *Kurubere*	3. *Ve-ton-na-masa*
Old nobility, chief slave-father,	builder, intercessor,	master intercessor, intercessor for the young,
intercedes, firstborn, founder,	redeems, firstborn, founding firstborn, friend of the outcast, chief slave-father friend of the poor.	
intercessor as God.		solid as a spear, "Daughters, regard him!" the one the young women admire or mourn.

Finally, we have the particular attributes of the image or symbol of the chief: As chief in the community, as firstborn, founder and builder of the village, he intercedes for all, especially the young, and is the one who practices friendship with slaves and the poor, solid as a spear.

For us, then: we have three faces (images) of the elder brother/child, or firstborn: Founder, builder, and initiator. The village elder as initiation elder (chief or master) is founder, builder, and intercessor.

Elder (root *vo*) designates the authority of the village chief (*kirevoo*), the initiation chief for youth (*yèlèvoo*), the chief of the *Do* religion (*Do-Voo*), and the land chief (*lagavoo*).

The village chief and initiation master are two officials, delegates of the families in charge. They are both chiefs, elders. They found and direct the village, continuing to build it, aided and assisted by the other two.

The elder, chief, or master is the firstborn, the big brother, the delegate. He may be the chronologically eldest (*gwere-yi*) in space and time. Or he may be of the first rank (*zin-te, zegete*). He is especially the one who has most matured in age and experience (*pra-yi*) and the one most confirmed in that experience (*fan-yi*).

The reader will notice here that the word or notion of chief/master implies siblingship; the notion of siblingship suggests otherness in identity, but never in equality (*ye tala, ye sra-sra ga*).

Without being untrue to this tradition in its profound conception, we might say that it sees the chief as an elder child/brother: as someone first in humanity, in siblingship, in filiation, in dignity, and in service. His role is that of "founding the community, building the village, and interceding as God himself would do."

The cultural face of Christ, image of the invisible God, firstborn of all creation, is grasped through fundamental, but still underground, images. Here they are, set in relation to the letter to the Colossians:

Mask,	visible (difficult to see) image of the invisible God,
ancestral,	things visible and invisible both created in him,
old nobility,	he is the beginning,
eldest in God,	first born of all creation, child of his love,
eldest in humanity,	firstborn from the dead,
child and sibling,	(same origin, same condition: Heb. 2:10-18),
worthy servant,	(taking the condition of servant: Phil. 2:7),
servant of slaves and the poor,	
founder,	to hold in all things the first rank,
builder,	by the blood of the cross,
intercessor,	reconciling all, establishing peace,
God.	all fullness abiding in him (John 1:16).

The image of Chief, the eldest who makes common cause with the slave, of the rank of slave as he appears in the songs of the Servant and in the sini genealogical traditions, is absent here, in Colossians. But the letter to the Philippians (2:6-8), which also speaks of the face of Christ (2:7), and the Second Letter to the Corinthians (8:9), which speaks of his poverty, readily fill this void.

Christ, ancestral mask, old nobility, firstborn before all creation, child of God's love, coming into our humanity, to be the firstborn of mortals, child of the human being, first big brother of human beings (Heb. 2:10-18), come as a worthy servant who takes the condition of a slave, with the distorted face of the sinner, friend of the poor and even of poor sinners, you who cherish the poor in their poverty, you hold first rank in all things, having founded all things by the blood of your cross: you can reconcile all things and establish peace, you the sole intercessor, the sole mediator (1 Tim. 2:1-6), in whom God dwells in all fullness.

The poems of the Suffering Servant, the hymn of Christ's kenosis (Phil. 2:6-8), the canticle to Christ as head of the universe (Col. 1:12-23), can all be commented on and understood from within our *sini* cultural tradition, and of being rooted in an authentic Chalcedonian vision. In the tradition of the *sini*, the important thing is to take account of the image and truth of Christ, true God and true human being, without mixture or confusion.

NAMELESS FACE?

Show me your face, tell me your name! How many of the friends of God utter this cry today! As the face reveals the person, spelling the name procures purchase on that person and his or her face.

To see the face of Christ, to recognize his African face, is to find an African name for him.

As we know, there are a number of translations that transpose the Latin, Greek, or modern languages into the tonality of the African languages (*krista, sakrama, batemi*), without sufficient effort to translate the roots.

The tradition of family genealogies was the reservoir of names attributed to families and their members. It provided proper names both for families and for individuals. To receive a name at initiation, or even at birth, was a sign that one was a full-fledged member of a particular family. To ask for a name was to express the desire to be acknowledged as belonging to a particular extended family.

A name and a face tend to designate personal and relational identity, personal being and social being. That is, they seek to express personal being in its social bonds—in its social, communitarian dimension.

In the tradition of the genealogies, a Christian-and-African genealogy ought to be discovered for Christ, in order to root his face and name. It would be possible to do this from a point of departure in the "ancestral mask" that we have made of him for ourselves.

The most current formula, from the catechism, is that Jesus Christ is the Son of God who became a human being. True God and true human being: this is the teaching of the church.

But no one has gone to God and seen and heard God. Therefore God has neither face, nor image, nor altar, nor name. There are only attributes, pronounced according to the circumstances in which God manifests the divine activity.

The only thing left is to go to God's envoy. One can know the name and face of this human being whom the nameless, faceless One has sent.

By what routes?

In terms of the dynamic content of the passages cited from Isaiah, Philippians, and Colossians, and rooting them in the tradition of the genealogies, three ways are open to us: the negative way, the kenotic way of abasement, and the way of inclusion.

THE NEGATIVE WAY

He had neither face nor beauty. We translate: his face no longer corresponded to the image that we make of him for ourselves. "They have disfigured his human face, and he was insignificant (nonsignifying) for human beings. . . . He could not be looked upon" (Isa. 53:3, 53:2).

Faceless and nameless go together. Nameless, without an inheritance or a posterity: it all comes down to the same thing. To have a face (*zin gun*, to win priority or primacy), to be acknowledged as present, is to hear one's name called in a positive tone. It means having a name, hoping to be prolonged in one's children.

The tradition of the genealogies proceeds not by the negative way, but by the interrogative. Who is that one, that we should call him chief? What does he do that shows that he is the chief? Nor is this kind of interrogative absent from Isaiah. (Who has believed . . . ? To whom has the arm of the Lord been revealed? And so on.)

TO "EMBRACE THE CONDITION OF A SLAVE"

The second way or avenue of approach situates the person in a degree or rank indicating social condition.

He was master and Lord—he became a servant. From the condition of Chief, he became a slave. From the rank of God he passed to the rank of human being.

We might think that each of the two assertions relativizes the other. But on closer examination, we see that the terms are correlative.

These situations reveal the unseen, the unheard, through what one sees and hears (Isa. 53:10).

This translates into the fact that

> Our master is our servant.
> Our chief is of the same rank as we, his slaves.
> Our God is of the rank of human being.

The *sini* tribal poems express this interrelationship by calling the chief the lover of, or saying that he is in love with, the poor. Thus we have a circumincession of condition and name: a transference without loss of the benefit of either term.

WAY OF INCLUSION

The third way uses the secret resource of all communication in the relationship of the "I" to another, of the "we" to "you."

"You" and "we," in my native language, are never the majestic "you" or "we," but those of inclusion, in which the speaker makes common cause with the interlocutor.

And so the collective, inclusive name springs into being. The inclusive "we" is posited between two interlocutory subjects as embracing the cause of the one to whom it is addressed.

This platform includes solidarity, participation, and mediation, all taken together.

In other words, the mutually exclusive "we" and "you" here enter into solidarity, through a bond implying and including authority, mediation, by virtue of some foundation or right.

Christ's face, Christ's name, are to be understood by us on this level, not as a "we" above and outside, beyond reach, but as implied to be within. It is what the letter to the Hebrews suggests when it presents Christ as the first elder brother of human beings: "Here I am, I and the children that God has given me" (Heb. 2:10-13).

In an effort to fix Christ's *name* and *face* in a particular tradition, we have taken into account the images and names proper to that culture, which will now lead our steps, concretely, onto the terrain of initiation.

JESUS, MASTER OF INITIATION?

Here we are, evening pilgrims finally come to this place where Jesus is being kept.

Bending down like John to peer into the tomb, or following Peter there, we see that everything, even the shroud, has been folded and placed to one side. The generations that have followed, since that day, have placed labels on everything, to arrange everything in good order and classify it all: a careful inventory and list. What can be said of Jesus of Nazareth that has not been said? Images, icons, drawings, films, paintings, and sculptures—everything has been tried, everything done, to transmit the best of this face, to deliver the secret of its beauty.

"JESUS ANCESTOR, JESUS MASTER OF INITIATION"?

What stranger is this, this latecomer, this evening companion come to trouble the disciples of Emmaus in their joy?

Yes, we are of the race of this stranger, the only person in Jerusalem not yet to have understood what everyone else in his cultural universe is seized by. We, too, cry out, and beg: "If it is you who have taken him away, tell us, and we, too, shall go take him!"

But without any pretensions whatever. Our particular tradition, too, touched by the universal element of grace, will have to be modeled from within. Reached in its particularity, it will be able, in this cultural particularity, to seek to express the universal dimension of this blessed face. It is what we call "evangelizing the particular tradition of initiation."

A LEGITIMATE RIGHT

Two thousand years of manifold readings by hearts and eyes eager to understand the truths of faith have opened many a way leading to the Lord. By what right may one see in Jesus a chief of initiation? Does such an image of the Savior make it bearable to look at him? Is this not rather to disfigure, to mutilate him? Perhaps indeed. But our intention deserves a hearing: for us it is a matter of presenting the Savior under other aspects (Mark 16:12), to lend him other faces, in cultural humanities that he surely could not refuse.

Such an approach, theoretically legitimate, can be supported in our case by plausible references.

For example, according to the letter to the Hebrews, which may serve as our guideline, Christ is our guide to salvation. It was fitting, then, that, as he wished to lead to glory a great number of children, he—for whom and by whom all things are—perfected by sufferings the Chief who was to guide them to their salvation (Heb. 2:10).

This passage evokes a progressive dynamics proper to initiation, and present from the first pages of the letter (cf. Heb. 1:1-3).

Salvation stands for the final state of things and persons. To lead them to this final perfection, and bring to a good end what is already begun, a master is needed, a teacher, a chief who will set those who are to be saved gradually and dynamically upon this path. The initiatory dynamic can be conceptualized as the beginning of a journey, as a gradual undertaking, and as the acquisition of the perfection that constitutes the goal. At each step, so to speak, the master of initiation is present.

On this score, to say that Jesus is Chief of initiation is to recognize in him, in our particular cultural tonality, the eldest sibling who guides to perfection those who have undergone their initiation—that is, those who, with him, have started down the road to the experience of the invisible through what is visible, to the encounter with God through the human being, to touch eternity through the symbol of the present life.

Are we not committing cultural transference when we refer initiation to Jesus, whose culture was Jewish, so different from the African traditions to which we seek to appeal?

One general response would consist in showing, by way of manifold examples seriously examined, the common ground that places biblical culture and African culture nearer to each other than Western culture (especially in its rationalistic, modern version) could be to either.

Another would be to ask: In what way would the pedagogy of initiation be unfaithful to the project of incarnation, that great plan of God who, instead of a full self-manifestation from the beginning, entered upon a progressive unveiling to the human being, all the way to the times of fullness?

This being said, according to the initiation tradition, Jesus cannot be promoted to master without having himself been subjected to the initiatory experience. The chief who presides as initiation master must himself have undergone initiation.

If we examine the matter attentively, we see that, from his birth to his burial, Jesus lived after the fashion of his people, according to the tradition that had been given him. That tradition, while availing itself of the mediation of the Book, was above all contoured to the fundamental rhythms of biological and social life. It is very often through this received tradition that Jesus introduces surprising novelties—for example, the Eucharistic meal, whose setting is the traditional Passover meal. Thus was Jesus initiated according to the tradition of his people, in their manner, and from out of their tradition. He was for us an initiation chief who introduces into every cultural initiation a radical novelty that does not pass.

To our view, the time has not yet come to justify the invocation of this legitimate right of ours. (We suppose it to be recognized.) Furthermore, it is the Lord who grants it to us—that Lord who wills to be manifested to us in the appearances, the faces, in which we are more apt to discover him.

Initiated into Humanity in His Own Tradition. According to the letter to the Hebrews Jesus is the one who leads saved humanity to its perfection, and this in a definitive manner. The initiatory rhythm that he inaugurates is that of his entire life. To be born, to grow, to suffer, to die, and to be buried with the desire for an endless happiness—here is an experience found inscribed on the horizon of all human beings. In Jesus' experience, these stages assume the sorrowful aspect of the Cross, but proclaim the glorious Resurrection.

When Jesus says, "It is consummated," we recognize that he has completed his human initiation. All has come to the final term designated by the Father.

The same letter (Heb. 10:14) plunges us to the heart of our undertaking, when it declares: "By a single oblation, he has perfected forever those whom he sanctifies." Christ's oblation, his total gift by the sacrifice on the cross, is the act of initiation for himself definitively, and it is valid with regard to all human beings. It is the visibly foundational act of the Redemption.

A more careful reading of this passage clearly reveals not only a vocabulary of initiation, but also the stages of the initiation experience. Jesus enters upon these stages of his own free will (Heb. 10:7) as eldest child. In the footsteps of this initiation master so full of constancy and perseverance, the disciples race to the fore, catching what he says word for word, desirous of beholding what he delineates in draft, hoping to arrive where he leads.

Here we should like to call attention to certain major propositions in all of these considerations.

Initiation is always performed from a point of departure in a given, culturally or traditionally situated, humanity. It comprises or supposes a dimension of creation and incarnation: in Jesus' case, that of having come into humanity, having been born of a woman (Gal. 4:4, John 1:14) and being of the race of David.

Initiation, established by the ancestors and proceeding according to the spirit of their tradition, is the deed of a subsequent generation. The candidacy of the initiated is regarded as that of children born of one and the same life, albeit in a hierarchy of siblingship.

We strongly feel this bond of siblingship with Christ. He is the child in the house of his Father (Luke 2:49, John 8:35). He chose the path of initiation as a child seeking to obey a Father. He who has not known the sin of rebellion in solidarity with his siblings, will know what it costs to obey on behalf of the one who has deserted the Father's house (Heb. 2:14-18, 8:11, 2:10-11).

We find here one of the functions of siblingship in initiation: that of mediation. According to this tradition, one of the sibling candidates, most likely the eldest, the chief candidate, represents the group. He is the group—for better or for worse. We readily understand that he would be regarded as "intercessor as God himself would do." After all, "he intercedes for the poorest."

Christ plays this role as elder brother, acknowledging a multitude of siblings. He is the first elder brother of human beings (Heb. 2:9-18). In solidarity with them he accepts all of the trials of human existence, accomplishing, first on their behalf, and then with them, the dolorous path of return to the house of the Father. He does so as master and sovereign.

Here he exercises a type of authority proper to initiatory societies. He is indeed chief, but as a brother. He is master, but as servant. He exercises an authority of siblingship.

Indeed, depending on the cultural tradition, the mantle of authority falls on the shoulders of father, mother, or brother. Without denying the parental authority exercised in the immediate or extended family, the initiatory tradition recognizes an authority to be exercised in the spirit of siblingship when it is a matter of groups born not of the will of flesh and blood but of the spirit of a tradition.

The basis of the community thus constituted is initiation, the spirit of the tradition presiding at initiation. The bonds struck among the members must be animated with the same spirit, inhabited by the same dynamism.

When candidates for initiation are advanced, it is not solely for the purpose of challenging them with the trials of initiation, it is also to verify whether what they experience among themselves and within the human community is in conformity with the spirit of this initiatory tradition.

We might say that the initiation-elder is at the service of the group as guarantor of this spirit, this manner of being a member of this community, learned at the fire of the initiatory path.

In the extreme case, it would suffice, in order for the group to live and perform its true role in the community, that this spirit of a responsible siblingship of solidarity be preserved.

It seems to us that, in the eyes of such a tradition, Jesus is an initiation-elder. Initiated after the fashion of his own, that is, initiated into humanity in the tradition of his people, what he has done more than anything else is to posit the act of redemption as the initiatory "great deed": for us, the mystery of his death and resurrection is easily deciphered in an initiatory context. He becomes the eldest child, the eldest sibling, the master in initiation, at once in solidarity with, and mediator of, his sisters and brothers.

But for us he is the initiation chief because he alone has carried to its term the hidden project at the heart of any initiatory tradition: that of leading a human candidacy to the full, authentic dignity and worth of children and siblings in the community of human beings. If until now the various initiatory undertakings, in their manifold rituals, have adopted so many initiation masters, we, for our part, know but one, and in his discipleship we are all siblings (Matt. 23:8).

Initiated through the Rites of Symbol. An imperfect being is called, in the course of an initiation, to be born or reborn. How does one go about this, when one is already old? We echo the objection of Nicodemus of long ago. (John 3:4).

Initiatory ritual is employed in the solution of this problem through recourse to a large number of symbols, very often recapitulated in a grand test of separation and detachment, of burial and return to life, of death and approach to a new mode of existence and knowledge.

A modern attitude will read, in these rituals, a pure symbolical, psychological game. This is understandable enough when a capital dimension is missing: experience. In the initiation experience, a being feels defenseless, adrift against the unknown. Subjects do not know whether they will emerge alive. They feel that if they do, in any case they will never be the same. The essence of the symbol consists in the receipt of life in the very act of dying. At that moment, human beings, conscious of their bodies, of all the pulsations of their being, cast themselves upon the invisible absolute concretized at this time in this place. They are alive, but in a way that strips and despoils them, a way that reduces them to the truth of their being. They experience a kind of "decentering" of themselves. Dispossessed of themselves, so to speak, they can now receive, in the truth of themselves, a seeming "extra": they become other somehow, while remaining basically themselves.

In this experience, symbol, as the living datum of contradictory realities, yields up the element of reality in life. Thus, Jesus' death is his resurrection, as in any initiatory rite; but just as this death seizes the whole of life, it is life that permits him to die, since it is life that submits the existent one to death. Before the life and death of Jesus, however, life submitted its subjects to death, and death called forth death rather than yielding life in fullness. Henceforward, however, death only delivers a greater life—that of the Risen One, who by his death has given life to the world.

The apostle Paul has kept the rhythm: Christ's death, burial, and resurrection (Rom. 6:1-11) as the symbol of the Paschal, baptismal experience, as well for the initiation of each baptized person as for that of the whole church community. Here is the acknowledgment that we receive a legacy common to every foundational experience of religious community and religious life, a community and a life seized by the invisible through the data of our visible horizon.

Finally, let us observe certain loci or symbols of this experience. First, the dimension of the body, locus of incarnation of the spirit. While it is true that the soul is in the world through a body, the fact remains that the spirit's first sign of manifestation is the body, which is progressively humanized, spiritualized.

Next, the name, as symbol of an individual and social person. The name expresses our personal identity while placing our own being within earshot of, subjecting it to, the call of others.

The third focus of the initiatory symbols remains the ritual itself. The ritual is a social legacy expressing a particular identity, but doing so through rites that themselves refer to a common humanity. Thereby the initiatory cultures, in defining for their candidates their manner of presence to the world, deliver to us a face of the human being that is not without an echo in the concern of the One who has willed the human being.

Must we say that the universal is manifested by the particular, or that the particular is reached by the universal? In any case, it is through these particular faces of the human that the universal is concretized.

We might wonder what the religious status of this common store is vis-à-vis definitive revelation, as compared with the special vocation of the Old Testament in this progressive revelation (Heb. 1:1-3). These considerations would call for a development of their own, and are beyond the purview of our present purpose.

For our own concern, then: Jesus has lived a human and cultural experience that makes him capable—humanly—of opening himself to other human and cultural experiences. This cultural humanity, assumed by him in the incarnation, serves as a mediation of redemption both to his humanity and to his role of adoption of all humanity.

This human being Jesus, assumed by the infinitude of the divinity, is capable of assuming all humanity, is open to all humanity, joining all humanities together in time and space to heal and save them.

Initiated in a Definitive, Decisive Manner. In what way is Jesus our master of initiation? He is that once and for all, in a definitive, decisive manner.

To be sure, all initiations seek to wrest from the invisible the secret of strength, of life, of power, and of all supreme values. Jesus, our chief of initiation, like any master in initiation, places these supreme values before us under the form of symbols.

He does so as firstborn, that is, as sibling of a multitude. He confirms the fact that the order of initiation is situated not on the level of conquest and possession, but on that of receiving and sharing. The child receives as firstborn, and shares with his siblings. Thus, among us, Jesus has the right to speak because he is the Word. Then he shares that Word, giving us life and access to his truth.

His filial condition, which he translated into an attitude of filiation and siblingship, is the foundation of his authority. He is heard by the Father and followed by his siblings like any true eldest sibling. This authority, received from the Father who has placed everything in his hands, is exercised by him as a sibling vis-à-vis his disciples. All that he has learned from the Father, he will give them to know—gradually, however—with the assistance of the Spirit. They, in their own turn, will enter into the secret of his life and his mission. Thus they will understand the secrets of the Reign, that vast project of God's love for human beings of which they will be the first witnesses.

His death on the cross will be the total, decisive symbol of his initiatory mystery. It ushers in the age of the Resurrection, by virtue of which is constituted the new community born of the gift of life offered once and for all.

Gazing on the wood of the cross, we behold the tree of total gift, the tree of the initiatory experience. The place of initiation is the space of the church, the meeting place of the visible and the invisible. The time of this world's duration is the time of the initiation of the persons and peoples who accede to the fullness of redemptive grace.

In the sacraments, we readily recognize the signs and symbols of this initiation. Through these actions, offered in ongoing fashion, the stages of life of the people of God and its members are caught up, at regular intervals, into the total mystery.

Among the supreme values that Jesus leaves as symbol to his disciples is the radical novelty of the spirit of service. He is the Master become servant. Lord he is; servant he has become, constituting himself a permanent servant among his siblings, in a deed of gift that goes as far as love can go. Thus he will make the supreme sacrifice of his life, giving us an example that he alone can give. Happy are we if, after the fashion of young initiates, we set off in the footsteps of the master to do likewise, in our own place.

The new commandment of love, the Reign and its demands formulated according to the rule of the evangelical Beatitudes, are but expressions of this radical gift offered by the master of initiation to those who follow the way that he has trodden before them.

Unlike the masters of initiation proposed by humanity, Christ brings his initiatory itinerary to its completion. What he says, he entirely fulfills in his own example. He delivers not words alone, he delivers up his life, fully accomplishing the will of the Father in totally assuming his solidarity with his sibling human beings. Thereby Christ fulfills the desire concealed in every initiatory project—on the one hand, to make a beginning and gradual advancement, on the other hand, to direct and accompany the candidates along the right road all the way to the final goal.

In him and by him, we have the definitive model of initiation, in fidelity to our fragile human rhythm and our desire to attain the invisible infinite.

Propositions Concerning Jesus the Master of Initiation. First, by having recourse to the symbols and symbolical tradition of humanity, Jesus is seen to be an initiator who transcends the boundaries of his particular tradition. True, he belongs to a cultural tradition of his own, which he assumes; but through it he opens himself to the tradition of other humanities, to the tradition of the various peoples of the earth.

Second, Jesus leads all of these manifold traditions to unity. Through all of this diversity, he reveals to them that to which they all aspire: the secret of the Reign, which is not conquered but received.

Finally, he introduces into the fabric of this ephemeral, fragmentary pedagogy the decisive novelty that does not pass away: the mystery placed within our reach by the lowly deeds and rites of daily life, those signs of mystery, those signs of his total gift of his life and presence.

Thus, Jesus manifests a threefold claim to the title of Master of Initiation: what he is or becomes culturally with us, what he makes of the initiatory traditions in view of the Reign, and what he takes up by way of a pedagogy in order to give us a living experience and understanding of himself.

A CHRISTOLOGY IN SYMBOL

The traditional African has always known that every human face is a mystery, to be scrutinized and penetrated only if it spontaneously opens itself to deliver the spirit animating it.

The face of Christ is, par excellence, a mystery to which we make only gradual, humble approach. The initiatory method borrows this progressive, symbolic manner.

Among the elements of this symbolical approach, we have called attention, for example, to cultural images, the name, the mediation of various symbols, and the law of the initiatory rhythms in its Paschal phases of death, burial, and resurrection.

Now let us add a consideration of the expression of art.

We wonder whether entry by the doctrinal door is the true entryway for a christology that will be in keeping with the African mentality. Other monuments are available, age-old ones, more accessible to the Christian people. We refer to sacred images, statues, and even the places and materials of worship.

An art and a liturgy inspired in christology mold the prayer and ultimately the faith of our communities. The history of the larger church shows us the fundamental options between the imagery of the Western tradition and the iconography of the Eastern tradition.

However, these works of art and piety, received in liturgy, are rooted in a familiar symbolical system, a received symbolical store, a reservoir of customary symbols. We observe this in the images, paintings, and sculptures displayed, the statues venerated, the chapels and churches erected, the songs and melodies that gain currency. Each generation tells the next the name and face it gives to Christ Jesus.

Our argument for an authentically African christology postulates first of all an investigation into concrete symbols. What symbols would best translate what the heart of African converts feel on contact with the Risen One? What name do they give to Christ? To what tone of voice do they themselves "convert," turn about, to recognize the Lord and say: "Rabboni!" "It is the Lord!" "My Lord and my God!" What signs speak for them, what signs are meaningful to them?

A repertory of authentic names for Christ, an inventory of the works in which African symbology clearly translates the face of Christ, an attention to certain beautiful artistic creations in the service of the faith, could well facilitate the further creativity of our artists and open the way to theological discourse.

Unfortunately, the handicap weighing upon the African stock of images and symbolical expressions has not been altogether lifted. African art, like African culture, despised, commercialized, or condemned, has seen its cultural soul wounded to death. Rehabilitation is not easy, where the tendency has been to read only offensive imagery, fetishistic objects, and even vain idols!

Resurrection will not be easy, as the following true story of an African religious sister, who was an artist and profoundly Christian, reveals. When I first met her she was in her convent, contemplating, sculpting in wood and modeling in clay. She created statuettes of an altogether feminine fineness and expression. Robust of stature herself, she drew from this wood and this clay faces of Christ of the greatest beauty and freshness. She, too, was in quest of Christ in his African face.

"How do you manage to get such beautiful things from this wood?" I asked her. Her answer came at once, and I have never been able to forget it. "I look at it until I see the face of Christ. Then I cut away the wood, and there he is."

And there we have it. We can look at another as an object or a subject. We can look at this wood in the same way: for burning, or for drawing the image of Christ from it. Regarded as objects, others will never be seen as living. Regarded as subjects, they become, they are, alive. The contemplation of Christianized African communities is protracted and profound enough for an African face of Christ to spring from them!

To perfect the spontaneous art of this contemplative religious, she was sent to travel in the West, where she came in contact with another universe of forms—as we surely might expect! Our second meeting occurred after her return. Troubled in her cultural and contemplative soul, Sister no longer modeled, no longer sculpted. In her, art, contemplation, and the religious life had been the symbol of a single vocation.

At our third meeting, in one of our African capitals, she was like a withered plant. She had been transplanted from her contemplative and artistic vocation.

Let us repeat, then: to have a christology enriched with African values, we should have to have an art and a liturgy rich in African symbology, itself progressively rooted in faith. The presence of Christ in a cultural world determines a new human symbology, a new language, and a new manner of life among persons. But in order to express itself, this novelty will always take the path of the already-here. It will be from a point of departure in the ancient cultural images, then, that we shall fashion for Christ an African and Christian face.

Up to this point, as in the letter to the Colossians, the litanic genre has seemed to us the most felicitous expression of this approach. In the litanies we have both liturgical invocation and artistic, symbolical expression, as we strive to grasp the mystery of the Face of Christ and to give him a Name that will seal his Face. Here we find ourselves on the same track as the family genealogical traditions, the *sini*. At the confluence of these two attempts, the Face of Christ has these Names:

> Ancestral mask,
> of the regard transparent to the invisible divine,
> of the unique face of the servant Chief,
> unbreakable cord binding us to the gift of the Father,
> founder from the origins of the world.
> Master of the Word that initiates human beings,
> Holder of the secrets of the Reign,
> who bear the Name of names among the known
>   names of God.

An African face of Christ? Yes, on condition that we recognize that we are still on the threshold of a great hope. A christology that will take into account the contribution of the African traditions as a homage to Christ is yet to see the light. It will be born of the deeply Christian life of the

communities and of the fertile reflection of theologians who will have succeeded in contemplating the Verbum of life in order to translate the Face
of that Verbum through the rich diversity of African symbology. Humbly,
this essay concludes on the threshold of such a christology, for which we
long with all our heart.

NOTES

1. Ernest Sambou, "Une voie réaliste pour l'ecclesiologie," *Lumière et Vie*, no. 159, p. 32.

2. Texts in the Madarè language of the Bobos of the Burkina Faso (formerly Upper Volta).

3. Presentations suggested by the Greek roots.

4. (Ancestral) mask: in the sense of the masked person, who in tradition is supposed to be the revelation of the ancestor.

5. *Sini*: Hymns, genealogical accounts proper to the Great Families of the Bobo tribe of Upper Volta. See Lucas Kalfa Sanon: *Le chant du "Sini": une approche du Projet madarè de l'homme* (Abidjan: Institut Catholique d'Afrique de l'Ouest, 1982); see also *Projet d'un 'Sini' chrétien (Une lecture Madaré des chants du Serviteur de Yahvé)* (Abidjan: I.C.A.O., 1983).

7

Christ as Chief

FRANÇOIS KABASÉLÉ

For some two decades now, the word "Christ" has been translated into the Luba language, for liturgical uses, by the word *Mulaba*. This Luba word means "anointed." The missionaries had refused to translate it, preferring to retain *Christus* in its approximative Luba transliteration *Kristu*. Since the adoption by Bantu Christians of the word for "anointed" in their own language — *Mulaba* — the name Jesus Christ has become for them something more than just a proper name. It has become an assertion of faith that arouses their attention. And it has become a name that calls for explanation. With what is this person "anointed"? And why? It is easy to see how important this is for a maturation in faith. Just as Indo-Europeans once translated a Hebrew word into a word of their own, so now have the Luba authentically translated the Indo-European word "Christ" into their language.

The process thereby initiated has accelerated in recent years. It has manifested itself, for instance, in the attribution to Christ of several other traditional titles, among which the title of "chief" is by far the most frequently encountered. We shall see how, by way of the qualities, the demands, and the identity of the "Bantu" chiefs, Bantu Christians have conceived the proposition that Christ Jesus is the one to whom the title of chief properly belongs.

We shall begin with certain selected expressions from the daily prayer of our communities. In the interest of concreteness and precision, and in order to furnish a verifiable point of departure, we have taken the Luba Missal of the diocese of Mbuji-Mayi, which has the advantage of offering an original series of titles, and in the Luba language. Here, Latin prayers are no longer merely "translated into Luba"; they are rewritten, with one eye on the texts of the day, and another on the culture of those who pray —

their ancestral faith in the Supreme Being, the genius of their language, and so on.

In a second stage, we shall ask ourselves *why* these faithful call Christ their "Chief." In other words, what is it, in their traditions of power, that might lend authenticity to this appellation? Finally, we shall see how Bantu royal symbolism has been enlisted in the proclamation of the sovereignty of Jesus.

SOME EXPRESSIONS

First of all, Jesus Christ is called "Chief" (*Mukalengé*) by virtue of the primary denotation of this general word which designates someone who holds some authority and who governs a part of the people. The colonists were all called *Bakalengé* (plural of *Mukalengé*) because they held power. Missionaries and parish priests are called *Bakalengé* because they direct the parishes. Civil leaders are called *Bakalengé* because they direct the polity.

> *Chief* of human beings,
> may your body and blood
> give us to be heirs of your power,
> you the living God. . . . Amen.[1]

Along with this general title, we find titles of power attributable only to particular persons. A colonist, a missionary, a parish priest, a head of the new civil administration, could never, as such, lay claim to them. For example, we have *Ntita,* and *Luaba.* Let us examine these in their traditional contexts:

> *Ntita*-who-distribute-powers-and-principalities, you have fed us with the stores of your chiefdom (your kingdom, power, principality). Grant that we may remain ever in your service, you the living God. . . . Amen.[2]

The custom referred to in this prayer is that of the banquet offered by a new chief on the occasion of his enthronement. The whole people, along with neighboring dignitaries, were invited to this sumptuous repast. This was how the new chief proved his great power—one of the royal prerogatives being to be able to come to the aid of his people, to feed them (we shall return to this). In the prayer just cited, the body and blood of Jesus are compared to the stores brought forth by the new chief to spread forth the banquet of his enthronement.

But the title *Ntita* itself is only attributed to particular chiefs, those who, throughout an entire region, are authorized to initiate and enthrone other chiefs. It is sometimes attributed by extension to men who, without being chiefs, have charge of the royal insignia, and the prerogative of conferring them on the chief. They are regarded as "carrying the chief." This duty is often passed down from father to son. Since they "carry the chief," they are *as if* above the chief, like the *Ntitas*. The ideal Christian context, the circumstance in which this title resounds in all its power and glory, seems to me to be the feasts of Christ the King and the Epiphany, where Christ reigns above all other kings. Here is how it is used for Epiphany:

> Chief of chiefs, *Ntita,*
> hierarch of hierarchs,
> with the chiefs of the East we have come
> to prostrate ourselves before you and worship you,
> for your glory is supereminent,
> you the living God. . . . Amen.[3]

Luaba is another special title. It belongs to those who are destined for power, who strive for power, who are "indicated" for power. It is in the acceptance of "indicated for power" that it is attributed to Christ. In other words, Jesus is "altogether indicated for power." Thus, we have the following prayer, of which we cite only an extract.

> Lord God, . . . help us to be attentive
> to the voice of your word,
> after the example of the Anointed One, *Luaba*
> *and our Chief,*
> who vanquishes Satan and all evil,
> who has life and power
> unto ages of ages. Amen.[4]

The conjunction of the two titles *Luaba* and "Chief" suggests a tension that, it seems to us, is in keeping with the eschatological tension between the "already" and the "not yet." It is asserted of the same person that he is *Luaba* (not yet chief, but on his way to becoming chief) and at the same time "Chief" (actually). The Reign has commenced, but its plenitude has not yet been achieved.

TRADITIONAL SUPPORTS

But why have Bantu Christians placed Christ in the category of chief? Surely Christian revelation proclaims him such (Phil. 2). But there is something else. The prerogatives of a Bantu chief are seen to have been fully realized by Jesus Christ. Power belongs superlatively to Jesus Christ because he is a mighty hero, because he is the chief's son and the chief's emissary, because he is "strong," because he is generous, wise, and a reconciler of human beings.

Hero. Christ is called "Chief" by the Bantus first of all because he has conquered—because he has triumphed over Satan. The figure of the Bantu chief is closely associated with that of the hero. The latter indeed performs one of the roles of the chief, that of defender and protector of the people. Among the Luba, for example, it is the *mwadia-mvita* ("renowned combatants") who have inherited the power of the chief, not by a "coup d'état," but by election by the notables, or even on the initiative of a weary chief past his prime. Several titles are ascribed to these heroes. Here are the ones that occur in the prayers and hymns of Luba Christians as attributed to Jesus Christ: first, "*Cimankinda* of the countless arrows," who strides to the fore and leads the battle lines:

> *Cimankinda,* full of life and honor,
> you have delivered yourself to erase our sins:
> grant that we may do good,
> that we may be with you at your coming. . . .[5]

> Chief of human beings,
> Mulopu, *Cimankinda* of the countless arrows,
> by your word remove the evil of our hearts,
> you who are God. . . .[6]

He is also the *Cilobo,* that is, the hero who never flees before the enemy, but who always scatters them from before his face:

> Jesus the Anointed,
> *Cilobo* who never flees the enemy,
> accept the offering of our faith,
> and send it to the Father,
> you who have life and power . . . Amen.[7]

He is acclaimed as the *Kanda Kazadi,* that is, the one who wins victories, whom no one dares to confront. One often hears expressions of gallantry and valor in hymns to Christ. He is the *mpanga-wa-mananga-nanga,* that is, the ram of the mighty sinews and majestic carriage. He is the *mukokodi-wa-ku-muele,"* the one who never trifles with his hatchet, the one whose hatchet never fails to strike home. He is the "rainbow that ends the rain" (*muanzankongolo-lukanda-mvula*). The rainbow is one of the cosmic powers, but it has never been divinized by the Bantu. It is always associated with the image of the hero: as the rainbow arrests the most threatening rains, so do mighty persons thrust back the most redoubtable enemies. In civilizations in which iron played a role of prime importance for the manufacture of weapons, the names of precious work tools entered into the panoply of heroes' titles, such as the hoe and the axe:

Lord our God:
Maweja, Son of *Ciama,*
your only-begotten, has accepted death
to vanquish death,
he who is the "axe-that-fears-no-thistles"
and the "hoe-that-fears-no-soil."
Deign to give us courage
to accept suffering and death
that we may rise with your Son.
By the Anointed, Jesus, your Son himself. Amen.[8]

Indeed the iron of the axe fears no thorns (the "thistles" in the prayer), especially those that grow in palm-nut clusters. The latter, when they reach maturity, are surrounded with a kind of thistle, with menacing tips; the best tool to pluck the nuts from the bunch is precisely the axe, whose iron has no fear of penetrating to the heart of the thorns. It is the same with the hoe: the iron of the hoe pierces any kind of soil, even the coarsest. These two titles are often placed together in a kind of cross-reference, to represent the hero's courage and determination.

Along the same heroic lines, Christ is acclaimed as the *Kavunga-biombo,* literally, the "one who tightens the loops." The allusion is to the rings of the python, the mightiest of the serpents of our forest arcades and our savannas. Once the python has placed one of its loops around an animal or person, it is all but impossible to escape. The title *Kavunga-biombo,* then, recalls the python's heroic might: "You, who are God, *Kavunga-biombo,* you are our wealth and our [only] hope, for ages of ages. Amen."[9]

This same heroic power is also suggested in the title *mvunda-kavula-ba-madiba, cipepele-kavundakaja-bisosa,* which means, literally: "hurricane who strips those who wear the *madiba* [a garment of raffia fibers], wind who whips the grasses."[10] In this title, the energy of the wind and hurricane is a symbol of the power of Christ. The wearers of the *madiba* are nearly always helpless before the force of the wind; they are simply obliged to stop and wait for the wind to die. These cosmic titles are conferred by a civilization very close to nature, so careful of, so respectful of nature that it spontaneously discovers manifestations of the Beyond there. To be sure, the energy of the wind falls immeasurably short of the power of Christ. But this is simply the limitation inherent in symbol as such: it reveals what it signifies only in concealing it, and even at the risk of betraying it.

Finally, in the perspective of the hero, Christ is invoked under the title of "pillar." He is the pillar of support, *cipanda-wa nshindamenu,* the traditional title given to strong personalities who have played the role of support for their families or their villages. Luba Christians have added a new element to this traditional title: pillar "who watches for us" (*cipanda-mutui-manini*).[11] This addition, however, is along the same lines as the allusion to the pillar of support: the supporting pillar in a hut stands in the center of the hut, inside, standing guard like a sentinel. The tree that is sought out for the fashioning of the supporting pillar is always the one most resistant to ants, rodents, and so on. Furthermore, it is the smoothest trees that are selected, since the supporting pillar likewise serves for wiping the hands after a meal. Thus, we find this title of pillar accompanied by a circumlocution, "supporting pillar, you eat *nshima,* you wipe your hands."[12]

Chief's Son, Emissary. Christ is also called Chief because he is the child of the Chief, of God. That Christ is the Son of God, the Bantus have learned only through Christian revelation. But that God is the Chief of the universe, the ultimate recourse, they know by their ancestral faith. The theological discourse of the Bantu religions asserts this from beginning to end.[13] It is suggestive in this regard that one of the ancient titles of the Luba chiefs, and incidentally the most common, serves to designate God: *Mulopo.*[14] Among the Luba of Katanga (those retaining their ancient culture), "Chief Lasongo" is always translated *"Mulopo* Kasongo," while God is called simply *Mulopo.* And the Luba Christians have adopted without change this ancestral terminology[15] referring to the power of God:

> *Mulopo Maweja* of all goodness,
> sun too bright to behold
> —by whose rays the beholder is burned—
> behold us come to offer you our hearts:
> deign to accept our offering,
> you who live. . . . Amen.[16]

Since Christ is revealed as the Son of this *Mulopo,* the Bantu confer upon him, as well, in the logic of their conception of power, the title of *Mulopo*—or else of *Mulopo muana,* that is, *Mulopo* the Son. To take only one example:

> *Mulopo Maweja,* Son of *Cyame,*
> may your body and blood
> feed our weakened hearts
> and restore them forever,
> you who live. . . . Amen.[17]

Even emissaries of a chief are addressed as *Mulopo.* As *Mulopo's* special envoy, Jesus must be called God's *Mulopo.* Finally, the spirits, by virtue of their proximity to God, are called *Milopo.* Thus, this title will be verified of Christ par excellence. It seems to me that it is on account of the designation of the spirits close to God as *Milopo* that the necromancers or faith healers who are deemed to be inhabited by these spirits are called "Mothers of the *milopo,*" or "Mothers of a *mulopo.*" Here is an extract from a traditional hymn alluding to this proximity to God, entitled, precisely, *Mulopo.*

The oak that leans on God, *yo yo y'e,* the oak that leans on God.
—I am the mother of God [of the "Lord" or chief], in what place am I not known?
—Her skull was almost split with a reed! [irony]
—The mother of God [of the chief] can use no cosmetic [she who everlastingly coats herself with kaolin for the rites of healing!]
—she is like an oak, leaning on God [the chief].[18]

If the necromancer, "inhabited" by "spirits" close to God, enjoys such divine power (an oak that leans on God becomes even more solid) that she may be called "mother of *Mulopo,*" then Christ, Son of God, can only have the actual title *Mulopo.*

Chief by Reason of Strength. The Bantu chief represents an ambivalent figure.[19] On the one hand, he is the vessel of a life force that protects and strengthens the life of a group and its individuals, while employing a certain violence that constrains, punishes, and even destroys. On the other hand, he is supposed to be bicephalous, his this-worldly face concealing a region of the Beyond. This causes the Bantu chief to be placed at the intersection of the earthly and the Beyond, a sphere called by the Bantu the region of the "strong" (*bakolé*).

To be sure, a chief must be strong and mighty, active and energetic, solid and firm.[20] But his strength is not precisely a "muscular" one. It is rather the strength of a "participation in being." Thus, the sphere of the "strong" includes fortune-tellers, "mothers of a *mulopo,*" healers, initiators of various orders and social groups, manipulators of natural forces. These are regarded as "strong" because they see what we do not, they hear voices inaudible to "profane" ears, and so on. The world is a vast field of networks and circuits of interdependencies and mutual influences among beings. The "strong" are able to locate them and direct them to a particular end. Healers know the secret of the plants: thus, they can exploit their "strength." It is not enough for them to possess a technical know-how: they must also acquire a "disposition of being" that places them in dialogue with these plants before they deprive them of a bit of their latex or their bark.[21] And it is this disposition that will enable them to choose the opportune moment for the gathering of the required elements, which is of some importance where the anticipated effect is concerned. Finally, it will enable them to uncover the hidden, profound causes of the disease to be treated, whose complete cure will be effected only with the cooperation of the Beyond.

Such personages must be *initiated.* The rites work a transformation of being within them that extends far beyond any technical know-how (likewise indispensable). Thus, there is no such thing as an uninitiated Bantu chief. A chief belongs to the category of the "strong," by the fact that he is guarantor of growth of life in the social group, and the fact that, in virtue of his function as chief, he shares in the charge entrusted to those-beyond

(to the Ancestors). The Bantu chief does not "exercise" power—he holds
it in his hands!

> [He is] the receptacle of the forces at work in a given geopolitical and
> social space. Any serious disturbance will be imputed to him, to the
> point where, in certain cases, his existence can be suppressed for the
> reestablishment of the dynamic equilibrium of society.[22]

In the exercise of a like task, religion and politics are inseparably joined,
but in a different way, in both content and form, from the theocratic regimes
that so long tyrannized the West, or the systems dominated by religious
castes. Where the principle "Cujus regio, eijus religio" was the order of the
day, it was a matter of an abuse, in which religion was a means of establishing the power of the sovereign. Among the Bantu, the bond between
the political and the religious means that the chief must conform to the
religious ideals and practices of the people's ancestral experience, which
are at the same time their conception of life and their social ethic.

It seems to us that this aspect of "strength" constitutes one of the major
supports of the attribution of the title, "Chief," to Christ: his activity, his
thoughts, his mission have appeared to the Bantu such as to place him in
the category of the "strong." The Gospels surely present him as the one
who comes from on high (as in the Annunciation and the infancy narratives). Jesus says this of himself explicitly: he comes from the Father, and
is sent by him (John 8:42). Again, in Jesus the invisible is rendered visible:
God has shown himself:

> *Mulopo Maweja,* God whom none can see, our
>   Creator,
> you have willed to show yourself to us in the
>   Anointed, your Son,
> and thereby have given us the joy of attaining
>   salvation.
> Our union with him has joined us to you who are of
>   on high:
> this it is that most rejoices us,
> and is all that we desire,
> in Jesus' name, the Anointed, our Chief. Amen.[23]

"The Word was made flesh": for a Muntu, a flesh of this sort, a mirror
of the Beyond, can only belong to the order of the "strong," and conforms
perfectly to the identity of the chief.[24]

For the Bantu, Christ is confirmed as "strong" in the miracles that he
works, in the effectiveness and weight of his word. His words have a hidden
meaning: "Destroy this temple . . . I shall rebuild it in three days" (John
2:19). It sometimes took time for his words to be understood (John 20:9,

Luke 24:32-34). His words were enigmatic, which to a Muntu would readily suggest the words of a diviner, a healer, and so on. The "supernatural" is at play in words like these. The words that emerge from the mouth of the chief are received against this background, since power is essentially supernatural.[25] These words are, in a certain sense, of the order of "sorcery" — of good sorcery, that of the chief,[26] calculated to safeguard life, and therefore contrary to wicked sorcery, which is ordered to death and exudes hatred.

Chief by Reason of Generosity. The parallel between Christ and the Chief is verified in other qualities that the Bantu demand of their chiefs: for example, generosity, wisdom, the spirit of conciliation among human beings.[27] The chief is generous. He must be able to make life pleasant and prosperous for his subjects. He is the one who blesses, the very master of blessing.[28] We find "presence" to be a quality of this attitude: the chief is present to the people. An absent chief is never available to his subjects.[29]

Jesus is seen as the one who is present, Emmanuel (Matt. 1:24), the shepherd who abides with the flock. He is generous in the distribution of his gifts: he satiates the hungering crowd beyond its expectations. He addresses his call to all, good and wicked: on the hard-trodden path, among stones, amidst brambles, on good ground, everywhere. His generosity goes all the way to the gift of his life (John 10:18).

Among the Bantu, accession to power was never "automatic." Of course heredity weighed in the balance, but, among the candidates of various royal lineages, or even among the sons of a deceased chief, the notables chose the one who was seen to be wise, of whom one might expect good advice. Impulsive, ireful, and awkward princes were eliminated from consideration,[30] sometimes even in favor of a particularly well-endowed hero.[31]

To a Muntu, Christ appears as Wisdom itself, from the fact that he follows the will of the "Father," doing nothing that he does not see the Father do (John 5:19). Inasmuch as the Bantu see the Ancestors only in conformity to the will and desires of the Supreme Being (we shall return to this), a Muntu will replace "Father" with "Fathers." The Bantu chief does not what pleases himself, but what pleases them, and therefore they do not leave him solitary (cf. John 8:29).

The wisdom of the Bantu chiefs is also expressed in good judgment. They must not judge according to their own interests or caprices, or according to appearances. The chiefs must be dexterous and cunning, must know how to elude traps. They must not dupe others, as do the Kabundi, to whom power was refused,[32] but govern in the interest of all, and at the service of all. The Bantu are particularly struck by the way in which Christ was all of this to an extreme (we shall return to this apropos of certain points of discontinuity): "If, then, I have washed your feet, I the Lord and Master . . ." (John 13:14). Of course, the Bantu princes did not go as far as that. But the one who, while his royal father was yet alive, manifested tendencies to have himself served by his contemporaries, or who already treated them as slaves, thereby got himself eliminated from the scrutinies of the notables.[33]

Chief by Reason of the Ability to Reconcile. Finally, a Bantu chief had to be a *"cinkunku*-who-gathers-the-hunters." He was like a giant tree, in whose shade are found all who have taken part in a hunt, there to share the spoils and swap accounts of the adventures they have had.

When the Bantu hear the Gospels and notice that Jesus opposes the spirit of vengeance (Matt. 5:38, etc.), that he preaches forgiveness of offenses (Matt. 18:21, etc.), and that his last injunction before his death is love and union, they readily bestow on him the traditional title of *"cinkunku*-who-gathers-the-hunters," or of "mortar-who-gathers-the-grinders." These are titles that attach to Ancestors and chiefs, those reconcilers par excellence. In view of the principle of "vital union" (communion of life among the members of a clan, who all share in the life bestowed by an Ancestor and who are like links in a long chain), disunion among the people is the most pernicious of evils, and occasions the immediate decree of a "state of emergency."

Thus, the activity, personality, and words of Jesus, along with the Father's approval, confirm his sovereignty in the line of the Bantu traditions, with discontinuities and limits, of course, which we shall develop below. But just as, long ages since, the discovery of faith came only after the living experience of the first disciples, so also it is particularly interesting to observe that Bantu Christians, with an eye to traditions relative to the exercise of power, discover after the fact that Christ is Chief, and that his person is in perfect conformity with the very essence of Bantu power:

> Chief of chiefs,
> hierarch of hierarchs,
> Chief par excellence,
> we have eaten and been satiated
> with the food of the saints:
> strengthen in us the desire to serve you faithfully,
> God who live. . . . Amen.[34]

SYMBOLS

"Christ has no other hands, no other feet, uses no other words, or other images, than those of the believer."[35] Thus, the Bantu have used certain symbols taken from their royal traditions to express the authority of Christ. Here are some of them.

The Leopard Skin. Great chiefs, those who truly wield power, are called "chiefs-by-the-leopard" (*mukalenge wa nkashama*), or simply (among the Otetela) "leopard-mother," "of the belly of the leopard."[36] The solemn vesture of the chief, among most of the Bantu peoples, includes material taken from the leopard: two leopard skins, one before and one behind; or a headpiece in leopard skin; or a necklace of raffia fiber (or elephant hair) from which leopard teeth are hung. Among the Bashi (in Rwanda), it is believed that, after death, each individual undergoes a metamorphosis. The metamorphosis of the great princes or of the king is altogether special: with the king, the *cizunguzungu* (ethereal aerial projection of the inner vital principle, or else the soul-shade), transmigrates into a worm that emerges from him, which metamorphoses into a leopard before liberating the *muzimu* (soul-spirit).[37] Among the Luba, traditional chiefs on official excursion wear a piece of leopard skin attached to the belt, or on the right arm. Among the Bakongo, the chief-elect ascends the *myalu*, a kind of litter made with leopard skin, the leopard being regarded as *mbisi i kimfumu*, or animal of sovereignty.[38]

The adoption of the leopard symbolism by the modern civil authorities in Zaire is an indication of its persistence. With the coming of independence (1960), at Kasai, leader Albert Kalonji was seen to wear a leopard skin at his belt. At Leopoldville (now Kinshasa), Patrice Lumumba often wore a leopard-skin thong at his neck. Still more recently, President Mobutu and senior party officials wear leopard-skin caps.

We can understand, then, that Bantu Christians would wish to use leopard skin to adorn the tabernacle, for it is the abode of the great Chief.[39] After all, even God was traditionally invoked as the "leopard-with-his-own-forest."[40] Taking their cue from this traditional hymnology, the Poor Clares of Mbuji-Mayi[41] have made the liturgical vestment of a bishop of imitation leopard-skin: after all, the bishop is the *chief of the assembly,* the Christian assembly, and *presides at the constitution of the church.* The Mothers of Bethany pronounce their solemn oath of commitment before a cross erected above a leopard skin, recalling the traditions of swearing a solemn oath on a leopard skin as a symbol of the hierarchy of the universe, which is called to witness.[42] When these religious take an oath to bind themselves to Christ before a crucifix placed on a leopard skin, they thus proclaim that Christ is Sovereign of the universe and demonstrate that their commitment is to the service of this sovereignty.[43]

Axe, Spear, Elephant Stakes. The leopard skin is always found associated with other insignia, such as the axe, which the chief places on his shoulder or holds in his hands. Elephant stakes are often placed at the entryway of the chief's enclosure, accompanied by several spears. These emblems of combat are symbols of both fear and trust: the enemy's fear, and the trust of the people of whom the chief is the protector. It is through these same insignia that Bantu Christians express their conviction that Jesus Christ is their defender, in a world they still see as a vast battlefield of life and death. Thus, in churches (especially at Kinshasa) we often find two gigantic spears standing at either side of the tabernacle. At times the tabernacle spears are replaced by elephant stakes.[44]

Royal Necklace. Among Bantu chiefs, when the necklace is not of leopard teeth, we find it made of cowrie shells or rare pearls. In African symbolism the cowrie shell is a symbol of wealth.[45] This accords with the status of the chief as the people's purveyor and "supplier" par excellence. Christ, too, in certain sixteenth-century crucifixes fashioned by Congolese artists, wears a royal necklace of pearls and cowrie shells.[46] I was surprised to see them in a Palm Sunday celebration at Mbanza-Ngungu (in Lower Zaire). A Redemptorist missionary had collected them, here in this cradle of evangelization in Zaire. Preaching on Christ as King of the Universe, the missionary exhibited one of these brass crosses, with its corpus clad in the Kongo royal necklace and concluded his homily with these words: "You see, your sixteenth-century ancestors believed in the supreme authority of Jesus!"

NOTES

1. Missal of the Diocese of Mbuji-Mayi, published by Cimanga-Dipa-Dia-Nzambi under the title, *Didia dia Mfumu* (The Lord's Supper), Kinshasa, 1980, Year A, p. 232, Prayer after Communion. Translation and emphasis ours.

2. Ibid., p. 274, Prayer after Communion.

3. Ibid., Year C, p. 87, Entrance Prayer.

4. Ibid.

5. Ibid., p. 293, Offertory Prayer.

6. Ibid., Year B, p. 62, Prayer after Communion.

7. Ibid., Year C, p. 160, Offertory Prayer.

8. Ibid., p. 113, Entrance Prayer.

9. Ibid., Year A, p. 59, Entrance Prayer.

10. Ibid., p. 62, Offertory Prayer.

11. Ibid., p. 177, Entrance Prayer.

12. Ibid., p. 63, Prayer after Communion.

13. C. M. Mulago, *La religion traditionnelle des Bantu et leur vision du monde* (Kinshasa, 1973); O. Bimwenyi-Kweshi, *Le discours théologique négro-africain* (Paris, 1981).

14. L. Mpoyi, *Histoire wa Baluba* (Kinshasa, 1972).

15. Mbuyi Wenu Buila, *Bankambua betu* ["Our Ancestors"] (Kinshasa, 1972), pp. 29-33.

16. *Didia dia Mfumu* (Missal of the Diocese of Mbuji-Mayi), Year A, p. 217, Offertory Prayer.

17. Ibid., p. 205, Prayer after Communion.

18. Other translations render *Mulopo* "Seigneur," Lord. I think it should be translated "Dieu," God, unless followed by another proper name designating a particular chief. See Katende Cyovo, *Voilà la nouvelle lune, dansons!,* Ceeba (Bandundu, 1977), p. 11.

19. Doomo-Lola, "Lieux de l'expérience et de sens de soi," third cycle doctoral thesis (Paris), p. 73.

20. D. Biebuyck, *Hero and Chief* (California, 1938), p. 111.

21. Eric de Rosny, *Healers in the Night* (Maryknoll, N.Y.: Orbis, 1985).

22. M. H. Piault, *La notion de personne en Afrique noire* (Paris, 1981), p. 460 ("La personne du pouvoir ou la souveraineté du souverain en pays mawri").

23. *Didia dia Mfumu* (Missal of the Diocese of Mbuji-Mayi), Year C, p. 96, Prayer after Communion.

24. Ndaywel è Nziem, "Note sur les structures d'autorité chez les Ngwi et leur origine," *Revue Zaïroise des Sciences de l'Homme* 2 (1973):88.

25. A. M. D. Lebeuf, *Les principautés Kotoko (Essai sur le charactère sacré de l'autorité)* (Paris: C.N.R.S., 1969).

26. Ndaywel è Nziem, "Note sur les structures d'autorité," p. 101.

27. The following works may be profitably consulted: G. Balandier, *Sociologie actuelle de l'Afrique noire* (Paris: Presses Universitaires de France, 1963); H. Baumann and D. Westermann, *Les peuples et les civilisations de l'Afrique* (Paris, 1967).

28. Biebuyck, *Hero and Chief,* p. 111.

29. Ndaywel è Nziem, "Note sur les structures d'autorité," p. 94.

30. A frequent allusion in traditional songs. See Katende Cyovo, *Je désire danser,* Ceeba, no. 49 (Bandundu, 1979), p. 39.

31. Cf. the legend of the hero *Mikomb'a Kelewo:* Katende Cyovo, *Source,* Ceeba, no. 72 (Bandundu, 1981), p. 91.

32. Ibid., pp. 31-33.

33. L. Mpoyi, *Histoire wa Baluba* (Kinshasa, 1972). See the accounts of power dispute among the princes, etc.

34. *Didia dia Mfumu* (Missal of the Diocese of Mbuji-Mayi), Year A, p. 267.

35. A. Vergote, "La réalisation symbolique dans l'expression culturelle," *Maison Dieu* 111 (1972:112).

36. Doomo-Lola, "Lieux de l'expérience," p. 30.

37. C. M. Mulago, *Religion traditionnelle des Bantu,* pp. 42, 43.

38. Van Wing, *Études Bakongo* (Brussels, 1921), pp. 138-47.

39. In the chapel of the Novitiate of the Soeurs Thérésiennes at Mbuji-Mayi.

40. The leopard constellation is detailed by O. Bimwenyi-Kweshi, *Discours théologique négro-Africaine* (Paris, 1981), chap. 8.

41. P.O. Box 76, Mbuji-Mayi.

42. Mbuyi Wenu Buila, *Bankambua betu,* pp. 191-93.

43. F. Kabasélé, "A travers des rites nouveaux, un christianisme africain," *Bulletin de Théologie Africaine,* no. 10, vol. 5 (1983), pp. 235-36.

44. In the chapels of the Bishop's Residence of Mbuji-Mayi, the Carmelites at Citenge, and the Poor Clares of Mbuji-Mayi.

45. Engelbert Mveng, *L'art d'Afrique noire* (Rome, 1964), p. 31.

46. *Cahiers des Religions Africaines,* nos. 31-32, vol. 16 (January-July 1982), pp. 137-47.

8

Christ as Ancestor
and Elder Brother

FRANÇOIS KABASÉLÉ

Jesus said to Thomas: "I am the way, the truth, and the life. No one goes to the Father but by me" (John 14:6). These words recall to a Muntu's mind the persons who are the *source of life* and *obligatory route* to the Supreme Being: the Ancestors. The figure of the tree (or the vine) used by Jesus to represent the way in which his life passes to the disciples reminds the Bantu of the importance of ongoing contact with the Ancestors for the maintenance of life. Unless one remains grafted onto them, one dries up and wastes away, like a shoot fallen from the stock (John 15:5ff.).

The parallel between Jesus and Adam in Christian preaching establishes the image and suggestion of the Ancestors on the figure of Jesus even more solidly.

> Adam, figure of the one to come. . . . If by the transgression of one, the multitude has died, how much more are the grace of God and the gift conferred by the grace of one man, Christ Jesus, poured out in profusion on the multitude! (Rom. 5:14b,15b).

The interdependence among the members of a Bantu clan reminds one of *vases communicants*: the pressure exerted on one point of the liquid is integrally transmitted to all other points. In the Bantu conception, life is comparable to such a liquid: the individual receives it from the first vessel, which represents his or her Ancestor, and with which the individual remains in ongoing communication. Everything that later enhances the degree of participation in life is of the highest interest to the Ancestors, and has repercussions on all other members of the clan. Jesus Christ comes to inaugurate a new equilibrium and new networks of communications among the vessels: he likewise brings them an "over-fullness," which fills the vessels to new levels. He is the "last Adam, . . . who gives life" (1 Cor. 15:45b).

Most of the movements of spiritual awakening in black Africa are marked by an acute sense of the concept of the intermediary.[1] By way of a single example, *jamaa* offers a very hierarchized spirituality, positing Christ as the new male Ancestor and the Blessed Virgin as the new female Ancestor. For *jamaa*, Jesus and Mary furnish models, and supply new channels, for the deed of salvation. In emulating the love of Jesus and Mary, a couple increase the love within their home and thereby their married life as well.

> Jamaa spouses have recourse to Christ and the Virgin Mary as to their Ancestors, whose communion they seek. Like the traditional Ancestors, they are part of the family universe. . . . Christ is the Ancestor par excellence, present today among his own . . . . [He is] the New Adam, . . . and Mary . . . the new Eve, . . . his associate by superabundance of love.[2]

Certain catecheses of the era of "adaptation" made a special effort to explain the worship of Jesus Christ in terms of Ancestor worship.

> And so Jesus Christ is above all spirits. He is our own Spirit [Ancestor], because we have been . . . born a second time by baptism. We are human beings, but we are also of the race of God, by our baptism. *Thus we have two lines of Ancestors.* The great spirit [Ancestor] is always Christ, God's child, who died and who rose again. He is the firstborn from the dead. *After Christ, we can rely on other founding spirits.* First, [we have] the Blessed Virgin Mary. . . . Then let us not forget our departed. . . . If something has gone amiss in our homes, let us come together in church. Let us go there with all of our relatives, even our pagan ones, let us go there with the elder ones of the village. . . . For now we have a sacrifice that is better than all of the old sacrifices. . . . Let us offer this unique sacrifice in the celebration of the Mass.[3]

This is how Bantu Christians express themselves. Let us delve deeper into the relationship they strike with Christ as their Ancestor, first in the light of what the Ancestor represents for a Muntu, then by applying to Christ the various tonalities in which the relationship of a Muntu with his or her Ancestor is expressed.

THE BANTU ANCESTOR

It was to the Ancestors that God first communicated the divine "vital force." Thus, they constitute the highest link, after God, in the chain of beings. But they still remain human beings. In their death passage they have become more powerful than other human beings—in their capacity to exert influence, to increase or to diminish the vital force of earthly beings. In their present state, they behold both God and God's subjects. Not just anyone accedes to the rank of Ancestor. It is not enough to die; one must have "lived well"—that is, have led a virtuous life.

They must have observed the laws—have incurred the guilt neither of theft nor of a dissolute life. They must not have been wrathful persons or quarrelsome ones, or have dabbled in sorcery. They must have been a leaven of unity and communion among human beings.[4]

They must have left descendants on earth. Life received must be communicated. The more life there is, the stronger it is. The Ancestor must have been no curb or obstacle to life. If one has had no progeny, how can one be a sign, play the role, of the mediation of life—the role par excellence of intermediaries between human beings and the Supreme Being?

To have "died well," and to die well, means to die a "natural" death, full of years, after having delivered one's message to one's own, and to have had a funeral and burial.

Of course, the appellation "ancestors" can be extended to the deceased who have not fulfilled all of these conditions. But the role of mediation of life between God and human beings is played only by those who have fulfilled them. They perform this mediation in procuring fertility and health for their own who are on earth, prosperity in the enterprises of these latter (animal husbandry, business, agriculture, the hunt): in a word, in procuring a broad, happy life. They exercise it by the channel of lineage, consanguinity, because of the participation of all their descendants in the life handed down from them. It is always life that is asked, whether of God or of the apostles:

> God of the skies, Lord,
>   give me the strength of life, that I may be strong.
> Give me well-being.
> May I marry, may I have children.
> May I raise goats, chickens.
> May I obtain money, and goods of every sort.
> May I bloom with health and life.[5]

> Zira!
> It is true, God of heaven, you shed light.
> May you do so ever more!
> Receive this white cock, and give it to Grandfather.
> Zira, this is the white cock, yours, that I am giving
>   you.
> It is you who dwelt in this house: I came here and
>   found it built.

I give you this cock that you may well protect it [the
    house].
Protect your grandsons and granddaughters, your
    grandsons' wives.
Look upon me and protect me, night and noon.
Protect me in the marketplace,
    protect my wife when she prepares the food,
    when she goes to fetch wood.
Make there always be food in this house.
Reach out both hands and receive![6]

But how do the Ancestors live? According to the Bantu, they live in
villages like those of living human beings. They retain, in a mysteriously
spiritual manner, human needs. The worship rendered them provides for
part of these needs. The human is still a human being in the village of the
Ancestors. A woman is still a woman, a king is still a king; the rich continue
to be kings, and the poor to be the poor. But their life is now endless and
has changed its aspect. Earthly beings who have known them no longer
recognize them. When they appear to them, it is "under the form of a
vaporous body, a vaguely shaped shadow," they "pass like the wind."[7]

Recourse to them is made not only to ask some favor, such as a cure or
the satisfaction of some need, but also, simply in order to remember them —
as a memorial, to perpetuate a memory, a history of deeds and words, an
experience of the victory of life over death. Recourse to the Ancestors,
whatever its motive or occasion, is always a source of blessing. Thus, all
important events in the life of the Muntu become either an epiphany of
the activity of the Ancestors or an occasion of renewing contact with them,
like closing ranks before a battle. For the more "devout" among the Bantu,
all acts of daily life must be steeped once more in this presence of the
Ancestors. Before taking a drink or tasting a plate, the devout Muntu will
pour a drop on the ground, in token of deference to and participation in
the life of the Ancestors. If such a one happens to sneeze, he or she will
speak the name of an Ancestor, as if asking for a blessing. When surprised,
the devout Muntu will utter an Ancestor's name, as if to say, "Be surprised
with me!"[8]

APPLICATION TO CHRIST

The figure of the Ancestor is quite complex. Indeed, the various aspects
so converge that any attempt to dissociate them will deform this noble
figure. But circumstances oblige us to do so. We shall list various elements
of the ancestral figure under certain major headings, and then, in the light
of these aspects, sketch the main lines of the application of this Bantu
figure to Jesus Christ.

LIFE

"... And that by the power over all flesh that you have conferred upon him, he may give everlasting life to all whom you have given him" (John 17:2). The primary datum concerning the Ancestors is found in the role they play in the transmission and safeguarding of life. A person's life comes from an elsewhere that is God, who, as some Bantu say, is "mayi mfuki'a mukele"—the "water the salt comes from." But it has come by way of our Ancestors, upon whom God has conferred a power over their descendants.

Thus, the Ancestors are in some way our "origins," those from whom we emerge. One can perform the role of Ancestor only if one has given life. The greatest curse, for a Muntu, consists in dying childless. To live is to give life. The more one gives life, the more one increases one's capacities for being. To love life is to *give* it. Elsewhere we shall observe the necessary reservations in this respect. For the moment, let us confine our inquiry to what precisely is meant by life—a life at once biological and spiritual, since among the Bantu these are intimately bound up with one another. When a person fosters communion in a social group, when a person sows peace, joy, love, that person is *allied* with life, is a "giver" of life. But this gift attains its fullness only with its biological aspect.

Christ came to give "life" and to give it in abundance. On his account we become heirs to the life of the Father. This life is the gift of the Father, but it comes by way of Jesus. That Christ centered his moral teaching on love is perfectly consonant with the ancestral Bantu ideal: without love, there is no suitable milieu for life to spring up. Christ is the source of life by his word: "Man does not live by bread alone, but by every word that comes forth from the mouth of God" (Matt. 4:4). Those who live in Christ have life; even should they die, they shall live (John 11:25). From within the one who believes in Christ shall flow streams of living water (John 4:14). Christ gives himself to us as food of life: "The bread that I shall give is my flesh for the life of the world" (John 6:51). As the Ancestors watch over the life of their descendants and continuously strengthen it, so does Christ continuously nourish the life of believers.

PRESENCE

"And behold, I am with you always" (Matt: 28:20b).

The Bantu Ancestors are not dead but alive. This, with perhaps a bit of exaggeration, is the whole difference between the European ancestor and the Bantu: the former is a memory, the latter is a presence.[9] One *remembers* the former, merely—in recounting the family history, in remarking that this or that family member has traits similar to those one recalls in such and such an ancestor or in what is told of that ancestor. But the Bantu Ancestors are *invoked*, on every important occasion. One converses with them, one shares with them the food and drink of the communion meals of family or clan, which are often held in their honor.[10]

The Ancestors are the principal "allies" of earthly beings. Ever attentive to all of the dangers that lie in wait for their descendants, they fight at their side, their mighty champions, for the triumph of life over death.

THE ELDEST

Christ is the Ancestor in the sense of Elder Brother, as well. The Bantu notion of eldest child, eldest sibling, focuses on the notion of anteriority. The Ancestors, these elder siblings, are closer to the sources and foundations. They came first. The prime analogy here is God. The very name of God in the Luba language is revealing: *Mvidi-Mukulu*—literally, *Mvidi*-Eldest.

The literary translation of *Mvidi-Mukulu* as "Spirit-Elder" neglects the material aspects of the notion of *Mvidi*. The word *Mvidi* denotes a category of trees that multiply through their seeds, their roots, and their branches. Their bark secretes a white, viscous latex. In the dry season, these trees survive. Whan a Luba had experienced joyous events (abundant wealth, brilliant victories in combat, numerous, beautiful offspring), he planted a *Mvidi* before his home as a symbol of this happiness, and as a "memorial" (in the Deuteronomic sense) of what he had experienced. Henceforth the family communion meals would be held at the foot of this tree. And it would be whitewashed—white being the color of the Beyond, the color of the Ancestors.

The reason why God is called by the name of this tree, it seems to me, is to mark that God is the source of life, an overflowing life, a life ever constant and stable, and so on. But here it is the addition of the qualifying name "Eldest" that is of interest for our present concern. The combination, "*Mvidi*-Eldest," marks God's anteriority to all life, all being.

Christ, God's only Son, likewise receives the attribute of "Eldest." Among the Bantu, the children of the elder brother will always be "elder" vis-à-vis those of the younger. Even if the latter are chronologically older, the line issuing from the elder will always be "upstream." The other lines will owe it a corresponding deference and respect. The children of the eldest line will have the last word in clan reunions, as well as the initiative in convoking these reunions. They will have the right to ritual presents from those of the younger—after all, according to a Luba proverb, "it is never the earth that gives its gift to the rain, but the rain that gives its gift to the earth." Among the patrilinear peoples of Kasai (a region of Zaire), the respect due an elder brother requires a father who gives his first and second daughters in marriage not to receive their dowry for himself, but to make an entire gift of it to his elder brother or to the latter's sons. It is the same with a younger brother's first wages: they are handed over entirely to the eldest.

In this perspective, Christ is the Elder Brother par excellence: it is to him alone that offering must be made. Or again: once we know Christ, all of our offerings must henceforth be made through him. It is the eldest brother who makes an offering to the Ancestors and to the Supreme Being on behalf of all the rest. A commentary in the solemn profession of the Mothers of Bethany will show what we mean:

Christ first offered himself to the Father: henceforth he is the origin and end of all our offerings. And this, our Ancestors knew not; ourselves, we know it, and it is on this account that we must transmit all of our offerings through him. This is the intent of these religious sisters whom you have just seen bind themselves to God by oath. . . .[11]

Certain Christian communion hymns attribute to Christ the title "Eldest Brother of the anointed ones" (*Mulaba-Mukulu*), in the sense that he is the model according to which the others will be anointed. The Bantu eldest brother represents an example to follow, except in the case where he does not conduct himself as an "eldest brother." It is not enough to have seen the light of day before the others in order to have the above-mentioned prerogatives. Here, as in all social groups, there are individuals who fail to live up to the expectations of the community in performing the role with which they have been entrusted. We call them the "melancholy-eldest," as they have disappointed the expectations of their families. Those who receive a social charge are reminded of the dictum: "Do not do as the elder child who has been so longed for but who cuts himself with his axe." The expression "longed for" in this dictum adds an affective note to the figure of the eldest child: he is "so longed for," as the "first rain" after the dry season. Thus, he is often named *Kavula-mbedi*, "First Rain." And so the Luba sing their refain to Christ: "O our *Kavula-mbedi*, Give us vigor and strength!"—just as the first rain gives vigor and life-strength to the seeds that lie in the ground.

Christ is a true "eldest one," as he has disappointed neither our expectations nor those of his Father. His Father has restored and crowned him (in the resurrection). As for ourselves, Jesus has been our example: "I have given you an example, that as I have done to you, you also may do" (John 13:15): the eldest sibling discharges an exemplary function for the younger, or for the age group that follows. For the living, it is the Ancestors who have "founded" them, who have laid the foundations of societies, thereby permitting life to "rise" and be maintained. Accordingly, we must follow them if we would preserve our lives. Their will is sovereign.

In virtue of his function of exemplarity, the eldest child is charged with responsibility for the acts of the younger. For the Bantu, Christ has shown himself to be our eldest brother in taking responsibility for our wrongs, in performing expiation for us (Isa. 53:4-5, Heb. 8—10). This introduces us to the last aspect of the ancestral figure: that of mediation between human beings and the Supreme Being.

MEDIATION

Christ fits the category of Ancestor because, finally, he is the synthesis of all mediations (Heb. 8). First, then, let us mark out the notion of mediation in the Bantu context.

The importance of mediation in the spiritual quest of the Bantu arises from their very conception of the world, and of the role played by community of life in the individual's life journey. The African universe, especially the Bantu, as we have repeatedly observed, is a hierarchized universe: all beings share in the life of the Supreme Being on different levels according to their nature. The human being is the center and shares the life of the Supreme Being on the highest, fullest level, an altogether special level. But this participation is indirect. As the world is hierarchized, there are intermediaries between sectors. The Supreme Being, the world of Spirits, and the world of human beings are distinct, while compenetrating. And it is their distinction that requires a mediation for contact among the three degrees.

Another basis for the necessity of this cosmic mediation is found in the constitution of the human being in Bantu anthropology. The human being is an indissoluble whole, composed of the visible and the invisible. One has access to the unseen only through the intermediary of what one sees. The sorcerer or scoundrel strikes the human being only through the latter's material substrate—nails, perspiration in a garment from which one has managed to obtain a thread, and so on. Everything surrounding a person ultimately shares in that person's being—and becomes a conduit to that person's very being.

Throughout black Africa we find the conviction that, while no one has ever seen God, nevertheless God maintains contact with created beings. Contact with God is made by way of certain divine envoys and delegates, or intermediaries, who are precisely the beings closest to the Source of life—beings who, by a particular gift of God, have been endowed with a special communications network with God. These are the soothsayers, the "strong ones."

The reason why the community is of the first importance for black Africans is the African awareness of the community as the principal mediator of the individual's initiation to life. Not only can the human individual not do without the community of human beings, but his or her existence itself would be devoid of all sense and meaning outside the community. In the Bantu world, one lives by and for the community. Countless sayings and proverbs reflect this view of human reality: "What one has raised will be eaten by all,"[12] or "It is better to be covered by human beings than by straw"—straw representing things, wealth, which "burn up" as easily as straw.[13]

The "hardness" of the present life forces one to have recourse to the community: "It's hard down here, the tall grass and underbrush are *found already here*."[14] This being the case, it will be the part of the most elementary wisdom to have recourse to those whom we have *found already here*: "When you visit the Bakuba, do not immediately set your traps. First see how the Bakuba set theirs."[15] Those whom we have *found "already here"* constitute an indispensable mediation in our rapport with this world of ours, which itself was *found already here*.

In this mediating community, the Ancestors hold first place. They are closer to the Source, they know us more intimately. It is their relation to the Supreme Being and to those living on earth that places them in this special intermediary position.

> My father, my Ancestor,
> you in the region below,
> you with God and the earth,
> it is with you I speak.
> As for me, I see nothing, anywhere.
> Then receive this feather [this hen],
> and bear it to the Being whom you know, take it to
>   him.
> And may peace alone come upon me.[16]

Christ himself has proclaimed his mediation between human beings and his Father. He is the "door" of access to the Father (John 10:9). No one, he says, knows the Father but the Son! No one has ever seen God except Jesus, who has come down from heaven, and those to whom it pleases him to reveal God (Luke 10:22). For Bantu Christians, Christ performs the role of Ancestor, by the mediation he provides. He is the exemplar, Ancestor, who fulfills in himself the words and deeds of the mediation of our Ancestors.[17]

Is this to say that Bantu Christians no longer have recourse to their Ancestors? In other words, has Christ as Ancestor abolished the role of the Bantu Ancestors? It would seem not. Missionary catechetics had declared war on the Bantu Ancestors.[18] But it succeeded only in compartmentalizing the Bantu mentality. Anxious to resolve the conflict, some Zaire catechists have made an effort to reconcile the two. Here is an extract from one of their sermons:

> The tribe does not live on earth alone. It is divided into two parts, the dead and the living. All that happens to the living is also experienced by the dead. Everything is arranged in concert for the good of the tribe—arranged by the living, together with the spirits of the

ancients. The spirits are the dead. They have their village, they are alive. In another way from ourselves, of course. Under the earth, in the village of the Ancestors, everything is different from here. But they are alive, they are the spirits. . . . As Christians, we feel very close to all of this, and we have no wish to deny it. Is it not the *Ancestor of Christians* himself who has told us, "I shall not leave you orphans, I come to you"? . . . Our little spirit-hut should remain in our church. . . . We ought to draw a great tree of spirits on the altar where Mass is celebrated. Then, when we come into church, we shall think of our dead, and we shall honor their spirits. . . . The church is the house of the spirits, since it is the house of the Chief of Spirits, Jesus Christ. . . .[19]

Once more out of a concern to resolve the conflict, other catechists have attempted to include the Bantu Ancestors in the category of the Saints, just as ancient Christians did with the just of the Old Testament, who were deemed to have been led to heaven by Christ in the moment of his victory over death.[20] This seems to us to be rather too facile an attempt at the rehabilitation of our Bantu Ancestors, proceeding from a good intention — that of reconciling salvation by Christ and the goodness of the Creator, who cannot reject those molded by the divine hands and stamped with the divine image for the simple "ill luck" that has befallen them of not having encountered God's Son. For my part, I think that one could manage to reconcile the two without forcing the notion of "saints" in the church, and in taking care not to enclose Christ in structures, even when the latter have become Christian structures. In the Christian church, it is the martyrs who are the first object of the devotion to the Saints. The notion of *exemplarity for perseverance in faith in Christ*, then, is primary. The Christian saints are *witnesses* of the happiness experienced by the human being in being attached to Jesus Christ.

Not having known or experienced faith in Jesus Christ, our Bantu Ancestors can perform the role neither of witnesses of nor of exemplarity for attachment to Christ. They can, however, perform the role of exemplarity for values which, while not originally Christian, can become Christian, somewhat as a latecomer to the dining room takes a vacant seat — the one reserved for this late arrival. As new cultures encounter Christ, various "vacant seats" in Christianity will be taken. Thus, certain Bantu values, such as that of ancestor worship, will become Christian, by the fact that they will be experienced by Bantu Christians, in a synthesis that breaks neither with the Bantu nor with Christ, a synthesis over which the criterion of an unconditional, absolute love for God and our siblings ought to preside.

Our Bantu Ancestors have no need to be painted over as "saints" to deserve our veneration. Just as they are, they are founders of our societies and reconcilers of human beings. In a word, they are intermediaries, present to our daily life. The message of Christ has shown us that they, too, are *in via*, on-the-way to fulfillment. And this is perfectly consonant with Bantu culture, which represents these Ancestors to us as still in need of us, their happiness somehow dependent on an increase of life among their descendants. Thus, we have proposed to retain the offering of libations to the Ancestors.[21] Instead of simply replacing them with the Mass, we have decided to integrate them into the Eucharistic celebration, so that they may express that Jesus Christ is the fullness of being, that he is the very essence of Ancestor—in brief, so that our libation may signify that, without the body and blood of the Son of God, our Ancestors do not attain the fullness of life, and thereby proclaim that Jesus Christ is Lord, to the Glory of God the Father.

Just as Christ, the one priest, does not abolish human mediations, but fulfills them in himself,[22] so does he consummate in himself the mediation exercised by our Ancestors, a mediation that he does not abolish but which, in him, is revealed to be henceforward a subordinate mediation. And at all events, we need only observe that this mediation of the Ancestors permits Bantu Christians to approach, perhaps even to comprehend, the fullness of the mediation of Jesus Christ.

NOTES

1. The recent work reporting the Second International Colloquy of Kinshasa may be consulted with profit: *L'Afrique et ses formes de vie spirituelle* (Kinshasa: Centre d'Etudes des Religions Africaines, 1983).

2. Mukeng'a Kalond, "Spiritualité matrimoniale, cas de la jamaa," in *L'Afrique et ses formes de vie spirituelle* (Kinshasa, 1983), pp. 327-28.

3. Nkongolo wa Mbiye, *Le culte des Esprits* (Kinshasa: Centre d'Etudes Pastorales, 1974), pp. 18-20. Emphasis ours.

4. For more ample details on this subject see C. M. Mulago, *La religion traditionelle des Bantu et leur conception du monde* (Kinshasa, 1973). See also L. V. Thomas and R. Luneau, *Les religions d'Afrique noire* (Paris: Stock-Plus, 1981) 1:78-82.

5. Ibid., p. 65.

6. Ibid., p. 85.

7. Mulago, *Religion traditionelle des Bantu*, pp. 43-45.

8. A current expression of astonishment among Luba women is: ". . . we!" citing the name of the speaker's father.

9. A Greek friend recounted to me that he sometimes spoke with his deceased grandfather. The latter had been an Orthodox priest, and continued to visit his family (in dreams). However, this deceased person was not present to his family to the point of their feeling their lives dependent on him.

10. Mbuyi Wenu Buila, *Bankambua betu* [Our Ancestors], 4, (Kinshasa, 1972), p. 74.

11. Ngoyi-Kasanui, "Cifingu cia Bamamu ba Béthanie" (Consecration of the Mothers of Bethany), unpublished, Ngandanjika, 1981. Translation ours.

12. Luba proverb: "Ciadima unue ciadia bangi."

13. Luba saying: "Baakufinga bantu kabakufingi nsona."

14. Luba saying: "Panu mpakole, masela ne bilunda mbisangana bimena."

15. Luba saying: "N'uya ku Bakuba kudianji kuteya, wanji kumona Bakuba muteyateyabo." The Bakuba, a people of artists, founded great and powerful kingdoms before the colonial era.

16. Thomas and Luneau, *Religions d'Afrique noire*, 2:182-83.

17. R. Luneau and Jean-Marc Ela, *Voici le temps des héritiers* (Paris: Karthala, 1981), extract of a homily by the present author.

18. See esp. the periodical, *Nkuruse*, founded by the Scheut missionaries in Kasai. See also G. A. Sma. and J. Mbuyi, *Femme congolaise, réveille-toi*.

19. Nkongolo wa Mbiye, *Le culte des Esprits*, pp. 7, 20, 21. Emphasis ours.

20. Ibid., p. 11. See also B. Bujo, "Nos ancêtres, ces saints inconnus," *Bulletin de Théologie Africaine* 1-2 (1979):165-78.

21. "Du canon romain au rite zaïrois," *Bulletin de Théologie Africaine*, no. 8, vol. 5, pp. 227-28.

22. Think of the current among the Reformers opposed to the ministerial priesthood.

9

Jesus as Healer?

CÉCÉ KOLIÉ

When it comes to observing the face of Jesus as healer in the evangelical proclamation today in North Africa, I am tempted to think that it might be easier for African theologians to present Jesus as the Great Master of Initiation, or as the Ancestor par excellence, or the Chief of Chiefs, and so on. To proclaim Jesus as the Great Healer calls for a great deal of explaining to the millions who starve in the Sahel, to victims of injustice and corruption, and to the polyparasitic afflicted of the tropical and equatorial forests!

It is not enough, as an anthropologist of Africa says, "to win Jesus credit with our peoples, to legitimate his claim to be the sole mediator who leads one to life."[1] It seems to me that it can only be from the experiential advent of Christ in the vital problems of our communities that a coherent theological discourse will arise and not remain superficial.

Within a destructured, humiliated, exploited society victimized by all manner of corruption, a discourse of this kind calls forth a reply like, "Your little Jesus there—wasn't it only yesterday that he turned up here, while our Ancestors have been here forever?"[2]

HEALING AS A PRINCIPAL ACTIVITY OF JESUS

Were we to remove from the Gospels the passages dealing with cures of all kinds, little would remain (before the Passion) apart from the parables and the infancy narratives. Indeed, in his programmatic discourse, borrowed from the prophet Isaiah, Jesus presents himself primarily as a healer (Luke 4:18-19).

As we shall see below, the healing accounts in the Gospels are bound up with the overall meaning of Jesus' life and death. It is only in the passion/resurrection of Christ that we better understand them.

128

The evangelist Matthew writes that Jesus traveled all of Galilee, teaching in the synagogues, proclaiming the Good News of the Reign, and healing every illness among the people (Matt. 4:23).

And St. Mark will place these words on Jesus' lips, presenting the ultimate meaning of his whole life: "The Son of Man himself is come not to be served, but to serve, and to give his life in ransom for a multitude" (Mark 10:45).

Christ, St. John will say, is come that humanity may have life, and have it in fullness.

Let us also point out that Jesus' healing activity is indissociable from that of the proclamation of the Reign of Heaven. His cures constitute firstfruits, and his death/resurrection *the* firstfruits.

ORDINARY ILLNESSES

A study of the Gospel forms permits us to distinguish four categories of cures wrought by Jesus.

There can be no doubt that Jesus had the gift of healing and that he made use of this talent to bestow health on a number of persons. Of course, there was always a proliferation of healers in ancient Israel. By a simple intervention—a word, a sign—Jesus heals. It is only in a case like that of the sufferer at the pool of Siloam that Jesus uses an intermediate element between himself and the patient: water.

Thus it is by the very efficacity of his word, his deed, or his saliva, that he effects cures. It is enough, on occasion, to touch his robe. Nor will this fail to occasion astonishment and wonder among his contemporaries. Jesus' word is seen as a reappearance of the word of God that came to the prophets. In him is realized the historic encounter of the proclamation of the prophets with the people who awaited the fulfillment of the divine promises.

CURES IN RELATIONSHIP WITH THE LAW OF MOSES

With Jesus, lepers—persons struck by the Lord (Num. 12:9) and excluded from the liturgical community of the living—are rehabilitated. Jesus abolishes the boundaries between clean and unclean and restores the meaning of the Sabbath as made for the human being rather than vice versa. Contact with a woman with a flux of blood does not defile him, as the Law has said it would (Lev. 15:25). Rather it delivers her.

Jesus places himself in contravention of and contradiction with the Law. He heals on the Sabbath day, he has contact with blood and the dead, he takes meals with publicans and sinners. In acting in this fashion, he is seen to be the one who inaugurates a new manner of relationships between God and human beings. The new covenant has arrived.

Jesus will be asked in whose name he heals, God's or Beelzebul's. He will answer this question with his death. His cures will cost him his life. He will be seen to be weak—helpless to save himself. He will incarnate anew the passage of the Suffering Servant in Isaiah (Isa. 53). A priori, it is of course not directly by virtue of his suffering and by the efficacity of his passion that Jesus heals. We may say, with P. Beauchamp, that "his efficacious compassion is a foretaste of his efficacious passion."

Specific Cures: Exorcisms of the Possessed. Jesus commands the demons, and expels them from the sick.

His deeds are reminiscent of the power of God as displayed in the accounts of Jonah, the Flood, and the crossing of the Red Sea. He commands, and his words come to pass.

Let us observe that Jesus takes express account of the environment of the victim of possession who throws himself into the fire, as of that of the other sick: he is concerned with their social integration.

As with his other cures, Jesus' exorcisms are closely bound up with faith, prayer, and fasting. The apostles are nonplussed at their inability to expel a demon. Jesus responds that "this kind" is driven off only by prayer and fasting. Here Jesus' word is calculated to demystify, and its effectiveness cannot but arouse approval and disapproval, admiration and hatred, amazement and defiance, faith and doubt. "It is by Beelzebul, chief of demons, that he works these miracles!" the authorities will say.

Does not the image of the thaumaturge threaten to eclipse and dull the central picture of a Messiah awaited to restore social peace, and effect a harmony among the elements of nature? The wolf will dwell with the lamb, the panther will lie down with the kid . . . (Isa. 11:6-8).

However this may be, it is the risk and stakes of faith to be willing to see a reformation of one's expectations, and this in their very fulfillment. Jesus requires this faith of his patients. For that matter, let us recall that Jesus himself is struck with admiration for the *pagans*. They have no equal in Israel, he says, when it comes to placing one's trust in God!

Catechetical Cures, Resurrections, and Social Reintegration. Paralytics, the dead, rise up. "Rise and walk": the deed of the One of Easter morn.

Jesus also works miracles in "the context of his teaching." Thus, the miracle becomes an illustration of the Gospel message.[3]

In his cures Jesus *always takes account of the social environment* of his patient. He integrates the leprous and the hemorrhaging into the milieux of their origin. They have been excluded, placed apart, marginalized by reason of their illness; Jesus resocializes them in healing them. He accomplishes numerous miracles of charity: seven cures[4] plus the raising of the daughter of Jairus, two multiplications of loaves, the calming of the storm, and so forth.

When Jesus heals, *he requires a gift in return*: faith, gratitude (the ten lepers), going to show oneself to the priests, and so on. In other accounts, especially those reporting miracles of charity, he asks nothing. In the case of spiritual cures, where sin is regarded as the cause of the bodily affliction,

Jesus encourages the patient to sin no longer and to believe more.

As any healer can attest, Jesus quickly perceives that his healing activities cause an increasingly *crucial problem on the level of his own social integration and recognition*. We observe that, very quickly, he becomes the victim of the same accusations as the other healers of his time: he is said to be in league with Satan (Matt. 12:24).

The deontology of Jesus' therapy is articulated upon acts and deeds calculated to alter social relationships. Jesus is aware that it is never on the physical level alone that one is deaf or blind, and that consequently neither can healing and salvation remain on that level. The evangelists, as well, were concerned to present us with a Jesus solicitous both for the suffering to be healed and for the evangelical proclamation to be heard. The two are not disconnected in his eyes, and the deaf, the blind, the mute, the crippled or paralyzed whom he cures are ample testimony to this.

But precisely, the conjunction of this activity and this proclamation do not long fail to arouse a number of reactions which go beyond surprise and envy to declared hostility. God has given him a power! He might become king! He will finally be arrested and crucified. And they will call out to him, "You have saved others, save yourself! Come down from the cross and we shall believe!" He will then appear weak and powerless. He will have no other recourse than to call upon "his Father" to deliver him from death.

While he brings more well-being to those he cures, the healer also troubles the social order. He is thereby exposed. He is a subversive, and this renders him vulnerable. While he seeks the good of others, and actually achieves their good, of those at any rate who are in the most need, he risks a great deal, he risks *everything*, himself.

To do the work of a healer is *to give a part of one's own humanity to those in need of the same*. It is a matter of something one receives "over and above," something one has received for the benefit of those in need.

The upshot of the gift of self is in fusion with the patient. The healer, however, fuses, merges with the "ill-ness," so to speak, and the therapeutic enterprise of the healer is necessarily pathogenic for himself, otherwise the therapeutic relationship of fusion cannot take place.[5]

The healer must undergo a symbolic death. Why?

The development of the healers' therapeutic capital is a process by which the simple "gift" of healing power becomes, in the course of the magical therapeutic relationship, an act of healing power.[6]

The gift of self cannot be an anodyne act. It is not gratuitous, it implies risks, it can be refused.

If Jesus is weak to the point of being one of us, to the point of going to ask for baptism, it is not because he seeks a way of concealing himself, or of confounding himself with the masses. It is his way of being in solidarity with us to the hilt, in all things except sin. He enters wholesale into the healer-patient logic. He is healer and patient at once. His role of healer quickly changes to that of being one of the sick. He passes from the pole of the healer in relationship with the sick, to the opposite extreme of the polarity and functions in the relationship of the sick toward the healer. Perhaps this is the Christian style.

As our purpose is to see how we might present the face of Christ in Africa as that of a healer, we must take a closer look at sickness and healing as it is found on that continent.

SICKNESS AND HEALING IN AFRICA

According to the World Health Organization, health is a "state of perfect physical, mental, and social well-being." Brief as it is, this laconic definition is not without its pertinence. However, it neglects an essential dimension: health as the state of a particular social *group* living in a given economic and political situation. Defined in the latter terms, the concept of health becomes less abstract: it is seen to be dynamic and becomes easier to approach and grasp.

Fundamentally, for the African person, being ill is an alteration in the equilibrium of the human organism, but it is also, and especially, a rent in the social fabric.

The body social and politic is also subject to this law of degradation; and not only in the person of the sovereign, but on the level of empires, it makes an effort to elude the erosion of time. Thus, the king figures on two lists: that of the physical, mortal body of an individual, and that of his mystical existence as incarnation of the people. As the latter, it is fitting that he should have a power that is exempt from death. The demise of the king is not announced until his successor has been designated.

In this fashion, the sovereign escaped the natural law of decay. He was strength and vitality in eternity. When he became helpless, he was made away with. In the interregnum it was not royalty that was suspended, but time. Farming activities, fishing, hunting were forbidden. The collective political and social imagery thus permitted an ensnaring of time. It is in this context that we shall attempt to approach health and illness in Africa.

For the black African person, the aspiration to *life*, to eternity, is so primary that the persons called to administer it hold a place of eminence. Soothsayers and healers, medicine persons of all kinds, are the pillars of social life.

Accordingly, Islam and Christianity have, and will continue to have, credit with the African only to the extent that they share, side by side with the African person, *the struggle for life*. This *cult of life,* infelicitously christened "animism" in the pejorative sense of the word, also explains the proliferation of the sects in Africa today. Their common denominator, which is at the same time their strong point, is the following: their serious attention to illness, and their prayers or rites of healing.

Traditional chiefs, masters of initiation, juridico-political institutions and rites, and so on, are on the wane in Africa. But soothsayers, seers, healers, abide. Surely this shows that the objective of life, from time immemorial, abides, as well: escape from the ravages of time.

The cause and meaning of illness are of far greater importance than their clinical symptoms. To be consistent, the development of a traditional nosology must not only begin with a general discourse on illness, but also, and especially, continue in terms of autochthonous socio- and ethno-clinical data.

THE BLESSINGS

Thus it is that, among the Kpèlè and the Logoma of Guinea, no ceremony, no assembly begins without a flurry of blessings and wishes for good health, happiness, peace, social harmony and concord, fecundity and productivity. This is the *luwô*. There are persons whose *luwô* is more effective than that of others, because they are upright. They have a "white belly," as the expression goes, and their blessings on the assembly or on a person come from the bottom of their heart. In a *luwô*, one expresses the wish for the death and total disappearance of the enemy par excellence, the sorcerer, whether the latter "eats or does not eat, drinks or abstains from drink," and so on. One expresses the wish, to the person being celebrated in the assembly (the newborn, the traveler, an initiate, someone deceased, and so on) that the vital principle of this birth be solid, that this departure be a source of cohesion and unity, that this arrival be a source of joy and peace for the community, as well as of benefits for all.

Here is the structure of the most current rite of this kind in the region of the Kpèlè.

1. Greeting: Inquiry whether the assembly be *well*.
2. Address: The one imparting the blessings assures the assembly that the brothers and sisters, parents and friends, who have sent the speaker, are *well*.
3. Blessings:
   a. Thanksgiving for the night, or the day, that has passed without *ill*, and wish that the times to come be *better*
   b. Wish that whatever is not *well* may not come to pass
   c. Exorcism bearing upon the *good or evil* that is the object of the assembly
   d. Curse of enemies and forces of *ill*: sorcerers, epidemics, famine, etc.
   e. Endorsement of the pledge that secures the assistance of the protecting Ancestors, the intermediaries between God and human beings
4. Conclusion: May all the wishes expressed be embodied in *health*, long

life, and vital power. Each wish concludes with the word *mina*, derived from the Arabic, by way of Islam, for "Amen."

AT PLACES OF WORSHIP

At rivers, on mountains, in forests (regarded as places of encounter with the Ancestors and with God), God is invoked through the Ancestors, that these may lavish on the village or clan the material and spiritual goods of which it has need for its well-being and equilibrium. These outdoor cathedrals have often been described in terms of "place-worship." Here is the meeting place of the living and dead members of a clan or family. They are called the "speaking places" of a clan or a family. This is our communities' altar of offerings, of requests, and of thanksgiving. Again, life is in rendezvous. In these high places of pilgrimage and popular piety, God and the Ancestors are invoked, honored, and consulted on the occasion of the important events of life: illnesses, social conflicts, natural disasters, deaths, journeys, births, initiations, and so forth. The divinity usually invoked on the occasion of these ceremonies is *Alla Tagana*, the Crossroads God of all good things and the rallying point of our lives and all life.

IN RITES OF BIRTH

The qualities desired in a newborn are size, strength, beauty, and a propensity to cry when there is danger. A "soft" baby, it is said, can be reared without thinking. From birth, the child is sheltered from evil spirits. Its hair and nails must be kept short, as it is these intimate items that sorcerers covet. As nascent life is fragile, pregnant women surround their condition with great discretion. The umbilical cord is buried with a kola nut, which will sprout and grow along with the child. No serious ritual among the Kpèlè dispenses with the kola nut. A sickly, dwarfish, mute, or albino baby "stays in the bath,"[7] is done away with at birth. From the first, a child must be surrounded with numerous blessings and rites, in order to have a powerful *magninèn*, a magnificent aura, an invulnerable double, and so have long life.

FUNERAL RITES

Funeral rites are calculated to demonstrate that a baby that dies was not meant to live just now. It will come back another time. But if a woman loses many children, the last will be called by some such symbolic name as *Vedeli* ("I have not called him") or will be referred to as grass, a thing, a dog, or the like, in order to discourage death from coming again.

An old man who dies full of years, leaving numerous children and good, respected by all, and so on, bids fair to become an Ancestor. His funeral will be the occasion of great feasting and rejoicing.

The death of a traditional chief also occasioned rites of ritual cannibalism, that his powers might be transferred to the heart of his successor and his children.

The African's greatest fear is not so much death as "dying badly"—from a sudden stroke, by drowning, abroad, in childbirth, by suicide, and the like. In these cases, burial will be hasty, without ceremony.

For the black African generally, a struggle with disease is not a struggle with death. The latter is not the opposite, the contrary, or the antidote of life. It is only another way of being in the world.

Since some deaths are the occasion of feasting (of the aged, or of warriors, for example) and others of sorrow (death in childbirth, suicide, the death of an unconfessed sorcerer, and so on), since there are births that cause sorrow (babies with severe handicaps or Down's syndrome, albinos, mutes, and so forth) so that the child is made away with at birth and the mother said to have had a miscarriage, we must say that the battle of African therapies is generally waged, on the one hand, against *ill-living*, and on the other against *ill-dying*. Ill living, as the Kpèlè say, is a failure, a life without *nwun na vie* (luck, basis for happiness, good fortune, success) or *magninén* (vital principle, basis of a human being's respect and glory). Ill-dying is the bad death that, like ill-living, is a shame for the subject and those around. Death is better than shame, we like to say.

The structure of healing therapy corresponds to that of the disease. In confrontation with the forces of evil are forces of well-being, which the activity of the healers will engage.

The activity of the African healer today is performed according to three modalities, described by the following authors respectively:

Marc Augé presents the figure of the *prophet* Atcho in Ivory Coast, in the face of the death of the traditional social order buried by a development mode of the capitalist type. Confronting the destructuring of the order of lineage and village, in order to afford his patients rebirth to the demands of a new world, the prophet Atcho declares that he is a healer, charged with restoring the African personality and the functioning of the traditional structure. He strives to discover the key of being to the new world of the African person.[8]

For five years, Eric de Rosny lived with the *traditional healers* of Douala, in Cameroon, the *ngangas,* and was actually initiated into their worldview. The path of initiation this Jesuit trod until he finally had his "eyes opened" to the source of violence in society was lengthy and authentic. The problems of sorcery illustrate, in an enlightening way, our African societies' underlying violence, whose control was once entrusted to soothsayers, seers, and healers.[9]

The third pole of the management of health is presented by another Jesuit, Meinrad Hebga, who recounts his own experience as a *charismatic healer*. As a theologian, philosopher, and anthropologist, he attempts to describe the phenomena of possession and divination. First he poses the question of whether certain phenomena regarded as paranormal and marvelous, even by persons of credibility, are always of irrefutable objectivity and authenticity. Might not the various phenomena presented under the general heading of sorcery be only a chimera, and a dangerous chimera? In a second book devoted to the activities of spiritual healing that he practices together with a team of laity, Father Hebga describes the services of healing, of deliverance, the laying-on of hands, the use of holy water, of crucifixes, of rosaries, and expresses all of his compassion for the sick and the possessed.[10]

Destructuring, violence, and possession are forms of illness in Africa. And healers seek to confront these three ills.

Just as with the West African healer, the traditional therapeutic practitioner has a broad knowledge of the history of family lines, of the origin of villages, of relationships between clans, of the psychology of each of the members of the community (relatives, neighbors, friends, allies), of conflicts past, present, and virtual, and so on.[11]

The most prestigious task of the *nganga* (the African traditional physician) consists in reconciling the social life of the village with the *jengu* or water genies, water Ancestors, reconciling the village with distant dead who have become active once more and who wander among the living. Père Eric de Rosny writes:

> It would be utterly foreign to a nganga to think of assigning neutral labels to mental disorders, as is ordinarily done in the West, where one speaks of mania, paranoia, hypochondria,. . . . He ranges these disorders according to the personal and maleficent forces that, according to him, have caused them: wind sorcery, cannibalism, the primitive intervention of water genies and Ancestors, the violation of taboos.[12]

DIVERSITY OF HEALERS

The spectrum of types of healers exhibits a wide diversity. Besides the figures we have already met, which range from the Douala *nganga*, to the prophet like Atcho, to the spiritual healer, there is the magnetizer; there is the radiesthetician with a pendulum; there is the traditional specialist of mental diseases who works with Fann Hospital at Dakar to reconcile the patient with the *rab* (spirits of the Ancestors) in the specific rite called the *ndoep*.[13] But we might also meet the chiropractic joiner who sets broken feet and arms; the elderly female specialist in childhood diseases; the general practitioner who quickly diagnoses and treats maladies of the genitals; the healer who delivers all those manipulated, asleep or awake, by *jinn*; and so on.[14]

The manner of transmission of all this knowledge can be open or closed. There are techniques and bodies of knowledge transmitted from father to son, from healer to patient, as well as others that require a secret initiation not open to all. In all instances, a healing gift demands a return gift in kind — a renunciation of living at home, or a sacrifice that may range from that of a he-goat to all or part of an element of one's life (continence, for example), or a state of unseeing or deafness. At all events, healers are generally the respecters of numerous taboos.

The deontology of traditional medicine appeals to very numerous duties and rules pertaining to relations between healers and their teachers, as between healers and their patients. Here we have space to cite only a few, and in broad strokes: the technique of socialization of the illness; interpretation of the accident, which may be fortuitous, in terms of one or (more often) several secret or social causes, such as ill luck; criteria of distinction between sufferers with whom one succeeds and those with whom one fails; relationship between victim and entourage; relationship with money; and so on.

Let us pause on this last point to indicate that money has become a major factor of perversion of traditional African medicine. In bygone times, cures were generally requited by an honorarium in kind. The substitution of money has rather banalized this stipend, making it a kind of calculation, a fee. There were various ways of celebrating cures. For example, we have what the Kpèlè of Guinea call *Gwêi yiliê*: the ritual meal after a cure, to congratulate the patient who has been restored to health. The pecuniary perversion of the traditional system of medicine springs from the fact that, at the hospital, everything is paid for in advance, even if the outcome of the disease turns out to be death. We shall return to this collision among medical practices. It is interesting to observe, in the coexistence of traditional and modern medicine, the behavior of tribes that have as yet accepted neither Islam nor Christianity.

THE HEALER'S "PANOPLY"

As for the manner of functioning of traditional healers and the instruments they employ, we can only mention in passing the elements on which they rely for their practice. First, however, let us observe that the African healer customarily functions in rapport with soothsayers or seers, who have, it is said, a third eye or ear, and who convey to the patients or their healers the demands of the Ancestors or the community consequent on, for example, the nonobservance of some taboo.

Inanimate objects such as horn, talisman, statuette, fly-chaser, kaolin, mirror are used. In phytotherapy there are barks, leaves, roots, and the pith of certain plants. Objects of the rite include eggs, kola nuts, rice flour, etc. To the healer, the objects used are either endowed with a directly therapeutic efficacy, or with an occult power, *mana*. These two types of objects are not to be dissociated, especially in their functioning, often in reliance on masculine and feminine symbolical numbers (three and four). According to the anthropologists, the symbolic effectiveness of these objects and rites proceeds from the fact that "the spiritual cause and bodily effect are mediated by meaning equivalents of what is signified, referring to another order of reality."[15]

This is better expressed in the usage of the *word* considered to be the locus par excellence of blessing and curse.

The word is an important element in therapeutic technique. For the African, disease and death always have another cause from the one indicated by clinical symptoms. Unlike the procedure of the Western physician, who has inherited an essentially analytical tradition of autopsy, that of the African healer is more synthetic and comprehensive. What is of supreme interest to the latter is the human being taken in his or her totality, including environment and social relationships. By utterance, the healer will attempt to bring it about that the patient contribute to being delivered from the disease by confessing to sorcery or by describing his or her dreams in order to submit them to interpretation.

Here African healers are reminiscent of Jesus. Their therapy includes an injunction to do no more evil (sorcery), and they seek first and foremost to reintegrate their patients into society when confinement has placed them outside the socio-economic circuit. Is disease in the West not primarily defined by the inability to work and thus by the inability to be useful?

Far from being a diabolic phenomenon, then, African holistic faith healing is a normal, regular, and recommended procedure, even today, in villages and cities. To the same purpose, in Paris, in the Eighteenth Arrondissement, one finds numerous West African mediums and marabouts who offer to resolve all manner of problems. Their clientele tends to be more interested in divination, however, than in therapy in the clinical sense of the term. The role of the traditional practitioner and soothsayer necessarily involves the oral or signed word. The efficacy of that role proceeds from the credit the therapist is confident of being accorded, e.g., "This marabout—everything he says, happens!"

Besides inanimate elements, and the word, the traditional doctor likewise makes use of the blood, entrails, and other parts of animals he or she kills or orders sacrificed (chickens, sheep, dogs, a cow, etc.). Thus, in Senegal, the rite of the *ndoep* makes frequent use of the intestines, stomach, and blood of an ox slaughtered for the purpose of treating a mental patient suffering the onslaughts of the *rab*, the spirits of the Ancestors.

We might sum up the activity of the African healer as consisting at one and the same time in phytotherapy, logotherapy, zootherapy, geotherapy (sequestration of the patient for protection from attackers), and so forth. But as we have seen, the healer is not content merely with detecting the causes of the disease. He or she is equally eager to stimulate the reconciliation of the principals in the conflictive relationship that lies at the origin of the illness. In this sense, the traditional healer is first and foremost a sociotherapist.

COLLISION OF MEDICAL TRADITIONS AND CULTURE SHOCK

Not content with failing to respect traditional structures, modern life in Africa has proceeded, and continues to proceed, to destructure economic and political life as well: in the economic area, monocultures, and mineral exploitation to the benefit of the local administrative bourgeoisie and the multinationals, and so on; in the political area, a dialogue of the deaf between traditional justice and a Roman jurisprudence, confiscation of power by dictators, and so on. Modern life thereby engenders new diseases (alcoholism, malnutrition, hypertension, abortion, venereal diseases, etc.).

Gift without return gift is alienation and paternalism. In relations between Europe and Africa, then, now become indispensable, it will be important to seek favorable ground for this cooperation.

The realm of disease and healing is the first concern of the African populations.[16] It could be here that Africa will contribute a great deal to Europe, and vice versa. As we know, European psychotherapeutic and psychoanalytic research is discovering practices that have always been known in Africa.[17]

The encounter between Western and traditional African medicine has taken place in a context of domination and the preservation of colonial interests. The creation of wealth in the colonies was dominated by the question of the work force. Infirmaries and hospitals, vaccination programs, and hygiene were all integrated into a comprehensive system of domination. The development of the colonies was nothing but the creation and maintenance of the work tools that were the peasants. We need only hear what Albert Sarraut, Colonial Minister, said in 1921:

Medical assistance . . . is our duty. But it is also, one could even say, our most immediate and most matter-of-fact interest. After all, the whole work of colonization, the entire task of the creation of wealth, is governed in the colonies by the question of manpower.[18]

The gendarme was the most useful medical assistant in the colonies. It is thanks to him that the populations were vaccinated against the epidemics of smallpox, the plague, and yellow fever. Health care was imposed, without instruction and without explanation. One obeyed without understanding. One was vaccinated because it was an obligation, without knowing why. I remember as if it were yesterday the times I spent hiding with my parents in the bush when vaccination sessions were announced. It was only health that we sought in this hiding-place—only, it was not the health our "masters" willed.

When all was said and done, the peasants were to be healthy without knowing it. Indeed, everything transpired as if the health of the natives were the white man's business—as were taxes, the circle commandant's collective fields, and so on.[19]

On the other hand, the medical missionary's work was not free of the ambiguity of benefaction, aid, and therapeutic effectiveness as confirmation of the excellence of the new religion. While there were those who had no intent of using their medical practice as a means of conversion to Christianity, conversion wrought by an evangelization bound up with medical aid did not fail to arouse diffidence in certain African milieus. In the colonial context, medicine and mission seemed to respond to one and the same purpose. In his book, *Kel 'Lam, Son of Africa*, Père Carré has his hero say:

> The whites are very smart, you see. After they have caused all this misery with their forced labor and their taxes, they make us feel good by sending us to their brother the doctor to treat us and their Father to tell us of God.[20]

MEDICAL PRACTICE IN THE ERA OF INDEPENDENCE

The era of independence has inherited systems put in place by the colonial master and his agents, interpreters, commissioners, gendarmes, and schoolteachers, the indispensable machinery of direct and indirect administration. Village hospitals and infirmaries are only stations created to treat the successors of the white colonials, especially in the burgeoning cities. Today the medicines available on the market are inaccessible to the popular masses, village hospitals and infirmaries are only centers for the distribution of prescriptions. Only the upper class can receive decent medical attention.[21]

While physicians leave their hospitals to make house calls for the colds or constipation of governors or ministers, hundreds of peasants walk for miles to the hospital, to be greeted with contempt and sent on their way with a prescription for something their meager purchasing power cannot obtain—if it exists! While the peasant masses have no drinking water or suitable shelter in the *potopotos*, the slums, CHUs are built that swallow the bulk of the health budget; when members of the senior administrative class (10 percent) fall ill they are sent to the hospitals and clinics of Paris, London, or Washington with the tax money collected from the ninety percent, the peasantry.

In a word, we are dealing with a medical practice confiscated by the hierarchy of political appointees. There are no popular health organizations. Foreign medical assistance in medicines and personnel, unfortunately, tends to maintain paternalism and underdevelopment. What good is treatment without health education at the grass-roots?

An ongoing misunderstanding prevails, then, between Western medicine and traditional medicine, not only in terms of their respective functional systems, but also by reason of the historical and political context, which has not been favorable to a reconciliation.

Asia founds its therapy on the balance of energies concealed in a person (yoga, acupuncture, meditation). The West uses the analytical principle of the autopsy of the afflicted parts. Africa practices a medicine based on the relational and symbolical functioning of the patient's environment.

POLITICAL POWER AND HEALTH

Not only is the health department a locus of the exercise of power; illness itself has become (if indeed it has not always been) a ground on which relations of force are put in play. The whole area of disease has become the battlefield for the expression of power—or better, perhaps, a mirror reflecting the various social categories.

The political functionary must be the first to be in good health. He belongs to both bodies, the individual and the social. Even if he is not in good health, he must present himself as blooming with health and strength. He is constrained to dissimulate his fatigue and illness. Someone has written: "These sick who govern us. ..." But since they are always in the forefront of the political scene, these sick must look fine, and seem to have "iron constitutions." Therefore they must receive priority medical treatment.

One need only pay a visit to the hospitals of Guinea—I have as yet been unable to establish precise statistics—in order to realize that diseases are divided by social category and that new diseases have made their appearance.

JESUS HEALER IN AFRICA?

The bipolarity of the religious loyalties of our baptized who carry a rosary in their hand and a "fetish" under their clothing leads us, by way of conclusion of this investigation, to ask whether Jesus can honestly be present in Africa as a healer. This past year, in the course of a meeting with community leaders of villages and quarters, along with catechists, I took the occasion to ask those assembled to list their own, personal names for Jesus. (It has been sixty years since Christ came to this region.)

They all gave titles taken from the Bible or missals. Not one of them came out with a term that translated his or her personal relationship to Christ. And yet you cannot spend more than a year in a black African community without acquiring a nickname expressing the type of relationship you have with the people. They all told me that Christ is the Savior, the Son of God, the man of peace, and so on. Certainly none of them told me that Jesus is a healer. And they would certainly not have been able to tell me why.

I ask myself more and more whether, on a different level, this is not the same thing that goes on with the majority of African theologians. Since their communities cannot name Christ personally without going to the Bible or catechisms, they do just the opposite, and attribute to Christ the traditional titles of initiator, chief, great ancestor, and so on, that they would *like* to see him given in the communities. Once more we impose on our fellow Africans the way of seeing that we have learned from our Western masters. Shall we be followed by our communities, when we have finally gotten the prayers of the missal translated into these titles for Jesus whose real effectiveness has not really been tested in Africa?

For my part, I think that to give Christ the face of the healer in Africa (even though this was his principal activity in Israel) will not be feasible until the manifold gifts of healing possessed by all of our Christian communities have begun to manifest themselves.

We often forget that the faith of the African person is expressed in a prayer that is precisely that of a person *in a situation* (drought, injustice, dictatorship, corruption, famine, social and family conflicts, fear, and so on). And we observe that, during this time, the established churches continue to function on this continent as institutions foreign to the fundamental problematic of the black person—a dominated person, the victim of exploitation and torture, racism, and contempt on the part of the established powers.

Our liturgies do not celebrate human beings fighting disease, or struggling so hard to get up on their feet, or striving to be free. Instead, our liturgical hymns sing the glory of the Sole Initiator, the Master of Life par excellence, or the Chief of Chiefs, while our spiritual exhortations by and large content themselves with saying, "Offer it up, this injustice, shoulder your cross daily, have confidence in Christ who has suffered as much as you!"

What can persons offer to God who have not yet taken up their pallets and walked? What courage can be asked of those who have known only the face of the Crucified One, and never that of the Risen One?[22] What confidence can be expected of persons in whom no one, least of all they themselves, has ever placed any confidence?

What was the meaning here, with regard to evangelization, of the context of the medical mission? Was it in the service of the mission or a means of proselytism? What can we conclude from this when it comes to the proliferation of the sects emerging from the established churches?

THE MEDICAL MISSION IN BLACK AFRICA

The achievements of the medical missionaries are impressive by any standard.

In 1956-57, in the Francophone territories of black Africa, there were 309 medical stations (18 hospitals, 270 infirmaries, and 21 leprosaria) supported by the Catholic missions, as compared with 125 supported by the French colonial administration. The Protestant missions, too, had infirmaries and hospitals, including outstanding clinics. Finally, every mission station had its dispensary hut or first aid room. We may recall certain towering figures here: Dr. Albert Schweitzer at Lambaréné in Gabon; White Father Goarnisson, at Ouagadougou, surnamed "Dr. Light," who restored sight of thousands of cataract or river blindness victims in the valley of the Volta, and who trained so many nurses and technicians; Dr. Lamplugh-Petit, the young Englishwoman of Birmingham who was converted to Catholicism at twenty years of age and who built a hospital in the interior of Southern Rhodesia (Zimbabwe) "with her own hands"; Sister Guido; Paul Aujoulat; along with many others.

The missionary significance of the religious medical undertaking is scarcely in doubt. For the missionary, it was a palpable expression of their desire, their will to "save the natives": physical health represented the salvation of the soul.

I was a Professor at the University of Strasbourg, an organist, and a writer. I left it all to become a physician in equatorial Africa. Why? It was my trust in the elementary truth incarnated in the fellowship of human beings marked with the seal of suffering that gave me the courage to found the hospital at Lambaréné.[23]

But that is just the trouble, of course. In evangelization, all African rites, including those of healing, were labeled "diabolical" and "pre-rational." This could only reinforce African dependence on Western medicine — especially when we know that the socio-political situation, with all its ills, was taken into so little account by the missionaries (apart from a few "prophets" who did not hesitate to denounce domination and corruption).

Thus, the health of the African person was confiscated, notwithstanding the gigantic medical enterprise.

Here again we are confronted with a problem of relations of force. The reaction would not take long to come.

THE SEPARATED CHURCHES: A RESPONSE TO THE AGGRESSION OF THE "SORCERY OF THE WHITES"

Indeed, the reaction was not long in coming! Very shortly after the beginning of evangelization in Africa, at the turn of the century, the independent churches, called, as might be expected, "sects," were born. There are nearly ten thousand in black Africa today, all issuing either from Catholicism, or especially, Protestantism. Their impelling notions: reaction against foreign domination, promotion of the power of the African person, confrontation with and attention to the more and more numerous diseases. Many of these "African Christian" churches practice spiritual healing. Besides the healing prayer itself, the warm, demonstrative rites (unlike the stiff, aseptic services of most of the established churches) are celebrated in communities of smaller, more human dimensions, with a fervent manner of prayer that fosters the inspiration of the individual and assigns an important role to the ministry of women, elsewhere so often thrust aside. The separated churches have a great concern for mutual assistance and lavish attention on the sick, through their healing rites. While some of these sects are purely and simply neopaganism, they offer a counterpoint to the insufficiencies of the established churches.[24]

A CRUCIFIED ONE AS A SYMBOL OF HEALING?

In order to be credible, our Gospel proclamation must strike root where human beings suffer, struggle, debate among themselves, and oppose the new forces of evil in Africa.

For ourselves, of course, we shall have to bring it about that the sick, too, be celebrated in our liturgies, and we must examine the case of the healing charisms of our ancestors, while maintaining contact with the Spirit of Pentecost.[25] But even more, we shall have to bring the church into the debate, perhaps even the struggle, for justice. After all, injustice is surely the source of the majority of the evils on this continent where, as the African film "Pétanqui" shows so well, embezzlement of public funds is no longer regarded as shameful, even during the most crying droughts and famines!

Jesus' credibility was not tied to miracles or cures—even if he did say: "If you do not believe in me, at least believe in the works that I accomplish." Not only does Jesus heal, but also, and especially, he gives a meaning to his cures, and consequently to suffering and evil. For Jesus, healing comes from God. It is not an end in itself, but a starting point. By his death, he draws the apostles from the spell of the miracle to taking his death seriously. He asks his disciples not to stand staring toward heaven and lose themselves in naive admiration, but to perceive the scope of the mission of the Suffering Servant.

> Death is not to be explained by fault. Life explains death. The Paschal mystery is joy not because it consoles us, or removes the weight of our guilt, but because it reveals life in death.[26]

In a basic way, disease and death for Africans are not the antechambers of nothingness or the antipodes of life, but loci of a new family cohesion, and of sources for a life harmony. With the Crucified One, suffering becomes a remedy for disease, and death a happy issue.

We are not making pious assertions. The symbolism of the empty tomb and the bodily reality of the Risen One bestow on the risks of human existence the fullness of their reality. They constitute, in their packaging, called faith, and their content, named love, a challenge to despair and the absurd.

In this context, on the basis of the conception of disease as *at one and the same time* a rent *and* locus of cohesion of the family fabric, and Christ's death-and-resurrection as a scandal to human reason, we can say that Christian salvation in Africa will necessarily reach the point of intersection of material happiness and absurd suffering. Just as in African tradition, healing will be much more than the simple effect of swallowing a medicine, even a magic one. It will take place in someone's name.

CHRIST'S DEATH-AND-RESURRECTION, LACERATION OF HISTORY

"We proclaim a crucified Messiah, a scandal to the Jews, madness to the Greeks" — and sickness to the Africans. For the person of black Africa, as we have indicated, the presence of someone ill in the family is a scandal. The entire family group suspends its activities. The author of the misfortune must be found: the sorcerer. Is it the patient himself, victim of a counterattack of the ancestors? Or does someone else wish him evil? And since the sorcerer who attacks a group can only be one of its members, the illness can only be revelatory of a syndrome of a social nature. As such, it must be subjected to radical therapy. One must find the scapegoat.

In Jesus' case, the African can blame his sentence and execution only on one of his own. Judas himself is at most the victim of a far broader conspiracy. The cause is too important for one individual to shoulder. And besides, did he not commit suicide? Is suicide not one of the "accursed deaths"? One must look elsewhere for the disciple or group of Christians who profit by this crime. The prosperity of the unrighteous alongside the suffering of the just is a first clue. And as a Kpèlè proverb says: "If he killed himself with alcohol or pimento, you find the corpse by the smell of alcohol or pimento." The second clue is the motive for which Jesus' betrayer hanged himself. Of what, or rather of whom, is the latter the victim? Inasmuch as the causes of death can only be metaphysical, one may not content oneself with listing organic causes purely and simply. Sin, then, being an abstraction from the notion of humanity in general, does not satisfy the African mentality in its quest for enlightenment as to the mystery of the death and resurrection of Christ. This does not mean a rejection of the role of sin out of hand. It does mean that a grasp of the precise role of sin in this mystery calls for in-depth considerations.

If Jesus is God, he cannot be the victim of a counterattack on the part of the ancestors in consequence of a transgression or fault of his own — especially since he rose from the dead, since this would mean either that the sorcerer had been found, or that he himself had acknowledged his fault. Neither thesis bears up under examination.

One must turn to God. But does not the non-Christian then face an impasse? Is the universe not now without its moorings? Above all, is it not a self-contradiction that a God who is Love would take gratification in seeing his Son struggle helplessly with suffering and death?

Our only recourse will be to begin with acceptance of the event, in order to receive its light and benefit after the fact. Otherwise the result will be psychosis and neurosis. Whether the death-and-resurrection of Christ is to be disease or healing will depend on our rejection or acceptance of that event—just as with a patient in confrontation with suffering.

However this may be, we are never merely on the threshold of illness, the threshold of drama, the threshold of sexuality, and so on. Life is a drama from beginning to end. The issue is a function of an option: serious involvement, or resignation. Black African tradition has understood and experienced this, in its rites of initiation. Through the symbolism of death and new birth in these rites, life is played out in a psychodrama staged for the assembled village. There the individual confronts the unknown, and by way of the struggle, the mask is vanquished by its own apparent victory over the candidate; the candidate overcomes an inner fear; and the social group "receives itself," becomes its own, through this collective psycho-drama, this general life-crisis.

Flung upon the ocean of life as newborn babes, we enter salvation history by taking up our own adventure—individually, collectively, and in relation with God. A person can live happily in a state of sickness only as a relational being. Just so, humanity can assume the drama of the cross only in confrontation with something or someone else. Otherwise only nothingness and absurdity prevail. The gulf created by the resurrection of a Galilean during the reign of Pontius Pilate can only be bridged in the taking of a position toward the Risen One. To be for or against the God found in history seems innocent enough, and yet it is (or is not) emergence from self to a commitment to that God in an adventure of which God alone is in control—the one to whom, to whom alone, worship is henceforward due.

HUMANITY HEALED IN JESUS' NAME

"The one whose sickness is called Jesus will never know healing" (Ibn Arabi, thirteenth-century Muslim mystic).

Many a one has been struck down by the "Jesus sickness" in the intervening centuries. As a black African I am ill with this second sickness. The first is my encounter with another world (the West) as a Kpèlè initiate, an encounter I had difficulty managing. Underdevelopment, unslaked desires, all manner of confrontation are the fruits of this encounter with Western culture. I can no longer be content with belonging to a village, a tribe, or even a country. The foreign causes a constant "questioning" in me and this questioning produces an inner disorder. The "sorcery of the whites" haunts me and my relationships. Here I can be attended to only with Western remedies, I can recover my health only in a reconcilation between the "lobbies" or spirits of my culture and those of the whites. As everyone knows, poison and its antidote are from the same root.

As we observe, this adventure is the spice of life, and it fills the monotony of daily routine. It is in the name of life that we rise from our hospital bed; it is once more in the name of life (after death) that we celebrate a funeral.

My second disease, a certain Jesus, is *what gives my life meaning*. No one lives, no one dies, in his or her own name, once that one lives for Christ. Thus, it is to Christ himself that we must appeal when we lose the *meaning of our life*. Disease, physical and mental handicaps, are contrary to life. But they preciously reveal our raison d'être. They are the meeting place, the intersection, of death and life. They represent a *crucial* point, a crossroads. As such, they are the rallying point of the forces of life for the struggle with the forces of evil. What our traditional chiefs in Africa fear is not death, but madness. And when a chief outlives his reason, one does him the favor of dispatching him to the other world. "Saya Ka fisa malo ye" — death is better than shame, a Bambara proverb from Mali has it. Our sages say that disease can have but two outcomes: restoration to health, or the graveyard. Far be it from us to mount a defense of euthanasia, but the underlying notion that there is a relentless attempt to effect physical healing, far from maintaining the balance and harmony of the social group, can have just the opposite effect: it can create a situation of permanent morbidity. What the black African person most fears is the coexistence of death and life: death in the soul, the presence of the dead among the living, the sudden apparition of ghosts in the street. Most of the sacrifices offered at the intersections of our routes are offered for the purpose of creating harmony not only among the living, but also, and especially, between the living and the dead. Our concern for the suffering sick is not only that they be consoled, but also that they be prepared for either reintegration into the family, or for entry into a new collectivity, that of the ancestors. The latter are invoked, and reprimands are addressed in their name—reprimands to the illness and its possible origins.

That which saves, in the Gospels and the Acts of the Apostles, is the name of Jesus. The name is the comprehensive being of a person, embracing the horizontal dimension of relationships in time and the vertical dimension of one's genealogy. It is not the Holy Spirit who heals in the New Testament, but rather the name of Jesus, the Lord. The fullness of the Christic presence can be obtained by the simple invocation of the name of Jesus. Why is this symbolical efficacy represented by this Galilean? Because in him is realized the unity of humanity and divinity. Just as the therapy for my cultural malady must consist in the drinking of a potion of Westernness and Africanness, so also the healing of the laceration of the resurrected Jesus must be by way of participation in his humanity-and-divinity. It is in this sense that the Crucified One, arms extended and body pierced, realizes the dream of humanity, and becomes a sign of salvation to past, present, and future.

The happiness Christ brings is that of attention to the suffering of the victim of disease. The cross enables us not to telescope the cries and lamentations of the widows and orphans in the name of a joy to come. It is reverence for the groans of the Man of Sorrows—that is, taking seriously his rebellion and his illness—that is the source of healing, and not analgesic words. The Good Shepherd knows his sheep and his sheep know him. What the disabled look for from their entourage is not sympathy, but recognition as full-fledged members of the human community.

CONCLUSION

The principal task of Christianity in black Africa is not so much to heal illness as it is to exorcise it, demystify it. But, for better or for worse, it happens that, on this point, it is not the West, today, that is in a position to give lessons to Africa. In Europe, death is conjured away, and you die amidst apparatus of reanimation. In Africa, by contrast, thanatic symbols tend to make death a rebirth, to ward it off by ridiculing it. In funeral rituals, derision and rites of inversion have the finality of occasioning a seeming disorder in the place of artificial order, and thereby play violence against itself, which frees up the energies that found the real order of society and life. For example, the rites of inversion suspend time at the death of the chief. Everything transpires as if the celebration of death were a therapy of grief and mourning at separation.

What does the resurrection of Christ teach us if not to "bracket" death, in order to hold it up to ridicule? "O death, where is your victory?" It will be the task of theology, in our lands, first to heal us of the new myths of the West and the local dictatorships, then to shed light on the salvation we celebrate without knowing it.

If Christian faith can enable African human beings to rediscover their deep roots in the life and message of Jesus of Nazareth who died and was raised, it will have contributed to the healing of myths and diseases. At the same time it will have enabled them to rise, take up their pallet, and go to their house, where they have a rendezvous with salvation. But if Christianity places the sacred groves, the places of worship, the fetishes, and so on, under suspicion and taboo, it will have thrown out the baby with the bath and march us down a blind alley. If it is true that human beings' current psychic drama resides in the monstrous proliferation of idols and the worship devoted to them, then what is at stake in the evangelization of our peoples depends on theology's ability to get them on their feet, to "receive themselves." We must bring it about that Jesus be named precisely by those who will have received and welcomed him. This Jesus will be Healer, Grand Master of Initiation, Ancestor par excellence, or Chief of Chiefs, not because I shall have declared him to be such, but because he will have wrought cures, presided over initiations, and given birth to a free person. His hosts will believe in him no longer on my word, but because they will have seen and heard them themselves, because they will have experienced the liberation he brings, the exodus he works. The heart of the matter will not be to seek to transfer to Jesus the uncontested and incontestable prestige of our ancestors. A like enterprise may shatter our Christians' sensibilities, but not their faith in the wisdom, security, therapy, and response of their ancestors when the problems of their lives are to be confronted. It is to be feared that a like presentation of Jesus may be a simple strategem of theological language.

We may ask ourselves whether, today, when the problems of the order of the day in Africa go by the name of famine, dictatorships, unemployment, emigration, corruption, embezzlement of public funds, and so forth, our theological culturalism is not still back in "negro" times. One has the impression of a gap between theological language and the current discourse or concerns of our peoples. At all events, meanwhile, we are surely obliged to acknowledge that the face of Christ in Africa today is more that of the ill than of a healer.

NOTES

1. Jean-Paul Eschlimann, "Ton petit Jésus," *Afrique et Parole* (Paris), no. 10 (November 1984): a "circular letter" from Tankessé (Ivory Coast).

2. Ibid., p. 2.

3. Luke 13:10-17, 5:17-26, 6:6-11.

4. Mark 5:1-20,24-34, 6:13,53-56, 7:24-30,32-37, 8:22-26.

5. Daniel Friedmann, *Les guérisseurs: Splendeurs et misères du don* (Paris: Anne-Marie Métaille, 1981), p. 113.

6. Ibid.

7. See Jean-Paul Eschlimann, *Naître sur la terre africaine* (Abidjan: INADES, 1982).

8. Marc Augé, *Prophétisme et thérapeutique: Albert Atcho et la Communauté de Bregbo*, Savoir (Paris: Hermann, 1975).

9. Eric de Rosny, *Ndimsi, ceux qui guérissent dans la nuit* (Yaoundé: Clé, 1974); idem, *Healers in the Night* (Maryknoll, N.Y.: Orbis 1985).

10. Meinrad Hebga, *Sorcellerie, chimère dangereuse?* (INADES, 1979); idem, *Sorcellerie et prière de délivrance* (Présence Africaine and INADES, 1982).

11. I. Sow, *Les structures anthropologiques de la folie en Afrique Noire* (Paris: Payot, 1978), p. 76.

12. De Rosny, *Ndimsi*, p. 287.

13. Cf. the film by Dr. Colomb, Ndoep-Dakar, 1986.

14. *Jinn*: word of Arabic origin designating an evil spirit.

15. See L. V. Thomas and R. Luneau, *La terre africaine et ses religions*, 2nd ed. (Paris: Harmattan, 1980), pp. 238-41, 308-18.

16. Cf. *Jeune Afrique*, March 12, 1980. A poll taken by this weekly reveals that the chief concern, ahead of family (48%) and job security (33%), is health (75%).

17. Gestalt therapy, group therapy, bioenergy, etc.

18. Cf. J. Suret-Canale, *Afrique Noire: L'ère coloniale (1900-1945)* (Editions Sociales, 1977), p. 305.

19. This paragraph takes its inspiration in manuscript notes of Cameroonese theologian Jean-Marc Ela.

20. Kindenque N'Djock, *Kel 'Lam, fils d'Afrique* (Paris: Alsatia, 1958).

21. At the C.H.U. of Abidjan (Cocody), the patient must furnish the gloves to be used by the surgeon!

22. Latin American popular piety celebrates Good Friday with more fervor than

Easter Sunday. Shall we be seeing the same thing in Africa? (NDLR).

23. Albert Schweitzer, *Ma vie et ma pensée* (Albin Michel, 1960), p. 215.

24. R. Luneau and Jean-Marc Ela, *Voici le temps des héritiers* (Paris: Karthala, 1981), pp. 133-35.

25. The case of Archbishop Milongo of Lusaka is symptomatic. Having discovered that he had gifts of healing, he was obliged by his fellow bishops and by the Roman authorities to abandon his healing sessions and his archdiocese (despite mass demonstrations by the faithful) for exile in Rome. Cf. Mana Mac-Millan, "Emmanuel Milingo, l'Archevêque guérisseur," *Informations Catholiques Internationales*, no. 566 (November 15, 1980), pp. 27-30.

26. F. Eboussi Boulaga, *Christianisme sans fétiche: Révélation et domination* (Paris: Préence Africaine, 1981), p. 67; English translation, *Christianity Without Fetishes* (Maryknoll, N.Y.: Orbis Books, 1984).

10

Christ the Liberator and Africa Today

LAURENTI MAGESA

Faith in Christ is a continuing process of insertion into what he signifies, insofar as our understanding of life, of human beings, and of the world allows. How shall we express our faith? By means of forms that are intelligible to us and represent our contribution to the deciphering of the mystery of Christ? [T]he humanity of Christ, which revealed both God and the response to human longings, is the bridge that gives us access to Christ. Admiration for him is the origin of all Christology. . . . Jesus-man is the ongoing critical memory of what we ought to be and as yet are not, and a permanent call that we be daily more so.

Leonardo Boff[1]

ADMIRATION OF JESUS: ROOT OF SOUND CHRISTOLOGY

According to the tradition and teaching of the Christian faith, the attributes of the God-man Jesus, the Christ or Anointed One of God, are comprehensive. They epitomize the perfection of the Godhead. They cannot therefore be realized exhaustively in this limited world. For to understand perfectly and to live out completely the demands of the Gospel— which is to say the concrete expression of these attributes in space and time—is to fully attain in this existence the Reign of God. But that the Reign of God has not been fully achieved is obvious enough from the present condition of the world. There is no evidence, furthermore, to suggest that the work of God proclaimed by Jesus will soon transform the world and remove pain and suffering from human experience. Christians in particular should know this. Moreover, they have to admit that with reference to their grasp of the life-orientation of Jesus—fundamentally, the complete but free acquiescence to the will of God for his life and ministry—theirs is an imperfect vision. As well, their resolution in the practical application of this vision fails them many times and in numerous respects.

Already in this admission lies the basis of the true and realistic Christian following of Jesus Christ, or Christian discipleship. Precisely because Jesus' qualities and life-orientation are beyond our full comprehension and complete emulation, they evoke our profound admiration. Jesus becomes in the life of the Christian the supreme exemplar, the ultimate beacon that anchors the faith, the courage and the hope to approximate in the circumstances of present existence what he was and what he stood for. But on our own we cannot manage to travel the road that he took and indicates in his teaching. We need his helping hand. It is here that the basis of the Christian profession of the continual presence of the saving grace of God through Christ in the world and in the church lies.

INTELLECTUAL AND PRACTICAL DEFECTS OF CHRISTIANS' VISION

It is important to be clear on this point. A central area in which the vision of Christians often fails is interpretation of Jesus' Gospel demands and their actualization. Biblical hermeneutics, for example, has never been cleverer than today in the admission of its own inadequacies. But it is not only biblical interpretation that is inadequate. Doctrinal and moral theology and all other branches of Christian thought suffer from serious defects as well. Shortcomings and failures in understanding the inner and true significance of the Gospel, however, obviously do influence the Christian following of the Master. Hermeneutical shortcomings in the entire field of theology are elements that limit our realization of the consequences of our commitment to Christ. Thus, they inhibit a more complete realization of the reign of God in the world.

Africa provides a concrete case where the need for the liberating grace of Christ in this area—that is, the power required to extricate ourselves from the intentional or unintentional falsification of the demands of the Gospel—couldn't be more apparent. That is why the African situation presents a challenge to Christian life and, of course, to theological reflection. The task at hand for African Christianity is to rise up to the challenge of death and resurrection involved in this situation. In the Fall, humanity was provided with the means of Grace, that is, the efficacious medium of salvation through Christ, who is called "the second Adam" in the Scriptures (cf. Romans 5:12-19; 1 Cor. 15:22). African theology must also trust that in such failures of comprehension and commitment lie the seeds of Christian growth. Faith sees in them a positive face. Defects in Christian understanding and commitment are at the same time a call to the followers of Christ not to be complacent. There is work to do.

St. Paul's letter to the Romans is a message of hope for the future. It is St. Paul's firm belief that through our adherence to Christ, the possibility is always open for us to be freed from servitude to the error of sin and death and to become agents of life through justice and truth (cf. Romans 6:16-23). If we as Christians have not been able to exhaust the demands of the Gospel of Jesus Christ in our comprehension here in Africa—much less fulfill them in action—there is then presented to us by that very fact a continual task to search ever more diligently, to try to understand ever more completely, to endeavour to live more perfectly our dedication to the very same Christ Jesus whom we profess. This we are called to do, following numerous factors or graces which deepen our vision of him and his demands. Isn't this what St. Paul meant with his injunction enjoining the Romans not to "conform yourselves to this age but be transformed by the renewal of your mind, so that you may judge what is God's will, what is good, pleasing and perfect" (Romans 12:2)? What is this effort of continual transformation wherever it is to be found?

THE DEMAND OF THE *KAIROS* FOR CHRISTIAN BELIEVERS

In judging the will of God and being transformed to conform to it by the renewal of our mind in space and time, that is, in the confines of our geographical-historical moment, we seize what the Scriptures call the *Kairos*. But the *Kairos* is for followers of Christ nothing short of a crucial point in a given time offered by Providence.[2] It is ignored at our peril. Paul writes to the Romans that they have to make the most of their privileged opportunity (the *Kairos*) by working to renew the world through being and doing good: "It is now the hour for you to wake from sleep," says Paul, "for our salvation is closer than when we first accepted the faith" (Rom. 13:11; also Eph. 5:16 and Col. 4:5). The acceptance of the liberating grace of Christ from sinful, inhuman situations is indeed an act of "waking from sleep." The effort to transform the world into the image of the reign of the just and loving God is to bring "our salvation closer."

Theologically and in our Christian behavior, our *Kairos* in Africa mandates that we discern our present socio-political and economic environment. This forms the infra- and super-structure of our understanding and following of Christ. To be fruitful, however, our discernment will not merely describe the environment in question, but it will endeavour to clearly and actually influence it, insofar as that may be possible at any particular time, through our commitment to and concretization of the most important characteristic quality of Jesus. This quality was perceived and actually proclaimed by Jesus himself to be the love-justice that generates freedom in and among people. The Christ-Event, the act of salvation or redemption of the human race by Christ, can be described in terms of liberty, the happiness of every human person, the breaking of every kind of chain that binds humanity—in a word, humanity's emancipation (cf. Luke 4:18-19; Gal. 5:1). Consequently, in Africa, the question for Christians must be posed straightforwardly: As followers of Christ, how do we participate in the advancement of the liberation that Christ is and brings?

LIBERATING CHRISTOLOGY IN AFRICA: METHODOLOGICAL CONSIDERATIONS

Involved in the question of participation in the advancement of the liberation of Christ in Africa are, indeed, massive and complex variables of historical and current realities of grace, faith, and human reason. Yet, with all the humility that is appropriate to our limited vision and horizon, we must engage ourselves in the discernment of the various structures, mentalities, and attitudes of our existence. At the same time, we have to commit ourselves to what we know is the way and action of Jesus Christ the Liberator on this historical existence. It is by doing this that we shall be true to our calling as *Christians*.

Drawing on the experience of the general mass of the African peoples, and also on the work of the various social sciences which have analyzed the codified experience, a theological examination of the socio-economic and political situation prevalent in Africa brings to the fore numerous ethical and moral questions.[3] These include questions of excessive wealth in the midst of dehumanizing poverty and vice versa; questions of exploitation of the majority of African peoples by internal and external forces; questions of political domination by domestic and international power brokers; questions of suppression of the African cultures by dominant conceptions of life by means of refutation and ridicule; questions of monopolies of power by ecclesiastical oligarchies at the expense of the liberty of the people of God; questions, in short, of instrumentalization and exploitation of the life of the African person. All of these are questions of suffering, issues of lack of freedom in its various aspects. Further problems to be seen all over the continent—problems of ignorance and preventable disease, of famine and ethnic wars, of class antagonisms and racial persecutions—are the direct consequence of ignoring this basic question of "unfreedom." They are a result of not confronting it in time with the active, liberating word of God.

What does this mean in practical Christian terms? It means mainly that there has been a failure in forming and pursuing concrete policies in favor of love-justice. W. Brueggemann has explained these policies to involve the political will, *"to sort out what belongs to whom, and to return it to them."*[4] This is the understanding that is required of Christian believers on the political and socio-economic level of their faith.

Such an understanding implies that there is a right distribution of goods and access to the sources of life. There are certain entitlements which cannot be mocked. Yet through the uneven workings of the historical process, some come to have access to or control of what belongs to others. If we control what belongs to others long enough, we come to think of it as rightly ours, and to forget it belonged to someone else. So the work of liberation, redemption, salvation, is the work of *giving things back*. The Bible knows that when things are alienated from those to whom they belong, there can only be trouble, disorder and death. So God's justice at the outset has a dynamic transformative quality. It causes things to change, and it expects that things must change if there is to be abundant life.[5]

Change in this respect will not be brought about merely by some mystical sentiment in us, nor simply by a well-argued and terminologically precise theology. The proof of our adherence to Christ (as Boff says, echoing Matthew 7:21) lies elsewhere. It lies in the field of active love-justice. "Christians are not simply ones who profess Christ with their lips, but ones who ... live the structure and comportment that Christ lived: love, forgiveness, complete openness to God ..."[6] This means that genuine commitment is expressed in the struggle for the integral freedom and well-being of all persons.

It may therefore be said with regard to Africa that the struggles for independence in the various regions of the continent in the late 1950s and 1960s were a concrete expression of the liberating will of God for the people of Africa because they promised precisely this integral well-being. It was in view of a better, fuller, more just life that the mass of Africa's marginalized children, propelled by the power of God in them, risked what little they had to join in the freedom struggles. Their desire to regain their humanity, to de-alienate Africa's wealth which had been alienated by long years of slavery and colonialism cannot be interpreted otherwise than that it was fundamentally the doing of God. He had heard "the cry of his people" and he was telling the colonial Pharaohs of the day, through the events of the independence struggles, "Let my people go, that they may serve me" (cf. Exodus, *passim*).

Implicit in those struggles was the hope of a transformed Africa, an Africa filled with abundant life for all. But looking back over these past three decades of Africa's political independence, the vast majority of Africa's sons and daughters are forced to ask with G. M. Houser the "somewhat cynical question: Was it worth it?"[7] Recall that during their sojourn in the wilderness, on the way to the promised land, the descendants of Abraham asked exactly the same question; they made the same complaint. In the midst of practical and painful situations, it is easy to be disillusioned about goals, however noble.

It is quite clear that the reality of Africa today cannot be said to be true to the aspirations that were raised and nurtured by the liberation struggles and by political independence when it was finally achieved. Bo Davidson's observations are to the point. This committed Africanist paints a sad but unfortunately very true picture:

> Thirty years ago, and more, the prospects that seemed likely to follow, even bound to follow, the anti-colonial liberation, the decolonization, of Africa looked bright, lit with hopes of solid reconstruction, of peaceful change, of many-sided human material progress. Today, those prospects—much more often than fulfilled—seem denied and even mocked. To affirm that Africa today is plunged into acute crisis, whether of institutions, of human relationships, or of material immiseration, is only to say what everyone knows to be true.
>
> ... And if one wished to epitomize Africa's fall from the moral and social assumptions of the liberation struggles we have known, what could be more convincing, more dreadful in its implications, than the recent political killings in Burkina Faso [to cite but one of many examples]? Boasting of their pure and progressive credentials, the colleagues—indeed, the close and intimate friends—of Thomas Sankara could evidently think of nothing better than to take up their guns and murder him. If the nationalism of Africa, with all its claims to be a liberating force, has been reduced to that level of degradation, to that grim caricature of the behavior of those expected to use the nation-state as a gateway to freedom, then indeed the central question cannot be avoided: Why this degradation, how has it come about?[8]

The liberation and independence problems have their origin in two areas. The first is the unbalanced socio-economic and political relationship between the economic North and South. The entire southern hemisphere is in a state of peripheral capitalism where it remains in a perpetual condition of dependency. The South is told to work harder, export more, make sacrifices. However, for its harder work and more export it continues to get back less or even nothing. For its sacrifices it is slowly strangulated and dehumanized. The sad behavior of Sankara's friends, noted by Davidson above, must not, and cannot, be properly understood apart from this general international environment.

The second more immediate cause of Africa's problems lies in the area of domestic politics. What Davidson touches upon is also a result of this. Colonialism was not interested in the development of the colonies, despite incidental benefits that may have accrued to them. According to the correct analysis of G. M. Houser:

> The colonial era was given to abetting the interests of the colonizers— not to the education and health of the people, nor to their economic development, nor to minimizing the more destructive aspects of tribalism. Racism was a concomitant of colonialism. Paternalism was the best an enlightened colonialism could produce.[9]

Yet, the colonial background provides only part of the explanation for Africa's contemporary challenges. Africans themselves have to deal with the problem of transforming their social structures to make them truly participatory, effective, and constructive for the welfare of their nations in particular, and of their continent as a whole.

From the Christian perspective, as again Houser says referring to the slogan of the liberation conflict in Mozambique, *a luta continua*, the struggle goes on. This slogan can be a basis of good politics as well as good theology. "The struggle for a better person, a better life, a better country and a better world never ends. Perhaps the moment of greatest freedom is found as we engage in the struggle to achieve it. And that moment is always with us."[10]

LIBERATING CHRISTOLOGY IN AFRICA: CONTENT

To consider Jesus Christ as Liberator in the African situation is therefore much more than just a metaphor. It is an attempt to present the only Jesus that can be comprehensible and credible among the African rural masses, urban poor and idealistic youth. In the long run, it is the only Jesus that can evoke the admiration of the rich and powerful of the land. This is the Jesus who actually calls individuals and peoples to freedom by his word and action. He does this through God's continual self-revelation in history, the Christian God being a God of revelation. In the process, he gives voice to the voiceless so that farmers, for example, can demand fair prices for their produce. He instills courage in the weakhearted so that industrial workers, domestic servants, and casual laborers can say no to the arbitrary exploitation of their person and labor. He provides hope to the prostitutes, parking boys, and sick and lame so that they may realize that in spite of their degradation, suffering, and handicaps, they are equal members of the society and children of God, with dignity in his sight. He confirms the idealism of the youth so that they may accept the challenge that the future belongs to them, that they can yet make the world a better place for everybody. To the refugees and other displaced persons he avails the opportunity to return home. Again, the list can continue.

At the same time, as a necessary corollary to the liberation of the poor (because his salvation is intended for all), Jesus is the Liberator of the rich, the proud, the intellectually conceited, the satiated. This also is in a real, rather than simply metaphorical sense. Through events in human history he pricks their consciences to conversion, attention, and dependence on Him. Sometimes he violently wrests their power from them to shame them. In the Scriptures, the song of Moses and the people after crossing the sea unharmed (Exodus 15:1-18); the song of Miriam, Aaron's sister, and the women (Exodus 15:21); and the song of Mary, the *Magnificat* (Luke 1:46-55), are particularly indicative of this fact. As I Peter 5:5 also has it, "God is stern with the arrogant, but to the humble he shows kindness." His sternness with the arrogant, however, is for the purpose of converting them, of showing them kindness as well, for salvation is for all. Paradoxical as it may seem, it is precisely in this process of God's sternness and kindness that we also find his conciliation and reconciliation.

Consider for a moment the historical Jesus. His life and ministry were dedicated to the promotion of awareness of the dignity of the human person as a child of God. It was simply a commitment or solidarity with the struggle to actuate this. Jesus identified himself, and God, with those who suffer under oppression and are rejected. By that same commitment, that solidarity, he called the perpetrators of oppression to conversion. Thus, the lamentation of Jeremiah (8:21-9:1) is also that of Jesus:

> The wound of the daughter of my people wounds me too,
>   all looks dark to me, terror grips me.
> Is there not balm in Gilead any more?
> Is there no doctor there?
> Then why does it make no progress,
>   this cure for the daughter of my people?
> Who will turn my head into a fountain,
>   and my eyes into a spring for tears,
>   so that I may weep all day, all night,
>   for all the dead out of the daughter of my people?

When we speak of Jesus as Liberator, then we refer to his assurance of solidarity with us, particularly but not exclusively as church, in the struggle—his struggle—to diminish poverty among the masses of the people. It is a struggle to prevent the untimely death of millions of children due to malnutrition, poor hygiene, and lack of medical care. We refer to Jesus' life example in cultivating a better person and a better world. We refer to his commitment to forming the rule of God by refusing to accept as right sinful structures of religious or civil domination, corruption, and tribalism. Christ is Liberator because he is at once the foundation, the inspiration, the basic reason, and the guarantor of the ultimate success of the struggle for the liberation of the human person, for development and healing— idealistically, through the church. Our Christology is thus also concretely ecclesiology: Christ as Liberator; the church as ideally the agent and articulator of Christ's liberation in the world. This is the sum of the content of a liberating christology.

COMMITMENT AS A BASIS FOR A LIBERATING CHRISTOLOGY

What, then, is the theological justification for our struggle in Africa for justice, human rights, human dignity, the just distribution of Africa's and the world's resources? It is the humanity of God in Jesus or, in other words, the incarnation of God in the midst of all humanity and, very concretely, in every person. This is the reason for giving due respect to every person however different he or she may be from us. It is likewise the foundation for letting every individual human being use what is probably the most fundamental resource-gift given to humanity by the Creator: the resource-gift of freedom. By the fact of the incarnation, of the joining together of humanity with the Godhead through Jesus Christ, all humanity is exalted because the Godhead has "emptied" itself so as to be filled up with the pain and tears of human suffering. In taking on "the form of a slave," the Godhead transforms pain and tears of the "lowest" humanity into joy and laughter. To the degree that this transformation is accomplished, to the degree that the "little ones" have access to full life, to that same degree is the Godhead itself exalted (cf. Phil. 2:6-11).

The self-emptying of God in Jesus (cf. Phil. 2:6-8) is a matter of commitment and solidarity. By becoming human in Jesus, God's dedication to the exaltation of the human race and all creation became manifest. The life and preaching of Jesus solidified this eternal dedication. The Holy Spirit works to keep this dedication alive in the world. The following of Christ and attentiveness to the Spirit demand it. The task is to renew the earth, to give it new birth by building bridges of friendship and justice among people, which is precisely what is meant by God's rule and order.

No wonder, then, that according to Luke the promulgation of the Reign of God is predicated upon such transformation. When the crowds asked John the Baptizer, just before the public ministry of Jesus, to tell them the meaning of true baptism (which means cleansing or purification and thus conversion or transformation),[11] he said in reply: "Let the man with two coats give him who has none. The man who has food should do the same." How about those in specific duties, such as civil servants and soldiers? For them also the requirements of transformation are no different. They are the same requirements of love-justice: Civil servants, "Exact nothing over and above your fixed amount." And as regards soldiers concerned with public order: "Don't bully anyone. Denounce no one falsely. Be content with your pay," or in other words, do not extort (cf. Luke 3:10-14).

If anyone should argue that all this does not apply to the contemporary African situation, then you cannot but wonder what signs of the times such a person is reading, or whether there is a reading of them at all. Another stronger objection may be that these are references to purely "material" concerns; but Jesus also had other concerns, the "spiritual" ones. What is his attitude in this respect?

It is not difficult to respond to this objection. The spirituality of the Scriptures is quite clear: Jesus' spiritual concerns were not different from the material concerns when it came to human beings' welfare. First of all, we ought to understand that for Jesus the dichotomy between the two hardly existed. His life's message was the liberty of the entire human person and all humanity in justice and love. Again, he was concerned about nothing other than building bridges of friendship and dignity among people. This was the salvation he epitomized in his own being. Where, therefore, the bridge of friendship would have been demolished by revenge, pride, questionable religious self-righteousness, oppression, and indifference, he counselled understanding, humility, tolerance, care, and charity (cf. Matthew 5-7), all this for the sake of mutual, holistic growth of all people and the perfection of creation. It is why, in the Beatitudes (at least quite clearly in the arrangement of Luke), Jesus condemns those who disregard the requirements of this transformation. They stay rich, full-bellied, and haughty at great loss to themselves and to the world around them. In the long run their attitude will merely cause suffering and humiliation to occur. But those who transform will bring about joy and fulfillment (Luke 6:20-26; Matthew 5:3-12).

Such are the dynamics of the transformation of humanity through Christ which alone will effect the emancipation of the world held captive by the powers of pride, selfishness, and greed. The powers of dehumanization in Africa are strong, but the Psalmist assures us that they cannot prevail if a concerted effort for justice and freedom, guided by faith in the just and loving God manifested by Christ, is made against them. What at first may seem a foolish dream will be vindicated as the work of God among us. With this faith the Psalmist can sing:

> When the Lord brought back the captives of Zion,
>   We were like men dreaming.
> Then our mouth was filled with laughter,
>   and our tongue with rejoicing.
> Then they said among the nations,
>   "The Lord has done great things for them."
> The Lord has done great things for us;
>   We are glad indeed. (Psalm 126:1-3)

For Africa, Jesus Liberator is the Master who brings about a new beginning, the acceptable time, the year of favor (cf. Luke 4:19). He will not obliterate the memory of the long, hard, brutal years of slavery and colonialism which is the memory of his own suffering. On the contrary, he will use this memory to urge forward the construction of redemptive civil, ecclesiastical institutions and structures which will no longer tolerate human degradation and exploitation. Through his apostles and prophets in the church and outside of it—courageous bishops, sisters, and priests; gentlemen and ladies of the press of all denominations and faiths or of none, but people who have the courage of their convictions; writers, lawyers, politicians, and teachers—through all of these people and others, Jesus Liberator will untiringly and unceasingly say no to hunger, torture, the muzzling of free speech, detention without trial, disregard of the common good, and the incitement of inter-ethnic hatred for selfish political ends. These are the features that enslave Africa. No messiah, no liberator will deeply, sincerely and lastingly be recognized and accepted as such in Africa today except as an enemy, in word and deed, of these and similar inhumanities. The true Christ is the one who breaks the binding power of these chains, the one who chooses the side of the powerless and delivers them from tyranny.

PRACTICAL ORIENTATION TOWARDS A LIBERATING CHRISTOLOGY

The church has often failed in its task as an ideal witness to the justice of Christ. This we have to acknowledge. Yet, elements for a total restructuring and renewal of society, and the transfiguration of the individual within society, that Jesus was promoting is contained in what has come to be known as "the social teaching of the Church."[12] Even though recently rediscovered and given impetus by the highest magisterium in the church, the identification of protology with divine socio-spiritual order[13] is clear throughout the Old Testament. As we have noted, the claim of the identification of the mission of Jesus (soteriology) with the re-establishment of this order goes back to Jesus himself. This is the one thing that the writings of the New Testament are clear and unanimous on. But the New Testament takes a realistic view: human beings must involve themselves in this soteriological work of Jesus, slowly transforming this world by humanizing their relationships, until God completes it in his own good time (eschatology). Protology and soteriology are, therefore, necessary and integrated movements towards the perfection of the eschaton to be effected by Christ.

For a long time, since the end of the first four or five centuries of the church, the original emphasis on practical redemption or transformation and transfiguration of the face of the earth (that is, of social relationships) as an integral part of the plan of creation and salvation was lost sight of. Circumstances and historical demands were different. Towards the end of the nineteenth, and especially twentieth century, however, it has been magisterially recaptured. And so, it is evident that quite a bit of the teaching of the church on society in modern times provides practical orientations to liberating christology and ecclesiology. Thus, in 1971, for example, a representative group of the bishops of the world, meeting in a synod in Rome, become very specific. Speaking in the name of and to the entire church they argue in the following meaningful terms:

The present situation of the world, seen in the light of faith, calls us back to the very essence of the Christian message, creating in us a deep awareness of its true meaning and of its urgent demands. The mission of the preaching of the Gospel dictates at the present time that we should dedicate ourselves to the liberation of man even in his present existence in this world. For unless the Christian message of love and justice shows its effectiveness through action in the cause of justice in the world, it will only with difficulty gain credibility with men of our times[14]

This passage of the synod provides a good summary of both the christology and ecclesiology of the documents of the church talking about the transformation of the world since Pope Leo XIII. This orientation places Christ directly in the midst of his brothers and sisters in the world, experiencing their joys and their frustrations, and leading them gently along the path of freedom. It places the church at the service of this freedom of Christ, to enhance it within itself and in the world at large. This is a christology and ecclesiology of social betterment and human uplift. As well as seeing Jesus as Son and member of the Trinity, it views him most prominently as herald of the Good News, healer, and liberator. Today, this latter is what the church, the visible body or sacrament of Christ, is required to project in Africa through its solidarity with all the temporal forces of genuine human freedom. These forces which, as Pope Paul writes,

> struggle to overcome everything which condemns ... [people] to remain on the margin of life: famine, chronic disease, illiteracy, poverty, injustices in international relations and especially in commercial exchanges, situations of economic and cultural neo-colonialism sometimes as cruel as the old political colonialism. The Church ... has the duty to proclaim the liberation of millions of human beings, many of whom are her own children—the duty of assisting the birth of this liberation, of giving witness to it, of ensuring that it is complete. This is not foreign to evangelization.[15]

In the present conditions of Africa, this is not unrelated to evangelization, it is the very core of the meaning and significance of Jesus Christ himself and his mission.

NOTES

1. Leonardo Boff, *Jesus Christ the Liberator: A Critical Christology for our Time* (Maryknoll, N.Y.: Orbis Books, 1978), p. 226. Original in italics.

2. For the use of this word in Scripture, see G. Kittel, ed., *Theological Dictionary of the New Testament* (TDNT), vol. 3, pp. 455-62.

3. Among the African theologians who have analyzed the situation from the liberation perspective are A. Boesak, *Farewell to Innocence: A Socio-Ethical Study of Black Theology and Black Power* (Maryknoll, N.Y. Orbis Books, 1977); T. A. Mofokeng, *The Crucified Among the Crossbearers: Towards a Black Christology*, Kampen, 1983; B. wa Ilunga, *Paths of Liberation: A Third World Spirituality* (Maryknoll, N.Y.: Orbis Books, 1984); J.-M. Ela, *African Cry* (Maryknoll, N.Y.: Orbis Books, 1986); M. A. Oduyoye, *Hearing and Knowing: Theological Reflections on Christianity in Africa* (Maryknoll, N.Y.: Orbis Books, 1986); H. Okullu, *Church and State in Nation Building and Human Development* (Nairobi, 1984); F. E. Boulaga, *Christianity*

Without Fetishes: An African Critique and Recapture of Christianity (Maryknoll, N.Y.: Orbis Books, 1985).

4. W. Brueggemann, "Voices of the Night—Against Justice," in W. Brueggemann et al., *To Act Justly, Love Tenderly, Walk Humbly* (New York, 1986), p. 5.

5. Ibid., pp. 5-6.

6. Boff, p. 247. Original in italics.

7. G. M. Houser, "Assessing Africa's Liberation Struggle," *Africa Today* 34:4 (1987), p. 17.

8. B. Davidson, "Thirty Years of Liberation Struggle" in ibid., p. 6. Besides T. Sankara, other African leaders who have lost their lives in a more or less similar manner include S. Olympio of Togo, T. Mboya of Kenya, and the former Secretary General of the Organization of African Unity, D. Telli of Guinea. In a different category are the leaders who met death in the midst of *hot* liberation struggles. Among them P. Lumumba, A. Cabral, H. Chitepo, E. Mondlane, and S. Machel.

9. Houser, p. 29.

10. Ibid., p. 32.

11. On the meaning of the Baptism see G. Kittel, ed., TDNT, vol. I, pp. 529-45. See also X. Leon-Dufour, *Dictionary of Biblical Theology* (London, 1967), pp. 28-31.

12. In modern times the social teaching of the church begins with Pope Leo XIII's Encyclical Letter, *Rerum Novarum*, of 1891.

13. On this question, see D. Dorr, *Spirituality and Justice* (Maryknoll, N.Y., 1985), and also B. Häring, *The Beatitudes: Their Personal and Social Implications* (Slough, 1976).

14. See the Exhortation from SECAM, *Justice and Evangelization in Africa*, Kisubi, n.d.

15. Paul VI, *Evangelii Nuntiandi*, no. 30.

11

African Christology in a Situation
of Suffering

JOHN M. WALIGGO

Theology, in all its branches, can best be understood when it is fully inserted into the cultures, times, circumstances, and concrete situations of a particular people. As the emerging theologies are trying to show, the main sources of theology include not only the Scriptures and church tradition but also the very people of each epoch with all their hopes and aspirations, their anguish and suffering.[1]

This essay tries to respond to the question: Who is Christ to the suffering people of Africa? From this central question we can derive three others: What image of Christ do the suffering people of Africa have? What image of Christ have the Christian churches and preachers presented to the suffering people of Africa? What should be the ideal and most relevant image of Christ to the contemporary suffering people of Africa? These questions are not at the periphery but at the center of meaningful christology, for as Monica Hellwig asserts: the first and all-inclusive question that Christians must ask and answer about Jesus is: What difference does Jesus make?[2]

Indeed what difference does Jesus make in the lives of the suffering people of Africa? What does faith in Jesus Christ bring to their suffering? What does *following*[3] Christ concretely mean within the African situation?

In attempting to answer the central question, five sources will be used: the present reality of suffering in Africa, aspects of historical Christian theology in Africa, biblical exegesis from an African perspective, the comparative studies of a few christological contemporary approaches and responses[4] of theological students to the theme studied.

Since the bisecting of Christian theology into quasi-autonomous branches has been a Western phenomenon, there is no intention in this paper to strictly follow the neat divisions in theology. While Jesus Christ is the center of our reflection, God the Father, the Holy Spirit, and the Trinity as a whole will be prominently featured as the discussion warrants. This approach is one of the ways of building a truly African theology which is not defined at the beginning but rather which naturally evolves as African theological thinking goes on.

NATURE OF SUFFERING

Suffering, as experience shows us, respects no age or condition, no place or human being. It is a reality which is ubiquitous. Only the causes, intensity, extent, duration, and attitude may differ.

For the sake of clarity, but at the risk of sounding a bit simplistic, I wish to place suffering under five categories. The first two categories should be constantly fought against in our lives and society, while the last three types ought to be positively and dynamically accepted and utilized as means to our growth to Christian maturity and to authentic and total human liberation.

SELF-INFLICTED SUFFERING

Much of the suffering we experience in and around us is self-inflicted. Through sin, misbehavior, ignorance, lack of self-control, laziness, narrowmindedness, and malice we inflict suffering on ourselves. A teenage girl who stubbornly refuses to take heed of her parents' advice against premarital sex may one day find herself suffering because of the "unwanted" and "unplanned for" pregnancy. From this single instance of self-inflicted suffering her entire life may become one vicious circle of suffering. Several years later, this person may forget she was the original cause of her own suffering and may refer to God as the source of all her suffering.

Self-inflicted suffering gives birth to many "if people." Such people live always to regret, but when it is already too late. It is to this self-inflicted suffering that much of classical christology was concentrated. It is a christology founded on the main message of Christ's preaching, namely, conversion. It emphasizes God's kindness and compassion. He is slow to anger and full of mercy. It is the christology of the parable of the prodigal son. It calls people to repentance and total conversion. In this christology, personal and individual sin is indeed the real cause of all evil and all suffering in the world. Against this claim, Monica Hellwig explains that:

[i]t is at this juncture that the plea arises, mainly from Third World Liberation theologians, for a soteriology and Christology that are concerned not only with contemporary experience of believers as *interacting individuals* but with the entire range of human experience of

suffering and hoping and surviving and transformation, which includes the political and economic dimensions of human life.[5]

Individual sin alone cannot explain the existence of evil and of suffering in the world.

SUFFERING CAUSED BY OTHERS

Much of the suffering we witness in the world at large and Africa in particular is inflicted on the innocent people by a few selfish individuals or groups or societies of people. In South Africa, a white minority which claims even to be "Christian" continues to support and use apartheid to humiliate, oppress, rob, and kill the black Africans. In Ethiopia, Sudan, Angola, and Mozambique, just to mention a few states, people continue to die of hunger, war, and want because of selfish leaders on either side who do not want to enter into dialogue and settle the existing conflicts. In the economic sector, a relatively limited number of people are continuing to amass wealth, a privilege not in practice open to the majority. In the cultural sector certain minority groups are being oppressed by privileged groups. In the religious sphere the same reality exists. Stronger religions attempt to suppress or entirely weaken the rest. This is most evident today within contemporary Islamic fundamentalism and its commitment to a general application of Sharia law.[6] In the political arena Africa has witnessed certain cases of dictatorial rule. These have caused suffering and even death to many helpless people.

Classic or traditional christology has provided answers to people who suffer because of the selfishness or sins of others. These answers, however, no longer satisfy the non-Euro-American Christian world. Jon Sobrino has suggested that "basically these suspicions come down to this: For some reason it has been possible for Christians, in the name of Christ, to ignore or even contradict fundamental principles and values that were preached and acted upon by Jesus of Nazareth."[7] Sobrino adds that classic christology reduced Christ to "a sublime abstraction."[8] Christ was also reduced to a pacifist Jesus "who does not engage in prophetic denunciations, a Jesus who pronounces blessings but who does not pronounce maledictions, and a Jesus who loves all human beings but who is not clearly partial towards the poor and the oppressed."[9]

Following the same trend of thinking but arriving at a completely different conclusion, Andrew Greeley, a sociologist, is critical of the view which is quite popular today that Jesus and his message are "irrelevant" to the problems of the modern world. The irrelevance of Jesus, however, Greeley emphasizes, "is not a new discovery. He was irrelevant to his own world too; so irrelevant that it was necessary for him to be murdered. The symbolism of his life and message was no more adjusted to the fashionable religious currents of his day than it is adjusted to the fashionable religious currents of our day."[10]

Greeley continues to explain that:

perhaps one of the reasons for the many controversies that have raged over Jesus of Nazareth is the difficulty in classifying him. For some, he seems a simple ethical preacher; to others, a mystical prophet; to others, an eschatological visionary; to yet others, a political revolutionary; and to still others, a founder of a Church. It is not merely the different presuppositions that we bring to our study of Jesus that create the confusion. He is a hard man to categorize. He does not seem to fit into any of our neat labels, and this problem of figuring out where exactly Jesus stands is not a new one.[11]

Greeley objects to the theology of revolution on two accounts: as a social scientist and as a Christian.[12] His objection, however, seems inconsistent with his christological analysis as portrayed above. When confronted with inhuman regimes, selfish dictators who deny people their fundamental rights, racist rulers (as in South Africa), the old classic christology of a pacifist Jesus can no longer be the answer. The christology here would be constructed on the central theme of Christ's message: the proclamation of God's kingdom of justice and righteousness, of peace and unity, of human dignity and universal brotherhood. This would serve as the model we use in repelling, resisting, destroying, eliminating the unjust sufferings caused by selfish or indifferent people. In such a model the theology of revolution occupies a central position. This theology is rooted in the theology of the *last resort*: when a prolonged tyranny, harmful to fundamental human values, has to be confronted by revolutionary methods.[13]

There is hardship in every endeavour to achieve a worthy goal, ambition, plan or liberation or transformation of society. The suffering involved in such hardship is only to be expected. The example of Jesus, in John 14, of the pains of childbirth for the mother is very relevant. Such pain disappears when a new child is born. It is replaced by intense joy for the mother. There is much pain in any struggle for justice, human welfare, and human dignity. The reward, however, of such struggle when it is completely or even partially won, is great joy.[14]

In accomplishing his mission of proclaiming and realizing the kingdom, it was inevitable that Christ had to suffer in order to achieve his goal. The joy he found in doing his Father's will forms a basis for a christology of this type of suffering.

SUFFERING ON BEHALF OF OTHERS

Nothing gives as much joy to a person as to suffer in sacrifice for one he loves. To share with one who has nothing demands a sacrifice, but one which brings joy to both. To sacrifice one's entitlements for another is a highly commendable act which enriches the one who does it. Every day people make sacrifices and suffer for those they love. This may be in terms of time, goods, energy or life itself. Maximilian Kolbe who during the Second World War sacrificed his life to save the life of a fellow prisoner is a contemporary symbol of such great love. All fighters for authentic liberation of peoples, such as Mahatma Gandhi, Martin Luther King Jr., Nelson Mandela, and others, are most appealing to the contemporary Christian mind because of their option. Many mothers, in critical situations, have made an option for their children to live instead of themselves.

This is exactly what Jesus of Nazareth did. He did it in his preaching when he said: "No one can have greater love than to lay down his life for his friends" (John 15:13). He did it in action by freely accepting suffering and death, death on the cross. Whereas, therefore, the cross is a sign of rejection, failure, and humiliation on one hand, it is a sign of extreme love, commitment, and liberation on the other. Since Jesus' death, many people have followed his example, giving support to this christology of extreme love which is tested through acceptance of suffering for a good cause.

Classic christology tends to shy from relating to Christ's death the daily deaths of men and women in sometimes justifiable struggles to liberate fellow human beings. It fails to draw out practical and concrete ways in which Christians can live and bear witness to this christology.

THE MYSTERIOUS SUFFERING OF THE INNOCENT

The conscience of the upright and innocent is revolted when the wicked or arrogant are the happiest, most successful, and most secure (Psalm 73). Questions arise in the mind of the innocent sufferer: What good and just God could do this to me? Was it useless, then, to have kept my heart clean, to have washed my hands in innocence? (Psalms 73:13). This is the suffering described in the book of Job. It is the suffering Jesus underwent. He had done good to everyone. He had spoken well as no one had before. He had committed no sin. He prayed for and loved his enemies and taught his followers to do the same. Why then the passion and the Cross?

The suffering of the innocent can make the victims lose Christian faith and faith in any God. The explanations given to them by some Christians resemble those given by Job's so-called friends. They add pain to pain, despair to despair. "You are suffering because of your sins, especially the hidden ones." "God is justly and openly punishing you, repent and accept your guilt." Such an approach is clearly unacceptable. Christ himself denounced it. Asked by his disciples: "Rabbi, who sinned, this man or his parents, that he should have been born blind?" Jesus' answer was brief and exact: "Neither he nor his parents sinned . . . he was born blind so that the works of God might be revealed in him" (John 9:2-3).

The type of christology for this kind of suffering which is abundant in

Africa must be built on the suffering servant, in order to contribute positively to the liberation and transformation of the world.

MAJOR ASPECTS OF SUFFERING IN AFRICA

To the outsiders, whose knowledge of Africa is obtained from the mass media, the most dramatized suffering in Africa is the lack of basic necessities of life that causes death to millions of Africans annually. These include hunger, famine, and malnutrition; insufficient and/or unclean water; lack of medicine and health care units; unsatisfactory living conditions; the large population of homeless people—the refugees, displaced peoples, orphans and widows. This type of suffering is emphasized abroad because it gives birth to compassion and stimulates humanitarian and Christian consciences to give relief to Africa. It is visible: the number of victims can be ascertained. Above all it is the type of suffering for which almost all world charitable organizations have been founded to alleviate. The philosophy, often unpronounced, which governs this approach, is to reduce the suffering without paying regard to the optimality of the structures of the societies in question.

Concentrating on this type of suffering has its advantages and disadvantages. Some victims of the above causes are assisted and saved from grim conditions and untimely death. The virtue of sharing in concrete acts of love for a faraway neighbor in need is instilled. A glimpse of hope is given to those in despair. The disadvantages include orchestrated mass media depiction of the levels of suffering and of the generosity of the donors. For the Christians giving assistance and the Africans receiving it, the image of Christ becomes that of a grandfather who throws some sweets to the starving grandchildren, a Christ who comes in the relief "container" or in the world food aircraft or the Red Cross vehicle. Such an image of Christ is no better than that of *fac totum, deus ex machina*. In this approach there is no desire to analyze the root cause, since such an exercise would lead to greater commitment and, "worse" still, to a clear taking of sides, which international charity organizations are not prepared to do nor allowed by their constitutions.

The second aspect of suffering is in the economic sector. Poverty has given birth to much suffering. It has made the continent appear sick, crippled, and begging. This poverty is primarily caused by unbalanced economic policies which favor the already rich and powerful nations of the world. This situation was established from the time of the African slave trade, through colonialism to the present-day neo-colonialism. In the first instance the "peculiar institution" of the slave trade took away over fifty million able-bodied African men and women to develop other continents.[15] The second phase of colonialism exploited African raw materials to develop the colonizing nations.[16] Neo-colonialism has made policies and rules which dictate the wishes of the powerful over the "weak and despised" continent.

All attempts to rectify this situation have failed, as UNCTAD can clearly bear witness.[17] The will to change and allow the less developed to arise is absent in the West. The present-day debt crisis is indicative of a sick world which pays lip service to the suffering majority of the world.[18]

Suffering brought by ignorance and illiteracy cannot be overemphasized. Africa has lagged behind in science and technology education. As a result most Africans cannot control or influence as profitably as possible their own environment and make it serve their needs and fulfil their aspirations.[19] In a world with so much knowledge and skills, it is a scandal that ignorance and illiteracy can be allowed to continue and dominate in Africa. From ignorance springs sufferings of disease, an inferiority complex, and feelings of helplessness.

Psychological and religious suffering in Africa is most felt in cultural oppression, racism, tribalism, and a feeling of being rejected. In this field both the colonial and missionary masters have done harm to the authentic African personality. An African Christian is a divided person, wishing to be true to both his cultural values as well as to the Gospel values—values which are often presented as opposed to each other.

Since independence, Africa has greatly suffered under the yoke of its own political leaders, many of whom adopted dictatorial approaches to government. Africa has witnessed over seventy military coups, most of which have claimed many innocent lives. There have been numerous military conflicts either internally or between nations, giving rise to millions of refugees, widows, and orphans. Funds meant to develop Africa have been placed in personal accounts in Euro-American banks by selfish African leaders. Such leaders had neither the capacity nor the intention to propose an authentic development programme for their people.[20]

Suffering in Africa is made worse through the feeling and prediction that so far there is no remedy to it; instead, suffering in all its aspects seems to multiply as years go on. The coming Third Millennium is not one of hope but rather of greater despair.[21] Despair has increased because the present situation threatens to be yet another vicious circle without a solution. As a reaction to such despair, numerous religious movements, both local and foreign, have sprung up to give assurance of *individual salvation* for the personal good of the followers.

WHAT IS THE ROOT OF AFRICA'S SUFFERINGS?

Many outsiders advance the root causes of Africa's sufferings as African tribalism, innate laziness, and lack of inventiveness or creativity. These are the easy and evident signs of Africa's backwardness to outsiders. To these, they often add corruption of the African leaders. Such people, however, fail to go a step further to ask why tribalism, why laziness and uninventiveness, and why corruption? To this category of people the redemption of Africa lies entirely in the hands of the Africans once they decide, as a community, to fight and eliminate those root causes. To me this explanation does not go deep enough.

Africans themselves are sharply divided on the root cause of their own suffering. Some advance exploitation of Africa by outsiders, an exploitation which enforces ignorance and poverty on the continent. Some suggest ignorance of science and technology which prevents Africa from competing with the developed countries. Other Africans see the root cause in the absence of total liberation of Africa and the Africans. Everywhere they argue that what can be seen is *partial* liberation which is not sufficient for the creation of the necessary attitudes and programmes for integral development. The Christian churches tend to interpret the entire suffering in a spiritualized manner which takes the presence of *sin* and the lack of *total conversion* to Christ as the root cause.

Unless there is some genuine agreement on the root cause, there cannot be an agreed-upon solution which can be undertaken with a unity of purpose.

After careful reflection, what I propose as the single root cause of Africa's suffering is *rejection*, both by powerful outsiders and powerful insiders. From this rejection come all attitudes which continue to oppress Africa and intensify suffering. From rejection there comes failure to seriously think of a lasting solution to the unnecessary suffering on the continent. It is on this theme of *rejection* that my christological reflections will be constructed.

When Christianity came to Africa towards the end of the fifteenth century, its theology soon sanctioned Africa's rejection by giving support to the enslavement of Africans.[22] This created a situation which was progressively to sanction rejection of Africans in many other instances.

After almost one thousand years of isolation, when the Western missionaries came in contact with Christian Ethiopia in the early sixteenth century, they utterly rejected its Christianity as heretical and listed hundreds of errors in it. This closed the door for cooperation between the Ethiopian church and Western Christianity. When the European Christian Nonconformists were prosecuted at home, they trekked to South Africa during the seventeenth century, and on arrival they rejected the blacks, the owners of the land, as the condemned children of Ham.

The nineteenth-century theology of the missionary movement rejected any value in the African traditional religions, despised many of the people's cultural values, and would not use them as a basis for Christian evangelization.

Throughout the colonial era Christian theology rejected African church leadership. This was even the case with the Anglican Samuel Ajayi Crowther who had been consecrated Bishop in 1864 at the insistence of the farsighted secretary general of the C.M.S., Henry Venn. The rejection of his church leadership came in 1890 when many of his African pastors were dismissed without trial on fabricated accusations, and he himself was succeeded by a white missionary bishop in 1891.[23]

When nationalist movements for independence first emerged in Africa in the 1920s and more so after the Second World War, Christian theology tended to reject them as communistic and Marxist. It remained to the Catholic Portuguese missionaries in Mozambique to outright condemn as evil and sinful the African aspiration for independence as late as 1973. Christian theology, as a whole, tended to support the *status quo* of colonial rule. Once Africans succeeded in their struggle for independence, Christian theology seemed to support the neo-colonialism, the control of Africa from afar.

In the late 1960s when African theologies were emerging, they were rejected by no less a person than the scholarly Jean Cardinal Danielou in a symposium organized in Rome in December 1967. Such theologies were considered as unorthodox and opposed to the one universal theology for all.

Western Christianity had been equated to Christianity itself. Western christology had been made equivalent to Christ himself. Even today, the very word *inculturation*, is still rejected in some Western and African circles. Instances of Africa's rejection within the history of Christian theology could be multiplied indefinitely.

When all such instances of Africa's rejection by Christian outsiders and their Euro-American theology are put together, some questions arise leading to several conclusions. What is the root cause of Africa's constant rejection? For some it is the very color, black, which is the common factor uniting all Africans within the continent and those living in the Diaspora. This color, which is God-given, happened to be a sign of dirt, sin, evil, sickness, malice, and aversion according to many Euro-Americans. It, therefore, created fear, dislike, and contempt among many of them.[24] Even artistic works by Euro-Americans depicting Africans still portray an African today as clumsy-looking with huge, red lips and unproportional in size. Some rejected Africans and their continent on the basis of a biblical interpretation which in their mind represented the Africans as the condemned children of Ham, who were to be slaves forever to the descendents of Shem. Still others rejected Africa because of the many myths which were told and written about the Africans and their land. One common factor uniting all such causes is the misconception that the Euro-American world is the center of the universe. It is the model of what is good, just, and holy. It is the center of God's love and presence. As a consequence it possesses superior knowledge and wisdom, culture and civilization, dignity and honor. When such a misconception is entertained for centuries and promoted in several ways, it becomes the heritage of the Euro-Americans. On the basis of such heritage, Africans look strange, unfamiliar, and dejected in appearance, behavior, environment, religion, and culture. Aspects of this heritage can be traced in Christian theology in relation to Africa. Missionary journals, diaries, and magazines are full of such assumptions. Christian prayer books and hymnals in Africa also show evidence of such prejudice.

It is basically such a picture and the attitudes it has generated that cause the contemporary African Christian and especially the theologians to ask themselves: Where does a church such as ours feature within the universal church? With the type of history we have gone through, what can be expected of us within the universal church? With the past attitudes of rejection still partially present within Christian theology, what should we do? What image and understanding of Christ can save us or bring us true assurance and not simply hope? As a woman theologian, Christine Reimers, recently asked: "Can a woman be saved by a male Saviour?"[25] So has one of the African people interviewed queried: "Can a white Christ accept and totally liberate the black Africans?"[26]

The perplexity and suffering of Africans would have been easier to comprehend had they come solely from the rejection by outsiders. As the post-independence history of Africa clearly shows, Africans have often been rejected by their own political, economic, and social rulers. Bad government in Africa has caused many deaths, forced many into refugee life, and created suffering for many people. Because of fear, self-interest, self-preservation, and sometimes ignorance, many of Africa's social, intellectual, and religious leaders have often overlooked the sufferings of their own people, allied with the rejectors, and supported the *status quo* in situations of suffering. To many ordinary African Christians, even the majority of African theologians are included among the "rejectors" of their own people. They appear to perceive that they have a monopoly of knowledge in religious and ethical matters. Instead of doing theology from and with the people and on issues of primary importance for the people, they concentrate on theological academic gimmicks which are at the periphery of people's living experience of suffering and hoping. Their theologies lack prophetic insights and witness; they lack a sense of urgency and relevance; and consequently they do not appeal to the people to whom they should minister.

Instead of succumbing to despair because of this double rejection from without and within, African Christians should look to Jesus who fully experienced rejection by the foreigners and by his own people. He certainly has something vital to say and do in the African situation and experience.

BIBLICAL INSIGHTS FROM AN AFRICAN PERSPECTIVE

It is with the above fundamental questions and emotional disturbance that a committed African theologian examines the biblical message to discover whether it also rejects Africa and Africans or whether it can liberate them. It does not seem right to think that a person reads or studies the Bible or prays without a specific bias dictated by upbringing, culture, circumstances, interests, and questions.

Certainly the Bible refers to non-Jews as Gentiles, a term that was derogatory. The Bible has also been used in history to give support to white supremacy and black inferiority. It is not an accident but a central theme in the Bible that Egypt, the land that enslaved God's people, is in fact in Africa. The entire movement of the Chosen people from slavery to liberation is portrayed as moving away from Africa to the land of milk and honey. It has, therefore, been easy for some African Christian intellectuals to reject the Bible outright, as a book of Jewish propaganda against the Africans and to warn their fellow Africans to reject being enslaved by the Bible.[27]

Once this initial temptation is overcome, however, African theologians, with all their background and sense of rejection, may be surprised at what they may find in the biblical message. In the Bible, the African theologian finds the line of the good people and the line of the evil people. The rejected are always traced back to the line of Cain, the first murderer, and to Ham, the first scandaler. The line of the godly rulers and godly people is traced to Abel, the innocent victim, and to Shem, the righteous vindicator of his father's shame.

The theme of rejection then becomes very important and indeed central in the entire biblical message. Joseph, the beloved son of Jacob, was rejected by his envious brothers and sold into slavery in Egypt. This rejected and long-forgotten son, taken for dead, one day became the saviour of his people who gathered around him in Egypt. It was around this formerly rejected person that God formed his future nation.[28]

Moses was rejected after his birth and thrown near the River Nile to die. This rejected child was saved and became the leader of his people from the land of slavery to the land God had given to his people.[29]

The story of David is not much different. He was utterly ignored by his father as the least likely candidate to be chosen by God. At the end, it was he whom the prophet anointed King of Israel. His line was to last forever, and from it the awaited saviour would come to liberate the world.[30]

Ezekiel's allegorical history of Israel as given in chapter 16 elaborates Israel's initial rejection and describes how the loving God came to its rescue, decorated it, gave it all good things to make it the most beautiful nation in the world. The entire Old Testament depicts God's liberation of his people, their constant rejection of that liberation, and his mercy and continual liberation.

In the New Testament the same theme of rejection becomes central in the life and ministry of the historical Jesus of Nazareth. At his birth, there was no place for him and his parents in the inn. And as John tells us: "He came in his own domain and his own people did not accept him" (John 1:2). Having spoken so well in the synagogue of his birthplace, his own people dismissed the message with disdain: "This is Joseph's son, surely?" They took him to the brow of the hill their town was built on, intending to throw him down the cliff (Luke 4:29). When he started calling disciples to follow him, Nathanael at first rejected him: "From Nazareth? ... can anything good come from that place?" (John 1:46-47). When he performed miracles, the Pharisees and Scribes attributed his powers to Beelzebul, the

Prince of the Devils. During his agony in Gethesemane, he was abandoned by his closest companions. When Pilate asked the crowd whether to release Jesus or Barabbas, it rejected Jesus and called for the release of Barabbas. On the cross, between two murderers, Jesus felt abandoned even by his Father and so He cried out: *"Eloi, Eloi, lama sabachthani:* My God, my God, why have you abandoned me?" (Mark 15:34). He died as a reject, a common criminal.

Such is Jesus of Nazareth, who in his historical existence experienced rejection on many occasions, was accepted only by a few, was despised and misunderstood, had several serious cases falsely brought against him; through envy, jealousy, ignorance, and malice he was done away with.

With these biblical insights the theme of rejection takes on new meaning. It is no longer the sinful, the evil, the enemies of God and people that are rejected, but usually the innocent, the just, and the God-fearing people. To the question: Why was Jesus killed? Andrew Greeley suggests that:

> [i]n the final analysis, it was for the same reason that all great men are killed: They bother us. Jesus bothers us immensely. He bothered his contemporaries and he bothers us now. His contemporaries killed him, but he didn't even have the good taste to stay dead. He continues to bother us. We evade him, distort him, attempt to turn him into a preacher or a prophet, a political radical or a serene moralizer. But his authenticity and his integrity are too strong for our attempt to categorize him. He keeps breaking those bonds even as he broke out of the tomb. There he is again, still confronting us with the demand that we should believe in the Kingdom of his Father.[31]

Had the life of Jesus ended with his death, the theology of suffering would be meaningless. It is with Jesus' resurrection that Christian theology receives its full meaning right from the Old Testament to Jesus' historical existence.

Before we suggest a christology that can be relevant and meaningful to the African Christians in their situations of suffering, it is most appropriate to give some samples from the responses to the questionnaire, most of which certainly advocate the real need to develop a relevant christology for Africa.[32]

The responses to the question: What image of Christ do the suffering people of Africa have? indicated the divergent views on the issue. The majority emphasized an image of Christ who is irrelevant and passive, remote and unconcerned with the situations of suffering: He "has little or no bearing on the actual life"; he "does not concretely suffer with the suffering"; he "is unable to intervene in the people's hour of need."

Many expressed an image of Christ who rewards the victims of suffering only in the life hereafter. He is concerned with only spiritual suffering but not material and psychological suffering. To some, Christ appears partial, allowing some to suffer terribly while others, mainly the rich and the powerful, live happy lives. The priests who, in the eyes of many people, represent Christ, do not seem to identify themselves with those who suffer.

Because of such images of Christ, respondents observed, many African Christians turn to Christ only as a last resort, when all other means have failed. In their daily sufferings, the majority revert to traditional religion and its deities and ancestors who are expected to "act immediately" to remove suffering and discover the causes thereof.

Among the positive images of Christ, informants stressed the Suffering Servant who experienced suffering and *silently* suffers with all his children. He is the consoler, comforter, and hope to those who trust in him. In some situations he appears as a "black Christ, economically poor and from a poor family." He was referred to as "that mysterious God who cannot be manipulated," "a mysterious Christ who is not understood but who is always very reliable." These images give perseverance to some African Christians in their suffering, convinced that Christ will not desert them.

The explanations of the images of Christ preached by the African Christian churches also fell into two blocks of opinions. Some informants felt the churches have stressed the image of Christ who "redeems only the soul" and usually at the moment of death. Christ is presented as an "abstract" with little practical relationship with the concrete realities of Africa. He appears as "a European who is opposed to African culture, religion and medicine." Some mentioned the image of Christ as a friend of the poor and the deprived whom he spiritually consoles while leaving them in their misery. Christ as a moral teacher demanding a very high standard of morality which few people can ever hope to achieve has been stressed. Much has been preached about the Christ "of turning the other cheek," who knows about people's suffering but simply calls them to perseverance, and who tells his followers that suffering is a necessary process for their purification from sins.

Others recognized that churches have presented Christ as a brother to all, one who has chosen to remain with his people, a judge, king, merciful God, and a powerful liberator of his people.

The image of Christ which respondents suggested as the ideal and most relevant to the suffering Africans can be summarized as follows: They want Christ who is the *liberator* in all dimensions of life, Christ who is the *healer par excellence* of all their diseases and anxieties. They desire an uncompromised Christ of the Bible who sets his people free in the here and now. They want "a sick Christ" amid the sick, "a fighting Christ" with the fighting, and "a deprived Christ" among those living in deplorable situations. In sum, the Christ identified is the tangible, functional, African, and dynamic Christ with whom they can fully and at all times feel at home.

African Christians, however, have also to face the classical challenge of Christians of all times, namely to avoid, as much as possible, creating *false images* of Christ which may be biblically, historically, and theologically unfounded.

IMPLICATIONS FOR THE FUTURE

The proclamation of Peter before the Sanhedrin as narrated in chapter 4 of the Acts of the Apostles gives the best link between the Jesus of Nazareth and the Risen Christ:

> Then I am glad to tell you all, and would indeed be glad to tell the whole people of Israel, that it was by the name of Jesus Christ the Nazarene, the one you crucified, whom God raised from the dead, by this name and by no other that this man is able to stand up perfectly healthy, here in your presence, today. This *is the stone rejected by you the builders, but which has proved to be the keystone.*[33]

This theology expounded by Peter was borrowed from the processional Psalm 118 and from Isaiah chapter 8 where it is stated: "It is the stone rejected by the builders that has proved to be the keystone. This is Yahweh's doing; it is wonderful to see."[34] "He is the sanctuary and the stumbling-stone and the rock that brings down the two houses of Israel, a trap and a snare for the inhabitants of Jerusalem. By it many will be brought down, many fall and be broken, be trapped and made captive."[35]

It is the same theology found in Matthew chapter 21: "I tell you, then, that the Kingdom of God will be taken away from you and given to a people who will produce its fruits."[36] Isaiah elaborated on the nature of this cornerstone in chapter 28: "That is why the Lord Yahweh says this: See how I lay in Zion a stone of witness, a precious cornerstone, a foundation stone: The believer shall not stumble. And I will make justice its measure, integrity the plumb-line."[37] In Peter's first epistle this theology was summed up thus: "He is the living stone, rejected by men but chosen by God and precious to him."[38]

The theology of the rejected stone is the theology of the historical Jesus, while the theology of the cornerstone is that of the risen Christ. When the two theologies are put together we get the one theology for all the rejected people of the world who, if they have faith in God and themselves, must one day become a key people. This theology is part and parcel of the liberation theology with one important addition in that it puts special emphasis on the reflection of the experience of rejection in order to amass the energy and strengthen the faith to fight for total liberation and thus become the keystone. It strengthens the theology of hope by giving concrete *assurance* using Jesus Christ's example to all the rejected people of the world. For *hope*, as Greeley defines it "is the belief . . . that tomorrow will be different. . . . It is the assumption that the universe is out to do you good, and therefore it's all right to do good to yourself."[39] Or better, as Sobrino asserts,

> Christian hope is the hope in the fulfillment of the universe, but it is not naive either. Rather than directing its gaze above and beyond injustice and death, Christian hope takes a stand against injustice and death. That this hope does not waver or grow weary is again part of the experience of gratuitousness. Without Jesus' resurrection, Christian hope could be skepticism or desperation, without his cross it could be mere optimism.[40]

Christian hope, according to Hellwig, "enables people to lay hold of history from the standpoint of a future with promise rather than from a present filled with misery. Christian hope believes in a utopia (a "no place") whose "place" is the resurrection and whose "no place" is the cross."[41]

The theology of the stone rejected becoming the keystone complements the theology of the compassion of God as suggested by Hellwig:

> The representation of Jesus as the Compassion of God seems to offer a mediation between those two perceptions of what is at stake in our practical response to the redemption, for Compassion is essentially non-violent, tending to communion and community, and yet is also essentially active, tending to redress injuries and injustices.
>
> The Compassion of God enables us to imagine the one God in dynamic ways; it relates God to the creation and to creatures as well as to the redemption of the human race and its history. It identifies Jesus with that outreach into creation which makes God present in it, participate in it, entering into human experience in solidarity with human suffering, history and destiny. It is a way of saying that in the person of Jesus, God truly enters into creation, into human dilemma in all its tragic dimensions.[42]

The theology of the keystone cautions the *rejectors* of God's people that they may be walking on slippery ground. It gives, on the other hand, great faith to the rejected that their moment of exaltation is near, in the here and now. It brings to preeminence God's almighty power which is going to turn things upside down, not only in the next world but also in this one, by making those who are first now last, and the last first.

Imbued with this theology the suffering Africans and indeed all the rejected people of the world can begin to see signs of the movement towards their liberation, their becoming the keystone. They can count the battles and wars they have won against all wise predictions, right from slavery to political independence. They can recall the lives of their heroes. They can see justice slowly being achieved in some of their countries. They discover the number of people determined to strive for justice increasing. They see that within the universal Christian church, their numbers are becoming significant and their presence being felt. The future of Christianity is indeed in the suffering Third World. Nothing can stop this movement. This realization creates concern among the rejectors, while it gives satisfaction to the formerly rejected.

Animated by this theology the suffering Africans will appreciate that it is possible to break the fetters of hardship and to unite, conscientize one another and join the victorious Christ, the keystone, to realize their liberation. The rejected Jesus of Nazareth being raised from the dead as the victorious Christ, to the great shame and dismay of his rejectors, is the Christ that is relevant to Africa. His final rejection lasted only three days and he broke out of the tomb victorious. This is the Christ who calls on all the suffering people of the world to throw away all that enslaves them as he did and start to live a life of victory, asserting their full dignity and equality in the world.

The practical task from this christology is to make this vision a reality. The surest way to achieve this is through preaching this dynamic Christ, to conscientize Africans, give them confidence, unite the scattered and animate them to work unceasingly for integral development. All this can best be done when Christianity has become their own, presented and understood in their own worldview. Christ then will be seen as fully African and black, fully one of them and on their side. It is this Christ that will lead the Africans to the achievement of the new earth and the new heaven. For as Leonardo Boff affirms: "In the important questions of life nothing can substitute for the human person: neither law, nor traditions, nor religion. People must decide from within, before God and before others . . ."[43]

Jesus affected human beings at their very roots, activating their hope principle and making them dream of the Kingdom, which is not an entirely different world but this world completely new and renewed.[44]

NOTES

1. Cf. *Gaudium et Spes*, nos. 5 and 58, *Ad Gentes*, no. 22.

2. Monica K. Hellwig, *Jesus: The Compassion of God* (Dublin, 1983), p. 21.

3. Liberation theologians like Jon Sobrino have made an important distinction between "imitating" Jesus and "following" Jesus. The latter, as Sobrino explains "is discipleship and takes into account the differences in Jesus' own time and our time." *Christology at the Crossroads* (Maryknoll, N.Y.: Orbis Books, 1978), p. 389.

4. The author distributed questionnaires to 130 theological students of Gaba National Seminary, Uganda, with 66 responses. Some responses are discussed later in this paper.

5. Hellwig, p. 26.

6. The present experience of war in the Sudan between the Northern Arabic Muslims and the Southern black Christians and traditionalists is a precise example of this.

7. Sobrino, p. xv.

8. Ibid.

9. Ibid., p. xvi.

10. Andrew M. Greeley, *The Jesus Myth* (New York, 1973), p. 18.

11. Ibid., p. 31.

12. Ibid., p. 188.

13. Cf. *Populorum Progressio*, no 31.

14. Cf. Ecclesiastes 3:1-8.

15. P. D. Curtin, *The Atlantic Slave Trade: A Census* (Madison, 1967).

16. E. A. Bret, *Colonialism and Underdevelopment in East Africa* (London 1973), L.H. Gann and P. Guignan (eds.), *Colonialism in Africa* (Cambridge, 1970).

17. UNCTAD Secretariat, *The History of UNCTAD 1964-1984* (New York, 1985).

18. *The Debt Crisis Network, From Debt to Development* (Washington, D.C., 1986).

19. Yoweri K. Museveni, "The historical task of development," a paper presented to the 4th National Theological Week, Katigondo, 9th January 1989.

20. Cf. D. Martin, *General Amin* (London, 1974); A. Mazrui, *Soldiers and Kinsmen in Uganda*, London, 1975; S.P. Panter-Brick (ed.), *Nigerian Politics and Military Rule* (London, 1970).

21. Adebayo Adedeji, *Can Our World Escape the Path of Mutual Injury and Self-destruction?* (Geneva, 1986).

22. Cf. Pope Nicholas V's Brief of 1452 to King Alfonso V of Portugal.

23. J. B. Webster, *African Churches in Yorubaland, 1888-1922* (London, 1964).

24. Cf. Jordan Winthrop, *White Over Black* (Baltimore, Maryland, 1969).

25. *Newsweek*, 20 February 1989, pp. 40-41.

26. Response no. 36 to the questionnaire.

27. Franz Fanon, *The Wretched of the Earth* (London, 1967).

28. Genesis, chapters 37 to 50.

29. Exodus, chapters 2 and 3.

30. 1 Samuel 16:1-13.

31. Greeley, p. 93.

32. Responses to the questionnaire administered by the author to theological students at Gaba National Seminary, Uganda.

33. Acts 4:10-12.

34. Psalm 118:22.

35. Isaiah 8:14-15.

36. Matthew 21:42-43.

37. Isaiah 28:16.

38. 1 Peter 2:4; 1 Cor. 3:11-13.

39. Greeley, p. 95.

40. Sobrino, p. 393.

41. Ibid.

42. Hellwig, pp. 122-23.

43 Leonardo Boff, *Jesus Christ Liberator*, p. 78.

44. Ibid., p. 79.

Contributors

François Kabasélé, lectures at the Theological Faculty in Kinshasa and works as a parish priest in Mbuji-Mayi, Zaire.

Cécé Kolié, a Guinean, works in N'Zerekore, Guinea.

Laurenti Magesa teaches in the Catholic Higher Institute of East Africa in Nairobi, Kenya.

Anne Nasimiyu-Wasike teaches at Kenyatta University in Nairobi.

Zablon Nthamburi teaches at Kenyatta University in Nairobi.

Charles Nyamiti, a Tanzanian, teaches at the Catholic Higher Institute of East Africa in Nairobi.

Efoé Julien Pénoukou, a native of Benin, teaches at the Institut Catholique d'Afrique de l'Ouest in Abidjan, Ivory Coast.

Anselme T. Sanon is bishop of Bobo-Dioulasso, Burkina Faso.

Robert J. Schreiter teaches at the Catholic Theological Union, Chicago, U.S.A.

Douglas W. Waruta teaches at the University of Nairobi in Kenya.

John M. Waliggo has returned to his native Uganda after teaching at the Catholic Higher Institute of East Africa in Nairobi.

Also from Orbis Books

HISPANIC DEVOTIONAL PIETY
Tracing the Biblical Roots
C. Gilbert Romero
Faith and Cultures Series

Hispanic Christian tradition is a rich blend of Native American, Spanish, and Portuguese traditions interacting with ancient biblical elements. Romero mines the social sciences, contemporary hermeneutics theory, and biblical studies to examine the biblical roots and the lived experience of four devotional exercises important to the Hispanic Catholics of the Southwestern United States. *Hispanic Devotional Piety* discusses the problem of relating "normative" biblical revelation and ongoing religious experience.

"As a Mexican-American priest and Old Testament professor, Father Romero has rare qualifications for showing how the narrative and symbolism of the Bible can mediate between Hispanic devotional piety and normative Catholic teaching. Skillfully interweaving materials from cultural anthropology, hermeneutical theory, and theology, this book helps to bridge the gap that sometimes separates popular religiousity from official Catholicism."   **—Avery Dulles, S.J.**
Laurance J. McGinley Professor of Religion and Society
Fordham University

175pp. Index. ISBN 0-88344-767-3 Paper

TRANSFORMING MISSION
Pradigm Shifts in Theology of Mission
David J. Bosch
The American Society of Missiology Series, No. 16

Seldom does one come across a truly magisterial book. This is one. Bosch examines the entire sweep of Christian mission, attending to the interplay of the *theological* and the *historical* as paradigms for the understanding and praxis of Christian mission. Treating the biblical epoch as a paradigm shift portraying human attempts to utter the divine concern for human salvation, Bosch shows us how the transcendent and the immanent are intrinsically linked.

Bosch grasps the radicality of the questions posed to Christian mission by both the Enlightenment and the onset of postmodernity. Overcoming modern skepticism and achieving a position that holds competing truths in dialectical tension, he helps us integrate the passion of Jesus' mission for God and the church's contemporary way of the cross.

650pp. Notes, bibliography, indexes. ISBN 0-88344-719-3 Paper
ISBN 0-88344-744-4 Cloth

UNITY & PLURALITY
Mission in the Bible
Lucien Legrand

In a truly creative, synthetic study of the biblical theology of mission, Legrand explores the Old Testament, with its twin ideas of "election" and "universalism," and the New Testament, retrieving an image of Jesus as missionary which is both historically and theologically convincing. In examining the primitive church, exploring the mission of Paul, and offering a close reading of the Gospel of John, he brings into relief the multi-faceted nature of mission in the Bible, in a way that illuminates both its variety of images and its dynamic center.

Unity and Pluarlity provides unique insight into the understanding and practice of mission throughout two millennia of biblical tradition. At the same time, it shows how that variety is at the service of the Mysterious One who comes to us—empowering, reconciling, challenging, renewing.

"While many hastily written works disappear quickly, this book will doubtless stand as a landmark in the development of missiology. Written with clarity, but without flaunting the author's learning, it deserves the attention of a wide reading public. It will inspire discoveries and sustain prayer."—*Esprit et Vie*
208pp. Notes, scriptural index. ISBN 0-88344-692-8 Paperback

TRENDS IN MISSION
Toward the Third Millennium
William Jenkinson and Helene O'Sullivan, editors
Introduction by Robert Schreiter

Major writings celebrate the 25th Anniversary of Dervizio di Documentazione e Studie (SEDOS), the joint research center sponsored by seventy-two Catholic mission societies. Contributors from the North and South, East and West, religious and laypeople, focus on key issues of mission today: the context of mission, models of mission and ministry, the future of mission today.
450pp. ISBN 0-88344-766-5 Paperback

MISSIONS & MONEY
Affluence as a Western Missionary Problem
Jonathan J. Bonk
The American Society of Missiology Series, No. 15

Drawing on his own Mennonite heritage and the dynamics of the gospel's profound ambivalence toward money, Bonk asks some hard questions. Do contemporary Western missionaries unwittingly subvert the gospel and hinder its inculturation because of their relative wealth? Does the wealth of the missioner eventually lead the indigenous peoples to feel hostility—consciously or unconsiously—toward the missioner? Deeply probing and insightful, *Missions & Money* calls Christians back to their roots, to the evangelical challenge to live simply and poorly.
200pp. Index. ISBN 0-88344-718-5 Paperback

UNCOMPLETED MISSION
Christianity and Exclusivism
Kwesi A. Dickson

As the church has spread throughout the world, Christians have contined to invite others to follow Christ. In most cases, the church accepts the converts with rejoicing but not their cultures and traditions. Kwesi Dickson, author of *Theology in Africa*, shows how the roots of this "exclusivism" lie within Old Testament Judaisim and the teachings of the church from the early apostles through the Reformation. Such exclusivism, which has become part of the twentieth-century mission movement, has mistakenly led the church to forget that God seeks communion equally with all peoples.

168pp. Index. ISBN 0-88344-751-7 Paperback